Predestination in Early Modern Reformed Theology

REFORMED HISTORICAL-THEOLOGICAL STUDIES

General Editors
Joel R. Beeke and Jay T. Collier

BOOKS IN SERIES:

The Christology of John Owen
Richard W. Daniels

The Covenant Theology of Caspar Olevianus
Lyle D. Bierma

John Diodati's Doctrine of Holy Scripture
Andrea Ferrari

Caspar Olevian and the Substance of the Covenant
R. Scott Clark

Introduction to Reformed Scholasticism
Willem J. van Asselt et al.

The Spiritual Brotherhood
Paul R. Schaefer Jr.

Teaching Predestination
David H. Kranendonk

The Marrow Controversy and Seceder Tradition
William VanDoodewaard

Unity and Continuity in Covenantal Thought
Andrew A. Woolsey

The Theology of the French Reformed Churches
Martin I. Klauber, ed.

Doctrine in Development
Heber Carlos de Campos Jr.

The Theology of the Huguenot Refuge
Martin I. Klauber, ed.

The Claims of Truth
Carl R. Trueman

Providence, Freedom, and the Will in Early Modern Reformed Theology
Richard A. Muller

Arminius and the Reformed Tradition
J. V. Fesko

The Roots of Reformed Moral Theology
Bruce P. Baugus

The Theology of Early French Protestantism
Martin I. Klauber, ed.

Predestination in Early Modern Reformed Theology
Richard A. Muller

Predestination in Early Modern Reformed Theology

Richard A. Muller

Reformation Heritage Books
Grand Rapids, Michigan

Reformation Heritage Books
3070 29th St. SE
Grand Rapids, MI 49512
616-977-0889
orders@heritagebooks.org
www.heritagebooks.org

Printed in the United States of America
24 25 26 27 28 29/10 9 8 7 6 5 4 3 2 1

Library of Congress Cataloging-in-Publication Data

Names: Muller, Richard A. (Richard Alfred), 1948- author.
Title: Predestination in early modern Reformed theology / Richard A. Muller.
Description: Grand Rapids, Michigan : Reformation Heritage Books, [2024] |
    Series: Reformed historical-theological studies | Includes bibliographical
    references and index.
Identifiers: LCCN 2024003934 (print) | LCCN 2024003935 (ebook) |
    ISBN 9798886861075 (paperback) | ISBN 9798886861082 (epub)
Subjects: LCSH: Predestination—History of doctrines—16th century. |
    Reformed Church—Doctrines—History—16th century. |
    Predestination—History of doctrines—17th century. | Reformed Church—
    Doctrines—History—17th century.
Classification: LCC BT810.3 .M855 2024 (print) | LCC BT810.3 (ebook) |
    DDC 234/.909031—dc23/eng/20240222
LC record available at https://lccn.loc.gov/2024003934
LC ebook record available at https://lccn.loc.gov/2024003935

Contents

Acknowledgments

I would like to express my thanks to my colleagues at Calvin Theological Seminary and to the graduate students who engaged in dialogue with me in the course of the several decades during which I developed my views and prepared the essays that appear in the present volume.

I am also profoundly grateful to the directors, librarians, and staff of the Hekman Library and H. Henry Meeter Center of Calvin Theological Seminary and Calvin University and the William Perkins Library at Puritan Reformed Theological Seminary for their efforts in gathering and maintaining the resources that have facilitated my research during the several decades of work that led to the essays in this volume, as well as several others. My thanks to Karin Maag, the director, and Paul Fields, the curator, of the Meeter Center for their help with resources over many years. The essay "Calvin on Predestination" owes its inception to their suggestion that I write a piece explaining some of the bibliographical issues endemic to the texts and translations of Calvin's main writings on predestination. I owe a special word of thanks to Raymond A. Blacketer, Andrew M. McGinnis, Jay T. Collier, and David S. Sytsma for their ongoing dialogue on the subjects covered in this volume and for their careful and insightful reading of several of the essays.

I am grateful to several journals and publishers for permission to include edited versions of the following essays in this volume.

"Predestination," s.v., in *The Oxford Encyclopedia of the Reformation*, ed. Hans J. Hillerbrand, 4 vols. (New York: Oxford University Press, 1996).

"The Placement of Predestination in Reformed Theology: Issue or Non-Issue?," in *Calvin Theological Journal*, 40/2 (2005), pp. 184–210.

"Calvin on Predestination: A Developmental and Bibliographical Essay," in *Hapshin Theological Review*, 8 (2020), pp. 81–107.

"Joseph Hall (1574–1656): Toward Peace in the Church and a Reformed *Via Media*," in *Calvin Theological Journal*, 53/1 (2018), pp. 9–31.

Introduction

The doctrine of predestination was hotly debated in the sixteenth and seventeenth centuries, not because it played the dogmatic role claimed by the nineteenth-century central dogma theories, according to which it was said to be the foundation on which the entirety of Reformed doctrine was based—indeed, deduced—but because in whatever form it took it raised the issue of the nature and character of the divine will to save sinful human beings and offered the basis for an explanation of why some are saved and others are not. Modern scholarship has often drawn highly negative dogmatic conclusions concerning the content and systematic role of the doctrine, sometimes portraying Calvin as the architect of a predestinarian metaphysic, sometimes attempting to rescue Calvin from the toils of later scholastic formulations on grounds of his purported "Christocentrism," often claiming that the mere placement of the doctrine in a theology radically altered its implication despite the retention of virtually the same definitions in the various placements of the doctrinal *locus*.

The decrees of God were understood and discussed in several ways by the Reformers and the Reformed orthodox. As essential to God, the decrees belong to the divine essence and are part of an answer to the question, What is God *ad intra*? They also, like various of the divine attributes, notably those identified as communicable, serve to identify and define the operation of God *ad extra*. As such, what is said of the divine attributes generally is also applicable to the divine decrees, and the decrees are to be understood as in harmony with the divine attributes—most notably in harmony and precisely expressive of the divine knowledge and will and in accord with the divine goodness, mercy, and justice. Further, following a distinction between the eternal decree itself and its execution in time, there was also Reformed discussion of the order or economy of the decree or decrees in the divine work of providence and human salvation.

The introductory essay, "Predestination in the Eras of the Reformation and Early Reformed Orthodoxy," originally entitled simply "Predestination," surveys the doctrine of predestination from the early Reformation to the Synod of Dort. I have substantively augmented and edited the text for the present volume, but have retained the original format with its selective referencing of relevant secondary sources, now placed in footnotes and updated with several more recent studies. I have not supplied footnotes to the early modern sources, many of which are referenced and analyzed in subsequent essays in this volume.

"The Placement of Predestination in Reformed Theology" offers a critique of some of the older scholarship on the Reformed doctrine of predestination, specifically, the scholarship that claimed Calvin had definitively moved the doctrine out of relation to the doctrine of God and into relation to soteriology, rendering it "Christocentric,"[1] only to have this wonderful new (and rather neoorthodox) pattern of exposition reversed by Beza who, based on a speculative and metaphysical approach to the doctrine, moved it back into the doctrine of God and set the pattern for later Reformed or Calvinist theology. The simple fact of the matter is that Calvin's doctrine of predestination is no more (and no less) focused on Christ than Beza's doctrine or the doctrinal formulation of the later Reformed orthodox.

Apart from the datum that Calvin never actually moved the doctrine and that Beza did not lodge predestination in his doctrine of God, this neoorthodox approach to the placement of the doctrine failed, in general, to ask the question of the relationship of the placement and structure of doctrinal exposition to the genre of the work under examination. It

---

1. Why this placement of the doctrine would render it "Christocentric" in the minds of proponents of the term as opposed to "soteriocentric" or even "pneumatocentric" remains a mystery. On "Christocentrism," see my essay "A Note on 'Christocentrism' and the Imprudent Use of Such Terminology," in *Westminster Theological Journal*, 68/2 (2006), pp. 253–60.

rather naively sought dogmatic answers to a question that is actually concerned with the genre and method of a document. These strictly dogmatic answers fail given that the doctrinal relationships on which they depend obtain wherever the doctrine of predestination is located in a theological work and that the definitions of the doctrine remain unaltered when theologians adopt different placements in works of different theological genres. For example, why do full bodies of divinity—in more modern parlance, "systems"—sometimes place predestination in relation to the doctrine of God, sometimes even placing the *locus* on predestination among the divine attributes? The most straightforward answer is that predestination is concerned with a divine willing located in eternity, prior to the creation of the temporal order, and that the doctrine was placed among the attributes or predications in response to the scholastic question, Can predestination be predicated of God? This is the case regardless of how the doctrine is defined. If one inquires into other locations of predestination, such as in the doctrine of the church, the answer is that, in addition to the theological issues of corporate election and the relation of election to the means of grace (which belong to the doctrine regardless of placement), the ecclesiological location is typically associated with commentaries on the Apostles' Creed or with catechetical works that include an exposition of the creed.

The third essay, "Calvin on Predestination: A Developmental and Bibliographical Essay," traces the development of Calvin's teachings on predestination from his earliest statements of the doctrine through his final nuancings of the doctrine in tracts and commentaries belonging to the years following the publication of the last edition of his *Institutes* in 1559. The intention of the essay is not to offer a full analysis of Calvin's doctrine—that would require a sizeable monographic study, and several such volumes exist. The study intends to identify in detail the locations and basis of Calvin's doctrine in numerous works written throughout his career. In doing so, it underlines the importance of examining Calvin's thought chronologically and contextually in his treatises, commentaries, and sermons, given that many of the major developments and significant details of his doctrine did not arise in the *Institutes* and are not registered there even when its several editorial strata are examined. The final version of the *Institutes* ought not to be viewed as the end point of Calvin's own theological development.

"Inclusive Supralapsarianism: The Heritage of Franciscus Junius and the Leiden Theology in Early Modern Reformed Thought" is a companion piece to my essay on the beginnings of Arminius' recourse to the concept of *scientia media* in his "Friendly Conference" or *Amica collatio* with Junius.[2] This essay examines Junius' approach to the order of the divine decrees, with emphasis on an unexamined issue in the discussion of supra- and infralapsarianism, namely, the issue of a third way of formulating the problem. This third way, a form of the supralapsarian doctrine that includes the infralapsarian position, given its presence in Junius' late sixteenth-century argumentation, may actually be the original pattern of supralapsarian argument. Be that as it may, it is a formulation that was present in the earliest debates over the Reformed doctrine of the ordering of the decrees and remained a form of the doctrine throughout the seventeenth century and into the eighteenth. It is characterized by use of the scholastic distinctions, drawn out of medieval sources, between the simple or absolute knowledge of God and the divine visionary knowledge, as well as assuming that such distinctions allow for a nontemporal sequencing of "moments" or "instants of nature" in the divine knowing and willing. Contrary to Arminius' claim, there was no misplaced or casual association between Aquinas' predestinarian formulations and Junius' patterns of argumentation. Junius himself denied the connection.[3]

Among the significant ramifications of this Junian supralapsarianism is that it explains, at least in part, why the seemingly infralapsarian definitions of the object of predestination do not by implication exclude supralapsarian definitions. If supralapsarianism were taken to mean, strictly, that the only way of defining the objects of predestination were as either "creatable" (*creabilis*) or "to be created" (*condendus*), it would

---

2. Richard A. Muller, "Arminius's 'Conference' with Junius and the Protestant Reception of Molina's *Concordia*," in *Beyond Dordt and* De Auxiliis*: The Dynamics of Protestant and Catholic Soteriology in the Sixteenth and Seventeenth Centuries*, ed. Jordan J. Ballor, Matthew T. Gaetano, and David S. Sytsma (Leiden: Brill, 2019), pp. 103–26.

3. Cf. Jacob Arminius, *Amica cum D. Francisco Iunio de praedestinatione per litteras habita collatio*, prop. vii, xxvii, in Arminius, *Opera theologica* (Leiden: Godefridus Basson, 1629), pp. 506, 609; in translation, *The Works of James Arminius*, trans. James Nichols and William Nichols, 3 vols. (Grand Rapids: Baker, 1986), vol. 3, pp. 86, 234; with idem, *Declaratio sententiae*, in *Opera*, pp. 110–16 (Calvin and Beza), 116–17 (Aquinas and Junius), 117 (infralapsarian); also, *Works*, vol. 1, pp. 641–45, 645–46, 648.

be excluded by an infralapsarian definition. But when the supralapsarian definition includes conception of the objects of the decree as also created and fallen, and therefore to the extent that it includes the confessional definition, it is not excluded by the confession. Ironically, the supralapsarian form is inclusive and the tightly defined infralapsarian form can become exclusivistic, as illustrated in the antisupralapsarian argumentation of such thinkers as Pierre du Moulin and Francis Turretin.[4] Influence of the Junian approach can be identified in a series of Reformed theologians extending from the time shortly after Junius' death in the work of Franciscus Gomarus and Johannes Piscator to writers of the late eighteenth century like John Gill and John Brown of Haddington.

The fifth essay, "Defending Dort: John Robinson and the Separatist Predestinarian Controversy," looks to the extended and highly sophisticated argumentation of a largely neglected English Reformed thinker. While in exile in the Netherlands because of his Separatist ecclesiology, Robinson encountered synergistic or Arminianizing directions in the theology of other exiled English Separatists and undertook the dual task of arguing both his loyalty to the Reformed views expressed in the Thirty-Nine Articles and his agreement with the Canons of Dort. Loyalty to the standards of the English church was necessary to securing right of passage from the English Crown to North America for his Pilgrim congregation. Agreement with the Canons of Dort was crucial to the maintenance of his congregation in the Netherlands. There has been some scholarly treatment of Robinson's doctrine of predestination, but it has not fully examined the details of his argumentation—and one study of the Pilgrim Separatists in the Netherlands has offered a distorted view of Robinson's work, claiming, quite contrary to his explicit statements, that Robinson failed to deny the divine authorship of sin, expressly "maintained that

---

4. Cf. Pierre du Moulin, *The Anatomy of Arminianisme: or the opening of the Controversies lately handled in the Low-Countryes, Concerning the Doctrine of Providence, of Predestination, of the Death of Christ, of the Nature of Grace* (London: T. S. for Nathaniel Newbery, 1620), xiii–xv (pp. 97–98); with Francis Turretin, *Institutio theologiae elencticae, in qua status controversiae perspicue exponitur, praecipua orthodoxorum argumenta proponuntur, & vindicantur, & fontes solutionum aperiuntur*, 3 vols. (Geneva: Samuel de Tournes, 1679–1685; 2nd ed., 1688–1690), IV.ix.

evil itself must be essentially good," and viewed the doctrine of free choice as heretical.[5] Examination of Robinson's own arguments place him in the line of English Reformed theologians that also includes Perkins and Ames and in accord with the Dutch Reformed thinkers of his time.

The final essay, "Joseph Hall (1574–1656): Toward Peace in the Church and a Reformed *Via Media*," examines the doctrine of predestination found in the works of a theologian of the Church of England who combined his loyalty to the Reformed direction of the Thirty-Nine Articles with adherence to the episcopal governance of the church and an advocacy of peace and union among Protestants, Reformed and Lutheran. Hall was awarded bachelor's and master's degrees after study at Emmanuel College, Cambridge. He subsequently served as chaplain to James I and as a delegate to the Synod of Dort. He was elevated to the sees of Exeter and Norwich, only to be expelled from his office by order of the Long Parliament in 1642. Hall also engaged, with John Dury, Samuel Hartlib, and others, in concerted efforts to find a ground of agreement and mutual cooperation between the Reformed and Lutheran confessionalities. Because of this effort and his irenicist tendencies, some scholarship has argued that his eventual *via media* placed him theologically somewhere in between the Lutherans and the Reformed or even indicated sympathies with Arminian thought. Specifically, some have argued that Hall began his theological career as a "Calvinist" and concluded it with only a few marks of Calvinism remaining. Against this reading, the present essay examines Hall's theological positions more closely and demonstrates his maintenance of an orthodox Reformed understanding of predestination, his willingness to seek "peace in the church" given agreement on the basic doctrine of salvation by grace alone, and his willingness to do so without requiring either side of the argument over predestination to sacrifice its more detailed theological constructions.

Hall's *via media* was not, in short, what *via media* came to mean in nineteenth-century Anglican theology—a stance between

---

5. Jeremy D. Bangs, "Beyond Luther, beyond Calvin, beyond Arminius: The Pilgrims and the Remonstrants in Leiden, 1609–1620," in *Reconsidering Arminius: Beyond the Reformed and Wesleyan Divide*, ed. Keith D. Stanglin, Mark G. Bilby, and Mark H. Mann (Nashville: Abingdon, 2014), pp. 39–69, here pp. 46–47.

Protestantism and Roman Catholicism. Rather, it was an attempt to end hostilities between the major Protestant confessionalities in view of their common ground in fundamental doctrines. If the line of definition associated with Junius, Mastricht, and others attempted to refine and elaborate the doctrine of predestination to render it inclusive of all Reformed variants, Hall's approach would look in the opposite direction, attempting to create formulae of agreement that set aside the detailed refinements of the dogmaticians, while at the same time allowing each confessional group to retain its distinctive explanations of the basic formulae. And as in the case of Junius' and Mastricht's definitions, neither did Hall's attempt at mediation bring about a resolution of differences or a conclusion to debate.

As whole, the group of essays illustrates the complexity and the refinement, as well as aspects of the development of early modern Reformed approaches to the doctrines of God and the divine decrees. Calvin's doctrine of the divine attributes, for example, as drawn not from the *Institutes* but from the commentaries and sermons, can be seen to observe a traditional understanding of both the essential nature of the divine attributes and the relationship of the attributes to the divine work in the temporal economy. This understanding stands in accord with the later Reformed sense of the essential *ad intra* identity and *ad extra* relation and operation of the attributes argued in a far more technical manner by the Reformed orthodox. Similarly, the view of divine permission that Calvin developed over the course of his career is echoed in John Robinson's treatment of predestination and the problem of sin.

Discussion of Reformed orthodox approaches to the essence and attributes of God offers examples of a complexity and refinement of Reformed doctrine in the era of orthodoxy that has often escaped the notice of writers who have sought to generalize about the Protestant scholastic theologies. The orthodox neither isolated the doctrine of the essence and attributes from the doctrine of the Trinity nor "privileged" one doctrine over the other. As with the various placements of the doctrine of predestination, the relative placement of the doctrines of divine attributes and the Trinity is seen to be related to clarity of argument and order of presentation rather than to issues of doctrinal importance. If one were to take the notion of "privileging" on the basis of order seriously, prolegomena would be the most important of doctrines and the "last things" the least, creation would be more important than Christology, and baptism more important than the Lord's Supper. The orthodox writers also evidence a refinement of argumentation concerning the way in which divine attributes relate to and define the divine acts *ad extra*. This over against facile claims that divine simplicity and immutability preclude divine involvement with creatures in the world order.

The several essays on predestination, taken together, illustrate the development of Reformed thought in different contexts and its complexity. This complexity stands in contrast to such oversimplifications as the reading of Calvin's thought solely from the *Institutes*, representations of supra- and infralapsarian debates as matters merely of a logical ordering of decrees, and views of Reformed theologians as so entrenched in their own dogmatic definitions as to be unwilling to engage in broader theological exercises. Reformed orthodoxy was clearly not monolithic. There were a series of editorial, organizational, and genre-driven placements of the doctrine of predestination, none of which were determinative of its doctrinal definition. But there were also a series of qualifications concerning the logic of the decrees, the proper objects of divine willing, and the relationship of the divine willing to the categories of divine knowing that were determinative of definition and therefore, also, of varieties of formulation among the Reformed. Junius' formulations and the arguments of those who followed him indicate a way of reconciling the supra- and infralapsarian approaches. Robinson's defense of Dort reveals a probable supralapsarian defending infralapsarian formulations against a synergistic adversary. Hall's irenicism looked toward still broader association—in this case with the Lutherans—while not sacrificing his own Reformed confessional identity.

CHAPTER 1

Predestination in the Eras
of the Reformation and Early
Reformed Orthodoxy

The doctrine of predestination inherited by the Reformation of the sixteenth century bore the imprint of Augustine's teaching and evidenced many of the fine nuances given to the concept of a divine decree or counsel by the medieval doctors. From the very beginnings of the Reformation, a pronounced doctrine of the entirely gracious predestination of certain individuals to salvation out of the fallen mass of humanity was evident in the writings of major magisterial Reformers, such as Luther, Bucer, and Zwingli. This teaching carried over into the thought of second-generation codifiers of Reformation theology and was developed particularly by Reformed thinkers such as Calvin, Bullinger, Musculus, and Vermigli, while among the Lutherans a movement away from the most strict Augustinian definitions of the doctrine occurred as Melanchthon's views interacted with those of Luther. By the second half of the sixteenth century, the doctrine had become a major point of controversy among Reformed, Lutheran, and Roman Catholic thinkers and had received a substantial elaboration and development in the hands of Reformed theologians and exegetes. Reformed thinkers in particular were responsible for a full, scholastic, and highly variegated development of the doctrine as they defended it against Lutheran and Roman Catholic alternatives and, eventually, against the internal threat of Arminian teaching.[1]

____

1. On the history of Protestant theology, note Otto Ritschl, *Dogmengeschichte des Protestantismus: Grundlagen und Grundzüge der theologischen Gedanken- und*

Early Reformation Views

Despite his opposition to many aspects of late medieval scholastic theology, Luther's views on predestination certainly stand in continuity with the strongly Augustinian teaching of his order, as evidenced in such scholastic thinkers as Giles of Rome, Thomas of Strasbourg, Thomas Bradwardine, Gregory of Rimini, and, above all, his mentor, Johannes von Staupitz.[2] Given this continuity, Luther's assumption that an unconditioned divine will was the foundation of salvation can be viewed as a significant motif in his theology from the very beginning of his opposition to the various aspects of late medieval semi-Pelagianism, whether its doctrine of grace or of free choice or of merit and indulgences. In the Romans lectures of 1515–1516, Luther clearly connected predestination with assurance of salvation, noting that were salvation dependent on the human will and human works, it would be utterly uncertain. Our very ability to will and to work the good depends on the grace and mercy of God.

The primary source for Luther's doctrine of predestination is his treatise *De servo arbitrio*, published in December 1525 in response to Erasmus' *De libero arbitrio* of the previous year.[3] Luther's treatise pressed the problem of the fallen will and its inability to perform the good—and, against the background of this problem, drew out a doctrine of the all-determining will of God as the counter to Erasmus' view of human freedom. Luther argues that God wills all things,

---

Lehrbildung in den protestantischen Kirchen, 4 vols. (Leipzig: J. C. Hinrichs, 1908–1912; Göttingen: Vandenhoeck & Ruprecht, 1926–1927); and see the arguments leading toward reappraisal of Protestant orthodoxy in Carl R. Trueman and R. Scott Clark, eds., *Protestant Scholasticism: Essays in Reassessment* (Carlisle, U.K.: Paternoster, 1999); Richard A. Muller, *After Calvin: Studies in the Development of a Theological Tradition* (New York: Oxford University Press, 2003); and Herman J. Selderhuis, ed., *A Companion to Reformed Orthodoxy* (Leiden: Brill, 2013).

2. See Gordon Leff, *Bradwardine and the Pelagians* (Cambridge: Cambridge University Press, 1957); idem, *Gregory of Rimini: Tradition and Innovation in Fourteenth Century Thought* (Manchester: Manchester University Press, 1961); Heiko A. Oberman, *Archbishop Thomas Bradwardine: A Fourteenth-Century Augustinian. A Study of His Theology in Its Historical Context* (Utrecht: Kemink en Zoon, 1957); and David C. Steinmetz, *Misericordia Dei: The Theology of Johannes von Staupitz in Its Late Medieval Setting* (Leiden: Brill, 1968), pp. 20–21, 75–88.

3. Robert Kolb, *Bound Choice, Election, and Wittenberg Theological Method: From Martin Luther to the Formula of Concord* (Grand Rapids: Eerdmans, 2005), pp. 38–43.

including human sin and error, yet in such a way that human beings sin by their own fault. Given the encompassing character of the divine causality, all things occur by necessity, although not by compulsion. In this context, salvation belongs entirely to the will of God, which alone can bring about human willing of the good. Luther insists, moreover, that we must not inquire into the secret will of God in an attempt to discern why God chooses some for salvation and leaves others to their own damnation—we must simply accept the revealed will of God and its election of some to salvation by grace alone.

Luther thus juxtaposes almost paradoxically the assumptions that all things come to pass necessarily by the decree of God's eternal will, that all human beings are foreordained to salvation or damnation, that God nonetheless genuinely wills (as Scripture states) the salvation of all people, and that those who are rejected by God are rejected for their unbelief. Any attempt to resolve such issues encounters the problem of the secret counsel or inscrutable divine good pleasure: some are elected to salvation, others are rejected, but the causes of the divine decision remain hidden and can never become the subject either of preaching or of legitimate theological speculation.

Melanchthon's views on predestination offer a significant counterpoint to Luther's. Although Melanchthon clearly rested election on the merciful will of God, he balanced his declarations concerning the cause of election with an insistence on the universality of the divine promise of salvation and with an assumption that the cause of reprobation is the sinful and willful rejection of the gospel. In his *Loci communes* (1543), Melanchthon cites Saul as an example of one who "of his own free will fought against the Holy Spirit when the Spirit tried to move him," and argues that, although the beginning of salvation lies with God, human beings must necessarily "hear, learn, and grasp hold of God's promises." The argument clearly echoes Melanchthon's famous dictum from the locus on free choice that good works are caused by "the word of God, the Holy Spirit, and the human will which assents to and does not contend against the Word of God."[4]

Melanchthon's development toward a more synergistic understanding of grace and predestination did not mark a turn away from

---

4. Kolb, *Bound Choice*, pp. 70–102.

Luther's more strictly Augustinian views on the part of all Lutheran theologians of the original Wittenberg circle. Nikolaus von Amsdorf retained the Augustinian model and early on developed a doctrine of double predestination. Although he did not publish direct criticism of Melanchthon's doctrine as it appeared in editions of the *Loci communes* following 1535, Amsdorf presided over a disputation on contingency that argued the ultimate divine control of all events as an absolute necessity to the exclusion of the necessity of the consequence. His work, however, exerted no significant influence on the development of Lutheran understandings of predestination and was unknown among the Reformed.[5]

The Reformed doctrine of predestination stands as a clear descendant of the Augustinian theology of the later Middle Ages and represents a spectrum of opinion rather than a monolithic doctrinal perspective: it moves between the concept of a single predestination to life and the concept of a full double predestination to salvation and damnation conceived in the mind of God prior to His permissive willing of the fall. Nonetheless, despite the emphasis placed on the doctrine by the Reformed, predestination cannot be understood as a "central dogma" or fundamental constructive principle in Reformed theology, whether that of Zwingli and Bucer, that of Calvin and his contemporaries, or that of later Reformed orthodox or scholastic thinkers of the late sixteenth century.[6]

Zwingli and Bucer both developed significant approaches to predestination, the former on a more dogmatic and philosophical level in his confession, the *Fidei ratio* (1530),[7] and in his treatise *De providentia* (1530), the latter exegetically and doctrinally in his massive *Metaphrases et enarrationes perpetuae Epistolarum D. Pauli Apostoli* (1536). Both adhere to the basic Augustinian pattern of the doctrine, with Zwingli

---

5. See Robert Kolb, *Nikolaus von Amsdorf (1483–1565): Popular Polemics in the Preservation of Luther's Legacy* (Nieuwkoop: De Graaf, 1978); and idem, "Nikolaus von Amsdorf on Vessels of Wrath and Vessels of Mercy: A Lutheran's Doctrine of Double Predestination," in *Harvard Theological Review*, 69 (1976), pp. 325–43.

6. Cf. Muller, *After Calvin*, pp. 94–98.

7. Translations of the *Fidei ratio* and of the other Reformed confessions noted in this essay are available, with introductions, in James T. Dennison Jr., ed., *Reformed Confessions of the 16th and 17th Centuries in English Translation*, 4 vols. (Grand Rapids: Reformation Heritage Books, 2008–2014).

tending more toward the delineation of an overarching divine causality of providence and predestination, with predestination understood by implication as *pars providentiae*. In Zwingli's formulations, God eternally determines all things and in so doing wills the creation, fall, and redemption of human beings, manifesting His goodness in the work of redemption and His justice in damning those not redeemed in Christ. Election to salvation rests entirely on the divine will.[8]

Apart from some differences in terminology with various later Reformers, Bucer's approach offers the clearer antecedent than Zwingli's for the teaching of Calvin and the other second-generation Reformed writers. Bucer defined predestination in the manner of Aquinas and other medievals as a positive divine willing to chose some out of the fallen mass of humanity and save them in Christ, by grace alone apart from anything in them. He specifically ruled out foreknowledge as the basis of election. Bucer also held for an eternally willed reprobation of the nonelect, but defined this predestination or *praefinitio* as distinct from predestination of the elect—arguing, in effect, double predestination.[9] Purely from a terminological perspective, Bucer is closer to Vermigli than to Calvin.

Calvin's doctrine of predestination was briefly stated with an emphasis on election in the first edition of the *Institutes* (1536) and in the early *Catechism* (1537/38) and developed at length in connection with the second edition of his *Institutes* (1539) and his commentary on Romans (1540).[10] Shortly thereafter he engaged in a bitter controversy over the doctrine with Albertus Pighius. Pighius' *De libero hominis arbitrio et divina qratia libri decem* (1542), dedicated to Cardinal Jacopo Sadoleto, Calvin's opponent in the debate over the nature of the church,

---

8. See W. P. Stephens, *The Theology of Huldrych Zwingli* (Oxford: Clarendon, 1986), pp. 97–106; idem, "The Place of Predestination in Zwingli and Bucer," in *Zwingliana*, 19/1 (1992), pp. 393–410, here pp. 393–401.

9. See Christian Krieger, "Reflexions sur la place de la doctrine de la prédestination au sein de la théologie de Martin Bucer," in *Martin Bucer and Sixteenth Century Europe: Actes du colloque de Strasbourg (28–31 août 1991)*, ed. Christian Krieger and Marc Lienhard, 2 vols. (Leiden: Brill, 1993), vol. 1, pp. 83–99; Stephens, "Place of Predestination," pp. 402–10.

10. Note Fred H. Klooster, *Calvin's Doctrine of Predestination*, 2nd ed. (Grand Rapids: Baker, 1977); further bibliography on Calvin's doctrine of predestination is provided in chapter 3.

argued the case for a cooperation between the human will and divine grace. Calvin's response came in two parts: in the first treatise, *Defensio sanae et orthodoxae doctrinae de servitute et liberatione humani arbitrii adv. calumnias A. Pighii Campensis* (1543), Calvin addressed the issue of free choice; in the second, *De aeterna praedestinatione qua in salutem alios ex hominibus elegit, alios suo exitio reliquit: item de providentia qua res humanas gubernat, Consensus pastorum Genevensis Ecclesiae a Jo. Calvino expositus* (1552), he addressed predestination and providence.[11] As the title of the second treatise indicates, it was signed by the pastors of Geneva and is sometimes identified simply as the *Consensus Genevensis*. The *Consensus* was not received beyond Geneva and, indeed, received a strenuous rebuke for some of its language from Bullinger.

The more politically bitter controversy arose when Jérome Bolsec, a former Carmelite monk, arrived in Geneva in 1550.[12] Calvin's God, he claimed, was hypocritical and more vile than Satan. Calvin, who was present, responded directly.[13] Eventually called before the consistory, Bolsec argued that God had elected some to salvation, but reprobated no one—a view of election with some parallels to that of Bullinger. Bolsec also maintained that grace was offered equally to all people and that the reason some are saved and others damned lay entirely in the human faculty of free choice. This point, Calvin argued, was utterly inconsistent with any genuine concept of election. In all of his treatises, as in his *Institutes*, Calvin argued the divine election of some to salvation by sheer grace, apart from any inherent merit, and the divine reprobation of others to their own sinfully merited damnation. His doctrine indicates a strictly defined double decree of

---

11. See A. N. S. Lane, "The Influence upon Calvin of His Debate with Pighius," in *Auctoritas Patrum II. Neue Beiträge zur Rezeption der Kirchenväter im 15. und 16. Jahrhundert*, ed. Leif Grane, Alfred Schindler, and Markus Wriedt (Mainz: Philipp von Zabern, 1998), pp. 125–39; also G. Melles, *Albertus Pighius en zijn strijd met Calvijn over het Liberum Arbitrium* (Kampen: Kok, 1973).

12. On Bolsec, see Gary W. Jenkins, *Calvin's Tormentors: Understanding the Conflicts that Shaped the Reformer* (Grand Rapids: Baker Academic, 2018), pp. 109–24.

13. See Erik De Boer, "The 'Consensus Genevensis' Revisited: The Genesis of the Genevan Consensus on Divine Election in 1551," in *Ad Fontes: Teologiese, historiese en wetenskaps-filosofiese studies binne reformatoriese kader, Festschrift vir Ludie F. Schulze*, ed. Victor E. D'Assonville and E. A. de Boer (Bloemfontein: Redaksiekantoor van die Universiteit van die Vrystaat, 2004), pp. 51–77.

predestination, leaning toward later infralapsarian formulations, insofar as he consistently referenced predestination in relation to the issue
of the redemption of sinners,[14] but without an argument for a strict
order of decrees. Over against the understanding of human freedom
as arising apart from the divine willing that was implied by Bolsec and
Pighius, Calvin understood divine permission as a category of divine
willing allowing the human act but also directing it toward an end
intended by God.[15]

Bullinger, who had voiced reservations about Calvin's views in the
controversies with Pighius and argued for moderation in debate with
Bolsec, nonetheless taught a doctrine of predestination in accord with
the Augustinian tradition. In his early *Oratio* (1536) on providence,
predestination, grace, and free choice, Bullinger appears to argue a
doctrine of double predestination, understanding both salvation and
damnation as belonging to God's predestination. The point is less clear
in his *Decades* (1549–1551) and *Confessio et expositio simplex orthodoxae
fidei*, or Second Helvetic Confession (1566), where predestination is
synonymous with election, reprobation is identified as a distinct divine
willing, and the damnation of the unfaithful as resting on their own
sinfulness rather than on a positive will of God, although in all cases,
Bullinger assumes a divine will to reprobate and damn as well as a
divine will to elect and save. The *Oratio* is significant for its rather traditional association of predestination with providence, for its pointed
condemnation of Pelagianism, and for its denial of any absolute necessity that would lead to the conclusion that God is the author of sin.[16]

---

14. Cf. John Calvin, *Institutes of the Christian Religion*, ed. John T. McNeill, trans.
Ford Lewis Battles, 2 vols. (Philadelphia: Westminster, 1960), II.xii.5, n5, where
McNeill declares Calvin to be tending in a supralapsarian direction, when Calvin's
text indicates that the eternal decree of election rests on the divine will "to heal the
misery of mankind."

15. Cf. Richard A. Muller, "Calvin and the Problem of Divine Will, Permission, and Contingency," in *Understanding the Divine in Early Modern Reformed Theology*
(Grand Rapids: Reformation Heritage Books, forthcoming).

16. Cornelis P. Venema, *Heinrich Bullinger and the Doctrine of Predestination:
Author of "the Other Reformed Tradition"?* (Grand Rapids: Baker Academic, 2002);
idem, "Heinrich Bullinger's Correspondence on Calvin's Doctrine of Predestination,
1551–1553," in *Sixteenth Century Journal*, 17/4 (1986), pp. 435–50; and W. P. Stephens,
The Theology of Heinrich Bullinger, ed. Jim West and Joe Mock (Göttingen: Vandenhoeck & Ruprecht, 2019), pp. 161–92.

Musculus, like Bullinger, counseled caution in the debate with Bolsec, although he was not opposed to a double decree of election and reprobation. In the definition of election in his *Loci communes* (1560), Musculus identified two related elective wills of God, one concerning the salvation of human beings, the other, God's choice of Israel as the bearer of the promise. The former concept refers strictly to the doctrine of predestination; the latter points toward Musculus's interest in covenant. Musculus indicates that all things predestinated by God are also foreknown, while not all things within the divine foreknowledge are predestined: God foreknows evil but does not cause it directly. Musculus drew on the notion of divine permission to argue that all humanity falls justly under the wrath of God and that the election of some to salvation and the reprobation of others to damnation belongs solely to the mercy and justice of God. Like Calvin and Bullinger, Musculus also grounded election fully in Christ who is both the eternal, creative Word of God and the Mediator of salvation. For Musculus, this christological ground of election connected God's original creative purpose with His ultimate redemptive purpose, the restoration of human beings in the image and likeness of God.[17]

Yet another significant voice in the framing of the Reformed doctrine was Peter Martyr Vermigli, whose *Loci communes* (1576) were gathered and published posthumously. The doctrine of predestination found in the *Loci communes* was drawn from Vermigli's commentary on Romans (1558) in which he set a doctrinal *locus* on predestination immediately following the exposition of Romans 9. There is also a shorter exposition of providence and predestination added in an appendix to the 1583 printing of the *Loci communes*. There is little evidence of influence on Vermigli from an earlier Reformer like Bucer, and no indication of any influence of Calvin on Vermigli. In view of his scholastic training, Vermigli's work provides a clearer index than the writings of other Reformed thinkers of his generation to the continuous lines of argument from the Middle Ages into the Reformation and from the Reformation into the era of orthodoxy—with

---

17. Note Jordan J. Ballor, *Covenant, Causality, and Law: A Study in the Theology of Wolfgang Musculus* (Göttingen: Vandenhoeck & Ruprecht, 2012); also Robert B. Ives, "The Theology of Wolfgang Musculus (1497–1562)" (PhD diss., University of Manchester, 1965).

the greatest influence deriving from the Thomist tradition.[18] Against Pighius, Vermigli argued that although God eternally understands and wills without past and without future, creatures are temporal and experience, in their own temporal order, a real foreordination. Even so, Scripture teaches a predestination that divides the elect from the non-elect prior to the foundation of the world. Although Vermigli includes all sins in the divine decree permissively and assumes that the wicked are formed by God as "vessels of wrath," he nonetheless argues that the positive act of predestination or election refers to the salvation of fallen human beings. Reprobation is a passing over of the fallen in their sin that is not, properly understood, "predestination." Vermigli echoes his contemporaries in arguing that election is to be understood in Christ, but somewhat more clearly indicates that the incarnation and crucifixion rest on the divine counsel and are to be understood, together with the salvation of believers in Christ, as effects of the decree. Arguably, given the detail and the scholastic clarity of his argumentation, Vermigli's influence on the later Reformed tradition was as great, perhaps greater, than Calvin's.

Predestination in the Era of Early Scholastic Protestantism

From a confessional perspective, the great difference between the Lutheran and the Reformed churches of the late sixteenth and early seventeenth centuries lies in the contrast between the Lutheran movement through bitter controversy toward confessional synthesis in the Formula of Concord (1577–1579) and the Reformed development of a large-scale confessional synthesis before the rise of internecine controversy on a large scale. Many Reformed theologians of the sixteenth century had, of course, debated key issues like the doctrine of predestination with a variety of adversaries, and there were differences over the definition of predestination among the various Reformed teachers.[19]

---

18. See David S. Sytsma, "Vermigli Replicating Aquinas: An Overlooked Continuity in the Doctrine of Predestination," in *Reformation & Renaissance Review*, 20/2 (2018), pp. 155–67; and Frank A. James III, *Peter Martyr Vermigli and Predestination: The Augustinian Inheritance of an Italian Reformer* (New York: Oxford University Press, 1998); also note John Patrick Donnelly, "Calvinist Thomism," in *Viator*, 7 (1976), pp. 441–55.

19. See Pieter Rouwendal, "The Doctrine of Predestination in Reformed

Theodore Beza, Calvin's successor in Geneva, is typically regarded as a major influence in the development of the Calvinist doctrine of predestination.[20] Nonetheless, the document usually identified as the basis of Beza's "predestinarian system," the *Tabula praedestinationis* (1555), neither constitutes a full theological system nor indicates the relationship between the doctrine of predestination and the doctrine of God.[21] Rather, the *Tabula* contains a presentation of the homiletical and pastoral use of the doctrine of predestination and a substantive discussion of the relationship of the divine decrees to the work of Christ. This christological emphasis is found also in Beza's *Confessio christianae fidei* (1558) and *Quaestionum et responsionum christianarum libellus* (1570), and even the *Ad sycophantarum* (1558), written in support of Calvin against Sebastian Castellio, offers a moderate, not particularly speculative presentation of the doctrine. Like Calvin, Beza maintains that no doctrine contained in Scripture should be hidden away—even the seemingly harsh doctrine of reprobation should be preached if only to teach the elect humility. He insists that the number and identity of the elect and reprobate cannot be a subject of speculation: believers must look to the testimony of Scripture that those who have been predestinated from eternity will be effectually called and, in God's own time, be justified, sanctified, and glorified through the grace of God in Christ. Although the elect are no more worthy of salvation than the reprobate, and the divine will is the sole reason for both election and reprobation, the human will remains the immediate cause of sin and the basis for damnation.

Orthodoxy," in Selderhuis, *Companion to Reformed Orthodoxy*, pp. 553–90; and idem, *Predestination and Preaching in Genevan Theology from Calvin to Pictet* (PhD diss., Vrije Universiteit Amsterdam, 2017).

20. John S. Bray, *Theodore Beza's Doctrine of Predestination* (Nieuwkoop: DeGraaf, 1975); and note the critique of Bray in Raymond A. Blacketer, "The Man in the Black Hat: Theodore Beza and the Reorientation of Early Reformed Historiography," in *Church and School in Early Modern Protestantism: Studies in Honor of Richard A. Muller on the Maturation of a Theological Tradition*, ed. Jordan J. Ballor, David S. Sytsma, and Jason Zuidema (Leiden: Brill, 2013), pp. 227–42, here pp. 232–40.

21. Richard A. Muller, "The Use and Abuse of a Document: Beza's *Tabula Praedestinationis*, the Bolsec Controversy, and the Origins of Reformed Orthodoxy," in Trueman and Clark, *Protestant Scholasticism*, pp. 33–61.

Although his views are somewhat more patterned, more strictly defined, and more indicative of the direction of later supralapsarianism than Calvin's, Beza did not argue an "order of the decree" or "decrees" in the manner of later supralapsarianism. He did, however, identify the divine decree as the highest cause above all other causes, and insisted that God's will to reveal His glory in mercy and judgment preceded His resolution to create human beings, and Beza interpreted the metaphor of humanity as a lump of clay (Rom. 9:21) as referring to the human race as to be created.[22] In his *Catechismus compendarius* (1575) Beza also linked knowledge of election to temporal effects of the decree, arguing the so-called practical syllogism, but he remained for the most part concerned to ground election and assurance in the work of Christ. Beza disappoints those who expect a strong association of the doctrine of predestination with a speculative doctrine of God and with the creation of a deductive, predestinarian system of theology. Since the identity of the elect and reprobate is hidden in God, Beza examines primarily not the decree but its effects, not the absolute will of God but the working out of election in the world. Beza does argue a full, double decree of election and reprobation, but he lessens the strict causal sequence of the decree by introducing a category of divine permission or permissive willing to deal with the problem of the fall, as had Musculus and Vermigli in the previous generation. Beza also insists that damnation justly results from human wickedness and from the obstinate refusal to accept the blessings of Christ.

More than Beza, the Reformed theologians of Heidelberg, Zacharias Ursinus and Girolamo Zanchi, were responsible for the transition from the Reformation to early orthodoxy and the development of the Reformed doctrine of predestination in the late sixteenth century. Both followed the infralapsarian tendency of definition, identifying

---

22. See Richard A. Muller, *A Dictionary of Latin and Greek Theological Terms: Drawn Principally from Protestant Scholastic Theology*, 2nd ed. (Grand Rapids: Baker Academic, 2017), s.v. "supra lapsum"; Raymond A. Blacketer, "'Meerly a Poynt of Logick': The Order of the Decree in the Early Reformed Tradition," in *Chosen Not for Good in Me: Unconditional Election in Historical, Biblical, Theological, and Pastoral Perspective*, ed. David Gibson and Jonathan Gibson (Wheaton, Ill.: Crossway, forthcoming); and Rouwendal, "Doctrine of Predestination," pp. 554–56, 590; also note my essay, "Inclusive Supralapsarianism," chapter 4 in this volume.

the act of election as an eternal act directed toward the salvation of fallen human beings in Christ, as generally reflected in the Reformed confessions, but without arguing an ordering of divine priorities in the decree.[23] Zanchi's Strasbourg controversy with Johannes Marbach, which occurred before his appointment to Heidelberg, provides both the outline of his views and an insight into the disagreement between Lutherans and the Reformed.[24] In 1561 Marbach began to inquire into Zanchi's doctrine, finding that Zanchi stressed the indefectibility of faith as a result of election. Although Zanchi's doctrine of predestination defined the elect as drawn out of the fallen mass of mankind, pointing toward the infralapsarian definitions of the later Reformed, Marbach found even this offensive because it was formulated in an *a priori* and not an *a posteriori* order and because it undermined the declaration of universal grace. Nor would Marbach allow a doctrine of perseverance: the elect, he insisted, could fall from faith.

Marbach accused Zanchi of teaching contrary to the Augsburg Confession. Zanchi countered by arguing that his views accorded with those of Luther, Augustine, and Bucer and proved the point in his *De praedestinatione sanctorum* (1561) with explicit citation, under each thesis, of Luther, Augustine, and Bucer. Marbach was not impressed and insisted that Zanchi had violated the confessional standard of the city not only in his doctrines of predestination and perseverance but also in his opposition to a doctrine of ubiquity. Argument had gone on for nearly two years when the debate was submitted for adjudication to the theologians of Marburg, Heidelberg, Zurich, Basel, Tübingen, and Saxony. The result of this consultation was mixed: Marburg, Heidelberg, and Zurich favored Zanchi; the Saxons divided on the issue, with the Melanchthonians opposing Marbach's ubiquitarianism and Zanchi's predestinarianism; Brenz at Tübingen held precisely opposite

---

23. Otto Gründler, "Thomism and Calvinism in the Theology of Girolamo Zanchi (1516–1590)" (ThD diss., Princeton Theological Seminary, 1961). Gründler mistakes Zanchi as a supralapsarian and has a negative view of Aristotle and Aquinas, but otherwise this remains a useful study of Zanchi.

24. See Christopher Burchill, "Calvin and the Strasbourg Controversy over Predestination, 1561–1563," in *Calvinus Servus Christi. Die Referate des Internationalen Kongresses für Calvinforschung vom 25 bis 28 August 1986 in Debrecen*, ed. Wilhelm Neuser (Budapest: Presseabteilung des Ráday-Kollegiums, 1988), pp. 165–72; and idem, "Girolamo Zanchi in Strasbourg, 1553–1563" (PhD diss., Cambridge University, 1979).

views from those of the Melanchthonians but hoped, as did the theologians of Basel, for conciliation. Finally, in 1563, Strasbourg adopted a form of agreement in which predestination was affirmed and indefectible perseverance denied. Zanchi signed the formula but expressed reservations concerning its treatment of perseverance and eventually left Strasbourg for a professorship in Heidelberg.

Ursinus' posthumous *Doctrinae christianae compendium* (1584), an edited transcript of lectures he had delivered on the Heidelberg Catechism, accepted the traditional view of predestination as a part or aspect of providence, but located the decrees under the doctrine of the church and, as is typical of the Reformed whatever the location of the doctrine, defined them primarily with regard to soteriological concerns and the constancy of the divine will. (Ursinus discussed providence in a prior location in the lectures, in connection with the creedal doctrine of creation.) His definition of predestination begins with the eternal, most righteous, and immutable counsel of God according to which human beings are to be created, permitted to fall, and then brought to redemption through Christ by grace through faith. Inasmuch as Ursinus makes no specification of precisely how the human objects of the decree are identified in this order, the doctrine cannot be strictly identified as either infra- or supralapsarian. Those who are not chosen for this salvation are to be left in their sins and ultimately condemned to eternal death. Ursinus' doctrine then is of double predestination, with the decree defined as consisting in both election and reprobation.

The views of Ursinus and Zanchi are quite similar. Both theologians assume that the eternal counsel or decree grounds all causality, including (under divine concurrence or permission) all free and contingent acts. Since human beings are locked in sin, election rests entirely on the free mercy of God while damnation arises because of human sin. The concept of a divine permission and concurrence that supports freedom and contingency distinguishes this view from a metaphysical determinism. Election, according to Zanchi's *De praedestinatione sanctorum*, is the special predestination of God: it is God's "eternal, most wise, and immutable decree, constituted by him in eternity, by which certain men in the trap of deepest sin and death, and one with all the fallen are, according to his merciful will, rescued graciously through Christ." This infralapsarian tendency appears still more clearly in Zanchi's *De natura Dei* (1577), where he sets predestination in the context of God's larger work of creation, salvation, and judgment.

In contrast to the Reformed position, the Lutheran doctrine of predestination codified in the Formula of Concord (1580) attempted to balance the themes of salvation by grace alone and the universal divine offer of salvation by affirming a divine election or predestination to salvation only, by identifying this election as the "cause of salvation," and by arguing that damnation rests not on a divine decree but in the wickedness of the nonelect, who refuse the grace of the Holy Spirit. Believers ought not, moreover, to seek out the doctrine in the eternal counsel of God, but in the gospel and, thereby, in Christ. The Calvinist concept of a special calling of the elect and an ineffectual calling of the reprobate is explicitly condemned, and the potential paradox of a God who wills the salvation of all, elects some, but permits others to damn themselves is left unresolved by either a use of Luther's own necessitarian language or of Melanchthon's mildly synergistic formulation.

In response to the Lutheran Concord, the Reformed compiled their own *Harmonia Confessionum Fidei, Orthodoxarum et Reformatarum Ecclesiarum* (1581). The section on predestination consists of the texts of the Second Helvetic Confession (1566), First Basel Confession (1534), Gallican Confession (1559), and Belgic Confession (1561), followed by notes to the places in the Augsburg Confession and Saxon Confession that touched on the doctrine. The briefest of the sections, that taken from the First Confession of Basel, testified to the early Reformation rootage of the doctrine: "We confess that God, before he created the World, elected all those, to whom he wills to give the inheritance of eternal blessedness." Sections taken from the other confessions, notably the Second Helvetic, offer further definition and a clearly infralapsarian direction.

In 1586, representatives of the two confessionalities came together at the Colloquy of Montbéliard initially to debate the question of the Lord's Supper, but as the colloquy progressed, the topic of predestination was added.[25] The principal interlocutors were the Lutheran Jacob Andreae, one of the authors of the Concord, and the Reformed

---

25. Jill Raitt, *The Colloquy of Montbéliard: Religion and Politics in the Sixteenth Century* (New York: Oxford University Press, 1993).

Theodore Beza. From the Lutheran side, Andreae argued that the sin and fall of Adam was in no way willed by God, that there was no absolute decree of reprobation, and that no one desiring salvation could be excluded from the benefits of Christ's death. Beza in response insisted that nothing occurs outside of the will of God and that therefore in some sense God must be understood as decreeing both the fall and the reprobation of some human beings—although God is neither the author of sin nor the cause of the damnation of the reprobate. Beza also insisted that only the elect are effectively converted and only they are the beneficiaries of the efficacy of Christ's satisfaction.

Beza's affirmation of the Reformed doctrines at Montbéliard led to controversy in 1588 in Bern, where Samuel Huber, a minister in the canton, condemned Beza's teachings as out of accord with the Reformation-era *Ten Theses of Bern* (1528). Huber took issue both with the doctrine of double predestination and with the limitation of the efficacy of Christ's satisfaction and proposed a doctrine of a universal intention of God to save all people. Huber was rebuked at a conference in Bern at which Geneva, Basel, Zurich, and Schaffhausen were represented. Beza and others at the conference pointed out that nothing novel had been said at Montbéliard, specifically nothing out of conformity to the various Swiss Reformed confessions. Huber broke his ties with the Swiss Reformed and departed for Tübingen.

Once in Tübingen, he began to press against the Lutheran doctrine as not responsive enough to a scriptural understanding of universal grace and the universal promise of salvation. The Lutherans, notably Aegidius Hunnius, objected on the ground that those who reject grace and fall into unbelief are obviously excluded from salvation: election must conjoin with faith, indeed, election referred primarily to that salvation which takes place on the grounds of the foreknowledge of faith (*praevisa fides*). The universal call of the gospel is maintained by this formulation, and damnation rests firmly upon stubborn unbelief. In addition, Hunnius' formulation permits a doctrine of single predestination and a doctrine of the immutability of the divine will and intention: God wills to save those who come to faith. The will to save all on grounds of faith refers to an immutable *voluntas Dei antecedens* whereas the predestination of some on grounds of faith belongs to the *voluntas Dei consequens.*[26]

On the Reformed side, the Heidelberg theologian Jacob Kimedoncius produced perhaps the most extensive rebuttal in three works against Huber, a preliminary *Theses de universali redemptionis et gratiae per Christum* (1591) followed by a major treatise, *De redemtione generis humani libri tres* (1592), and a *Synopsis de redemtione et praedestinatione* (1593) that also attacked Johannes Brenz's doctrine of predestination.[27] Portions of William Perkins' *Armilla aurea* or *Golden Chaine* (1590) are also directed against Huber's universalism.

During the same period, debate in England over the Reformed doctrine adumbrated the problems that would lead toward Arminianism and the Synod of Dordrecht. As early as 1581 Lawrence Chaderton had criticized the synergistic view of salvation held by a Huguenot professor of theology at Cambridge, Peter Baro. Controversy began in 1595, when Baro argued in favor of a conditional decree of election. Baro's position also looked suspiciously like the theory of predestination as *ex praevisa fidei* proposed by Hunnius or, indeed, like the views of the synergistic Danish Lutheran Niels Hemmingsen—and it set forth an order of divine willing much like that proposed a decade later by Arminius.[28] He was immediately opposed by William Whitaker, the regius professor of divinity at Cambridge, who vowed "to stand for God against the Lutherans." Archbishop Whitgift, who favored Whitaker's position, called a conference of theologians and churchmen at Lambeth in November 1595. A set of nine articles, drawn up by Whitaker against Baro, was debated and modified by the conference. These Lambeth Articles are uncompromisingly predestinarian and look directly toward the Irish Articles (1615) and the Canons of

---

26. See Gottfried Adam, *Der Streit um die Prädestination im ausgehenden 16. Jahrhundert; eine Untersuchung zu den Entwürfen von Samuel Huber und Aegidius Hunnius* (Neukirchen: Neukirchener Verlag, 1970).

27. See Nam Kyu Lee, *Die Prädestinationslehre der Heidelberger Theologen 1583–1622: Georg Sohn (1551–1589), Herman Rennecherus (1550–?), Jacob Kimedoncius (1554–1596), Daniel Tossanus (1541–1602)* (Göttingen: Vandenhoeck & Ruprecht, 2009).

28. See Keith D. Stanglin, "'Arminius *Avant la Lettre*': Peter Baro, Jacob Arminius, and the Bond of Predestinarian Polemic," in *Westminster Theological Journal*, 67 (2005), pp. 51–74.

Dort (1619).[29] The Lambeth conference, moreover, viewed their articles as definitive of the doctrine of the Thirty-Nine Articles—a view which would be the source of bitter controversy in the English church after the accession of James I in 1603.

Reformed theologians of the last decade of the sixteenth century and first decades of the seventeenth contributed and responded to these debates with statements of the doctrine of predestination that were both more elaborate and more precise. Notably, although Franciscus Junius, William Perkins, Bartholomaus Keckermann, Amandus Polanus, Johannes Scharpius, Lucas Trelcatius Jr., Antonius Walaeus, Johannes Maccovius, and Franciscus Gomarus used traditional scholastic distinctions concerning the divine essence and attributes far more than the Reformers and did use these distinctions to produce a more precise detailed statement of the doctrine of predestination, they did not develop the doctrine toward philosophical determinism. Of this group of theologians, Junius, Trelcatius, Maccovius, and Gomarus were supralapsarian, the others tending toward an infralapsarian definition.

William Perkins' doctrine of predestination, found in his *Golden Chaine* (1590) and *Exposition of the Symbole* (1595), exemplifies the English Reformed view of the doctrine that is reflected in the Lambeth Articles and established a supralapsarian direction for formulation.[30] Perkins' Ramistic version of Reformed scholasticism consistently balances divine and human will, primary and secondary causality, and places emphasis on Christ's work in the believer despite his supralapsarian definition of the decree as an election and reprobation before the creation of the world. His doctrine of predestination is also significant for its supralapsarian elaboration of the divine logic of election in precise causal relation to the *ordo salutis* and for its profoundly negative impact on the thought of Arminius. The logic can be seen in Perkins'

---

29. See John William Perkins, "The 1595 Lambeth Articles and the So-called 'Calvinist Consensus,'" in *British Reformed Journal*, 46 (2007), pp. 7–19; 47 (2007), pp. 6–11.

30. See Joel R. Beeke, "William Perkins on Predestination," in Joel R. Beeke and Mark Jones, *A Puritan Theology: Doctrine for Life* (Grand Rapids: Reformation Heritage Books, 2014), pp. 119–33; also note Dewey D. Wallace Jr., *Puritans and Predestination: Grace in English Protestant Theology, 1525–1695* (Chapel Hill: University of North Carolina Press, 1982); and John V. Fesko, "William Perkins on Union with Christ and Justification," in *Mid-America Journal of Theology*, 21 (2010), pp. 21–34.

discussion of a first and second divine "act" of predestination, with the second act distinguished into several "degrees," extending from the eternal saving purpose of God, to the ordination of Christ as Mediator, to the promise of salvation in Christ, to the application of Christ's work to the elect, their salvation, and ultimate glorification.

A generally infralapsarian tendency, less interested in arguing an order in the divine decree, is evident in the thought of Amandus Polanus. According to Polanus' *Syntagma theologiae christianae* (1617), the decree of divine good pleasure (*decretum beneplaciti*) itself remains hidden in eternity and can only be known as it is revealed in the Word of God (*decretum* or *voluntas signi Dei*), in the work of Christ, and in the order of salvation. While the *decretum beneplaciti* ordains all things to their ends, it does so in such a way as to respect the freedom and contingency of secondary causes. Unlike Perkins, Polanus does not argue an ordering in the decree, and typically identified election as the removal or salvation of some human beings from the common or universal destruction.

The Arminian Controversy and the Synod of Dort

The synergistic theology against which the early Reformers reacted remained a theological option in early modern Protestantism not only among the Lutheran followers of Melanchthon and the English, but also among the Dutch Reformed, most notably in the thought of Jacob Arminius. Arminius' theological training in Leiden and Geneva was confessionally Reformed. His education was not, as often stated, so rigidly supralapsarian as to produce a massive reaction against Beza's form of orthodoxy in the young Arminius. As his *Declaratio sententiae*, or *Declaration of Sentiments*, delivered to the States of Holland in 1608 indicates, Arminius objected not only to the more speculative supralapsarian definition of the decrees associated with Beza and his successors but also to the confessional infralapsarian direction of the confessions. The supralapsarianism that he found troubling, moreover, was not so much Bezan as it was the teaching of his immediate predecessors and colleagues in the theological faculty at Leiden—Franciscus Junius, Johannes Kuchlinus, Lucas Trelcatius Jr., and Franciscus Gomarus. Arguably, it was Arminius' polemical delineation of supra- and infralapsarian orders of the decrees, in an attempt to argue against what he took to be a Reformed theology potentially in conflict with itself, that sparked not only the controversies leading to the Synod of Dort but also the intraconfessional debates among the Reformed over the order of the decrees.

Arminius' mature view argues, rather than a single eternal decree and its objects, four decrees and an order of priorities in the mind of God that rests on a distinction between an antecedent, universal will to save and a consequent, particular will directed toward believers. In the antecedent divine willing, a first eternal decree appoints Christ as the Savior of the human race in general, a second declares the divine intention to save in Christ all who repent and believe, and a third establishes the means of salvation. Then, as the expression of God's consequent will, a fourth decree, resting on divine foreknowledge of belief and perseverance, concludes the salvation of believers and the damnation of unbelievers. From the Reformed perspective, this predestination was fundamentally synergistic and rested salvation on the choice of individuals to believe, rather than solely on the grace of God.[31]

When Arminius died in 1609 his supporters and followers had acquired enough strength to continue the controversy and to see the appointment of a successor in the university, Simon Episcopius, who could carry the debate forward. Whereas Arminius left no full system of theology but only a series of theses for disputation, Episcopius produced both the *Confessio pastorum qui Remonstrantes vocantur* (1622) and a massive, though incomplete, *Institutiones theologicae* (ca. 1640). Episcopius was also instrumental in the composition of the Remonstrance issued in 1610 to express the views of his party. The Reformed side immediately produced a Contra-Remonstrance. Debate polarized and led to the national Synod of Dordecht (1618–1619), which drew delegates not only from the Netherlands but also from the Swiss cantons and cities (Geneva, Basel, Bern, Zurich), the German

---

31. On Arminius' doctrine of predestination, see Keith D. Stanglin and Thomas H. McCall, *Jacob Arminius: Theologian of Grace* (New York: Oxford University Press, 2012), pp. 106–40; on his relation to Reformed confessionality, see Richard A. Muller, "Arminius and the Reformed Tradition," in *Westminster Theological Journal*, 70 (2008), pp. 19–48.

Reformed communities (Heidelberg and Bremen), and from Britain—including the bishops of Chichester and Salisbury.[32]

The Arminian Remonstrance is the necessary starting point for understanding the work of the Synod of Dort. Article one of the Remonstrance contains a distillate of the doctrine of predestination found in Arminius' *Declaration of Sentiments*: it defines predestination as the eternal purpose of God in Christ to save those who believe and to damn those who reject the gospel and the grace of God in Christ. Here already the implication is synergistic and the will of God is viewed as contingent upon human choice. Next (article two) the Remonstrance speaks of the universality of Christ's death: Christ died for all and the limitation of the efficacy of His death arises out of the choice of some not to believe. The third article argues the necessity of grace if fallen humanity is to choose the good and come to belief. In the fourth article this insistence upon prevenient grace is drawn into relation with the synergism of the first two articles. Prevenient and subsequent assisting grace may be resisted and rejected: ultimately the work of salvation, in its efficacy and application, rests on human choice. The fifth and final article of the Remonstrance argues continuing gracious support of believers by God but refuses to decide on the issue of perseverance.[33]

It was clear from the outset that the Synod of Dort would not receive these points for debate with a hope for compromise and the ultimate incorporation of some form of Arminian theology into either the Belgic Confession or a new confessional document.[34] The Remonstrant position was inimical to the confessional stance not only of the Dutch but also of the British, German, and Swiss delegates.[35] No compromise was possible—and in this sense, the synod could only result in the condemnation of Arminianism. The Canons of Dort mark the full

---

32. See Aza Goudriaan and Fred van Lieburg, eds., *Revisiting the Synod of Dordt (1618–1619)* (Leiden: Brill, 2011); and Anthony Milton, ed., *The British Delegation and the Synod of Dort (1618–1619)* (Woodbridge, U.K.: Boydell, 2005).

33. Cf. Rouwendal, "Doctrine of Predestination," pp. 570–71.

34. See Donald W. Sinnema, "The Canons of Dordt: From Judgment on Arminianism to Confessional Standard," in Goudriaan and Lieburg, *Revisiting*, pp. 313–33.

35. Cf. W. Robert Godfrey, "Tensions within International Calvinism: The Debate on the Atonement at the Synod of Dort, 1618–1619" (PhD diss., Stanford University, 1974).

confessional codification of early Reformed orthodoxy, not as an independent systematic statement of doctrine but rather as an interpretive codicil to the Belgic Confession and the Heidelberg Catechism in which the major deviations from the Reformed confessional consensus are outlined and refuted.

The first canon, "Of Divine Predestination," takes as its point of departure the fallen condition of humanity and the punishment of eternal death that will be visited on sin. In Christ, God has manifested His saving will and His promise of salvation to believers and has also graciously called sinful mankind to repentance and belief. Only those who fail to respond to the call of God receive His wrath. The doctrine of election arises as the answer to the question of how this salvation is possible and why some are able to come to faith and others are not. Against what many of the delegates viewed as Arminian speculation, the canons insist that there is only one divine decree, which includes the entire plan of salvation in both Testaments. In a thoroughly infralapsarian fashion, the canons define election as the unchangeable divine purpose, before the foundation of the world, to choose some people for redemption in Christ and to leave the rest in their sins to their own damnation. Since election does not rest on human merit or even on divine foreknowledge of faith but only on the good pleasure of God, it is unalterable.[36]

The canon on predestination is typically identified as infralapsarian—and it does, in line with the earlier Reformed confessional documents, identify the eternally known objects of election as belonging to the fallen human race, a definition which, if taken in isolation, coincides with the decree of election as defined by most infralapsarians. But the Canons of Dort do not set forth an order of divine decrees. Or to make the point from a different vantage, the canons do not determine an explicit ordering of the decrees to be confessionally normative

---

36. Cf. Donald W. Sinnema, "The Doctrine of Election at the Synod of Dordt (1618–1619)," in *The Doctrine of Election in Reformed Perspective: Historical and Theological Investigations of the Synod of Dordt 1618–1619*, ed. Frank van der Pol (Göttingen: Vandenhoeck & Ruprecht, 2019), pp. 115–34; idem, "The Issue of Reprobation at the Synod of Dort (1618–19) in the Light of the History of This Doctrine" (PhD diss., University of St. Michael's College, 1985); with Rouwendal, "Doctrine of Predestination," pp. 571–72.

for the Reformed. It is also the case that many supralapsarians held that one of the ways in which God knows the objects of His decree is as created and fallen.

After Dort: Patterns of Formulation among the Reformed

Following the predestinarian debates of the 1590s and in the wake of the Arminian controversy, three fairly distinct patterns are discernible in Reformed argumentation concerning the order of the divine decree or decrees: the infralapsarian, supralapsarian, and hypothetical universalist, each subject to variation in formulation. In each of these approaches, moreover, the underlying assumption of divine eternity and simplicity led to declarations that although the divine decree is and must be one, a nontemporal logical or "natural" ordering of priorities could be discerned, both from the explicit declarations of Scripture and by conclusions drawn from the temporal ordering of the work of salvation to yield an ordering of priorities that could be identified, from the human perspective, as subordinate decrees or as "degrees" belonging to the single decree of predestination. The three patterns of definition arose from different understandings of how to present that order.

The infralapsarian order of the decree takes confessional statements, like that of the Belgic Confession and, later, the Canons of Dort, that God's eternal election mercifully delivers some of the fallen human race and justly leaves the rest in their fallen state to their eventual damnation, as determinative of the definition of the objects of God's eternal willing. The position is characteristic of such writers as Polanus, Du Moulin, Wollebius, Wendelin, and Turretin—with Du Moulin and Turretin arguing its case not only aginst the Remonstrants but also, rather pointedly, against the supralapsarians. The infralapsarian assumption yields an eternal, nontemporal, logical order of divine willing according to which the will or decree to create the world and human beings precedes the decree to permit the fall, and the latter is followed by the decree to elect some of fallen humanity to salvation in Christ and eternal life and to reprobate or set aside the others to their damnation on account of sin. The majority of infralapsarians identify the object of the decree of predestination as humanity created and fallen (*creatus et lapsus*). Some others identify the object of the decree as humanity in the fall (*in lapsu*). On the assumption that predestination is a part of providence, two providential decrees—to create human beings and to permit the fall—precede the predestinarian decrees to elect some of the fallen human race and reprobate others, to send Christ as the Mediator and Savior of the elect, and finally, by means of the gospel and the work of the Holy Spirit, to call, justify, sanctify, and glorify the elect.

The supralapsarian order accepts the confessional statements that the elect are redeemed out of the fallen mass of humanity, but given the eternity and omniscience of God, raises the issue that the ultimate goal of God for humanity in the final salvation and glorification of the elect and the damnation of the reprobate cannot properly be understood as determined subsequent to the creation and fall of human beings. Creation, fall, and redemption must be understood as belonging to the order according to which God achieves His ends. If the argumentation for this ordering began among the Reformed with Beza and received further elaboration from Perkins and Junius, its full development and logic belongs to the thought of Gomarus, Piscator, Twisse, and Voetius in the seventeenth century. The object of divine predestination, then, is the human race, to be created and to be permitted to fall, for the end of the ultimate glory of God in demonstrating His mercy and justice. There are several ways, moreover, in which supralapsarians more specifically identify the initial object of predestination: either simply as possible humanity known eternally in the divine mind as creatable (*creabilis*); or as possible humanity known eternally in the divine mind as to be created (*condendus*); or as the mass of humanity eternally known as created but not yet fallen (*creatus sed non lapsus*). Quite a few of the more eminent theologians among the supralapsarians argue that, inasmuch as God eternally knows both all possibility according to His natural or necessary knowledge and all actuality that is to be according to His voluntary or visionary knowledge, the object of predestination must be considered as a creatable possibility, as a possibility to be created, as created but not yet fallen, and as created and fallen.[37] There is, accordingly, an order of the decree in which God wills to elect and to reprobate for His glory, then to create the world

---

37. Cf. Muller, *Dictionary*, s.v. "scientia Dei," and related definitions; and note my essay, "Inclusive Supralapsarianism," chapter 4 in this volume.

and humanity, to permit the fall, to redeem some in Christ, and mercifully to bring the redeemed to eternal salvation and glory while justly damning the reprobate for their sins.

The hypothetical universalist ordering of the decree, characteristic of the theologies of John Cameron, Moyse Amyraut, and Josue La Place, was an outgrowth of the long-standing assumption on the part of various Reformed writers that the sufficiency of Christ's satisfaction for all sin and the universal or indiscriminate call of the gospel to repentance and faith implied a hypothetical or conditional divine willingness to save all if all would believe. Such statements can be found in works of Bullinger, Ursinus, and Zanchi, albeit not directly associated with the doctrine of predestination or an ordering of the decree, and such views were present among the delegations to the Synod of Dort. The development of hypothetical universalism, understood as arguing an order of the decree, occurred following the Synod of Dort and belongs to the confessional controversies of the seventeenth-century Reformed.[38] Its chief exponents were followers of John Cameron in the French Reformed Academy of Saumur, most notably Moyse Amyraut, Paul Testard, and Claude Pajon.

Rather than rest on the distinctions in the divine knowing as Junius and various supralapsarians following his approach to the decrees, the hypothetical universalist argument was grounded in a distinction between the antecedent and consequent will or the absolute and conditioned decrees of God. It is characteristic of hypothetical universalism to distinguish the divine decrees into general and particular, absolute and conditional. There are two general decrees, one to establish Christ as the Mediator who makes satisfaction for sin and thereby also makes salvation possible for all human beings, another to call all human beings to salvation by means of the gospel. There

---

38. Cf. Muller, *Dictionary*, s.v. "universalismus hypotheticus." Note that there was also a largely English version of hypothetical universalism that maintained the older pattern of arguing a basic willingness of God that if all would believe, all would be saved: see Jonathan D. Moore, *English Hypothetical Universalism: John Preston and the Softening of Reformed Theology* (Grand Rapids: Eerdmans, 2007); Michael J. Lynch, *John Davenant's Hypothetical Universalism: A Defense of Catholic and Reformed Orthodoxy* (New York: Oxford University Press, 2021); and James I. Packer, *The Redemption and Restoration of Man in the Thought of Richard Baxter: A Study in Puritan Theology* (Vancouver: Regent College, 2003).

are also two particular decrees, one to engender faith in some human beings, and another to save those who come to faith. Of these decrees, the first three are absolute and the fourth is conditional.[39] The proponents of hypothetical universalism argued strenuously that, despite accusations of an Arminian tendency, their doctrine was in accord with the Canons of Dort, inasmuch as the elect are utterly graciously chosen from the fallen mass of humanity and only the elect are given the saving faith by which they meet the condition of salvation.

In the course of the seventeenth century, hypothetical universalism proved to be the distinct minority opinion, exonerated of charges of heresy by several French Reformed synods, subjected to ongoing polemic as tending toward Arminianism by infra- and supralapsarian Reformed writers alike, and ultimately ruled out, at least for the Swiss Reformed, in the Formula Consensus Helvetica (1675). The other two approaches to an ordering of the decrees, the infralapsarian and the supralapsarian, remained generally accepted options among the Reformed throughout the seventeenth century.

---

39. See Albert Gootjes, "John Cameron (ca. 1579–1625) and the French Universalist Tradition," in *The Theology of the French Reformed Churches: From Henri IV to the Revocation of the Edict of Nantes*, ed. Martin I. Klauber (Grand Rapids: Reformation Heritage Books, 2014), pp. 169–96; here p. 186 (Cameron's ordering), and p. 190 (La Place's ordering). Also see François Laplanche, *Orthodoxie et prédication: l'oeuvre d'Amyraut et la querelle de la grâce universelle* (Paris: Presses Universitaires de France, 1965); Brian G. Armstrong, *Calvinism and the Amyraut Heresy: Protestant Scholasticism and Humanism in Seventeenth-Century France* (Madison: University of Wisconsin Press, 1969); and Lawrence Proctor, "The Theology of Moise Amyraut Considered as a Reaction against Seventeenth-Century Calvinism" (PhD diss., University of Leeds, 1952).

CHAPTER 2

The Placement of Predestination in Reformed Theology

The Historiographical Question

The Placement of Predestination and the Assessment of Reformed Orthodoxy

It is certainly a commonplace in recent discussions of Reformed theology, and particularly, of Calvin's theology, to claim that the placement of the doctrine of predestination at different points in a theological system alters the impact of the doctrine on the system as a whole as well as the meaning of the doctrine itself. Edward Dowey commented that the location of predestination in the context of soteriology was so "essential to [Calvin's] conception" of the doctrine that "conceived in any other way, we no longer have Calvin's doctrine of election."[1] On the basis of Calvin's placement of predestination in the third book of his *Institutes*, following faith, justification, Christian freedom, and prayer, Dowey contrasts Calvin's thought with the theology of later Reformed orthodoxy, which frequently (although not exclusively) placed predestination in some relation to the doctrine of God. Thus, despite what Dowey calls Calvin's "supralapsarian" doctrine of the decrees, Calvin—in Dowey's view—assumed the soteriological context of the doctrine and unlike later Calvinists, "never [saw] the believer...as in direct connection with the precreation decrees."[2] In Brian Armstrong's view,

---

1. Edward A. Dowey, *The Knowledge of God in Calvin's Theology* (New York: Columbia University Press, 1952; 3rd ed., Grand Rapids: Eerdmans, 1994), p. 186.

2. Dowey, *Knowledge of God*, p. 186. N.B., the terms "supra-" and "infralapsarian"

Calvin's placement of the doctrine marks a "new methodology" on grounds of which Calvin most certainly "would have disapproved of the relocation of [predestination] in the doctrine of God as was done by the Protestant scholastics."[3]

Even so, the contrast between Calvin's teaching and later Reformed theology made on the basis of the placement of the doctrine of predestination is typically quite unfavorable. In Basil Hall's words, "It was Beza who reverted to the medieval scholastic device of placing predestination under the doctrines of God and providence—the position in which St. Thomas Aquinas discussed it—whereas Calvin has placed it eventually and deliberately under the doctrine of salvation. By doing so, although he was not alone in this, Beza re-opened the road to speculative determinism which Calvin had attempted to close."[4] It is worth taking a moment to note a series of problems in Hall's comment, particularly because it is simply wrong concerning placements of predestination by Aquinas and by Beza, as well as rather tendentious

---

are properly understood, in their purely doctrinal sense, as indicating the identity of the human objects of the divine decree, namely, whether God *eternally* considers the objects of his willing as *supra lapsus*, "above" the fall, i.e., not yet fallen; or as *infra lapsus*, "below" the fall, i.e., fallen. Neither view implies any temporality on God's part. The classic study of the doctrine remains Klaas Dijk, *De Strijd over Infra- en supralapsarisme in de Gereformeerde Kerken van Nederland* (Kampen: Kok, 1912); also note John V. Fesko, *Diversity within the Reformed Tradition: Supra- and Infralapsarianism in Calvin, Dort, and Westminster* (Greenville, S.C.: Reformed Academic, 2001). In the present study, the phrases "supralapsarian placement" and "infralapsarian placement" are used to indicate the formal location of the doctrine prior or subsequent to the fall in theological systems, as distinct from the supra- or infralapsarian implications of doctrinal definitions.

3. Brian G. Armstrong, *Calvinism and the Amyraut Heresy: Protestant Scholasticism and Humanism in Seventeenth-Century France* (Madison: University of Wisconsin Press, 1969), p. 162.

4. Basil Hall, "Calvin Against the Calvinists," in *John Calvin*, ed. Gervase Duffield (Appleford, U.K.: Sutton Courtenay, 1966), p. 27, citing as his proof of the point, Beza's *Summa sive descriptio et distributio causarum salutis electorum, et exitu reproborum*, from Theodore Beza, *Tractationes theologicae*, 3 vols. (Geneva: Crispinus, 1570–1582), vol. 1, pp. 170ff. See the general critique of the "Calvin against the Calvinists" approach in Richard A. Muller, *After Calvin: Studies in the Development of a Theological Tradition* (New York: Oxford University Press, 2003), pp. 63–102, et passim; and idem, *Post-Reformation Reformed Dogmatics: The Rise and Development of Reformed Orthodoxy, ca. 1520 to ca. 1725*, 2nd ed., 4 vols. (Grand Rapids: Baker Academic, 2003), I, 2.5 (A–B); 8.3 (A.1) (hereinafter cited as *PRRD*).

concerning Calvin's rationale in organizing the *Institutes*. Aquinas did discuss providence prior to predestination, as the whole to the part, arguably "under" providence, but he placed neither providence nor predestination "under" the doctrine of God. Rather, he placed both within the doctrine of God, among the divine attributes. As for Beza, in neither of his more systematic essays did he offer a similar placement: his *Confessio* juxtaposed predestination with Christology, and his *Quaestionum et responsionum* placed predestination with providence in an *a posteriori* position, echoing not Aquinas but the Calvin of the 1539–1554 *Institutes*. Hall's view of Beza's placement is the result of his misreading (echoing Heppe) of Beza's *Tabula praedestinationis* as an outline of a theological system.

Hall's concluding point is similar to Emil Brunner's view that Calvin had, rather definitively, lodged the doctrine of predestination in the context of "the Grace of God in Christ, the doctrine of Justification" while Beza placed the doctrine "at the beginning of his Dogmatics" and developed it "in connexion with the doctrine of Creation." Beza's approach, according to Brunner, "shows unmistakably that [predestination] is not derived from the Christian revelation, but from the process of speculative thought."[5] Such characterizations of the development of Reformed theology are almost commonplace.[6] Their basic thesis is that the placement of the doctrine is a virtually all-important consideration and that Theodore Beza, Calvin's successor in Geneva, was responsible for altering Calvin's biblically and soteriologically conceived placement. What is more, the thesis maintains, as evidenced by the placement of the doctrine (again based mistakenly on the *Tabula*), that Beza altered the relationship of predestination to the whole of Christian theology,

---

5. Emil Brunner, *The Christian Doctrine of God* (Philadelphia: Westminster, 1950), p. 345.

6. Cf. Peter Toon, *The Emergence of Hyper-Calvinism in English Nonconformity, 1689–1765* (London: Olive Tree, 1967), pp. 12–13; Dewey D. Wallace Jr., "Predestination," in *Encyclopedia of the Reformed Faith*, ed. Donald K. McKim (Louisville: Westminster/John Knox, 1992), p. 292, col. 1; Bruce A. Demarest, "Amyraldianism," in *Evangelical Dictionary of Theology*, ed. Walter A. Elwell (Grand Rapids: Baker, 1984), p. 41, col. 1.

indeed, was responsible for turning the whole of Reformed theology into a deductive, deterministic system resting on the decrees.[7]

Along similar lines, James Daane went so far as to claim that Calvin's placement of predestination "rescued" it from the problematic placement found in scholastic theology, namely, in the doctrine of God. This placement, moreover, in Daane's words, was associated with "the inclusion of election and reprobation as mere instances of a cosmic, wall-to-wall doctrine of predestination" that he viewed as characteristic of the older Reformed orthodoxy. Calvin's approach was soteriological, the later approach metaphysical and deterministic.[8]

This claim, with its several variants, is common enough, but there are several things about it that are quite remarkable. First, this is not a claim that appears to have surfaced before the mid-twentieth century. Nineteenth-century and early twentieth-century theologians and historians, like Alexander Schweizer, Heinrich Heppe, and Hans Emil Weber, who held that Calvinist or Reformed theology was a predestinarian system, made little or no distinction between the thought of Calvin and Beza, and certainly did not point to the issue of the placement of the doctrine as a key to understanding the implication of predestination for theology. In the view of Schweizer, predestination was a central dogma because of its fundamental function and interrelationship with other doctrines, not because of its placement in a theological system—and Beza is not described as the major interpreter of the doctrine after Calvin.[9] Heppe, who took Beza's *Tabula praedestinationis* to be emblematic of a predestinarian system, understood it to be in continuity with the teachings of Calvin.[10] Weber argued that

---

7. Charles S. McCoy, "Johannes Cocceius: Federal Theologian," in *Scottish Journal of Theology*, 16 (1963), p. 366; Basil Hall, "Calvin Against the Calvinists," p. 27.

8. James Daane, *The Freedom of God: A Study of Election and Pulpit* (Grand Rapids: Eerdmans, 1973), p. 38; cf. ibid, pp. 39, 42–43, 53–54, 60, et passim.

9. Alexander Schweizer, *Die protestantischen Centraldogmen in ihrer Entwicklung innerhalb der reformierten Kirche*, 2 vols. (Zurich: Orell, Füssli, 1854–56), vol. 1, pp. 5, 10–14, 367–72, 503–5; vol. 2, p. 44.

10. Thus, Heinrich Heppe, "Der Charakter der deutsch-reformirten Kirche und das Verhältniss derselben zum Luthertum und zum Calvinismus," in *Theologische Studien und Kritiken*, 1850 (Heft 3), pp. 671–72. See also the alternative readings of Beza in John S. Bray, *Theodore Beza's Doctrine of Predestination* (Nieuwkoop: De Graaf, 1975); and Richard A. Muller, "The Use and Abuse of a Document: Beza's *Tabula*

Calvin's doctrine was the source of the predestinarian metaphysic of "Calvinist scholasticism," indeed, of what he took to be the rationalistic tendencies of Reformed scholastic theology.[11]

The same assumption concerning order and placement, with a different understanding of the function of predestination in Reformed theology, is found in Bavinck's *Gereformeerde Dogmatiek* at the beginning of the twentieth century: Bavinck indicated that the order of the doctrine, whether *a priori* or *a posteriori* "in itself is not principial." Although, moreover, the *a priori* model had been frequently used by the Reformed orthodox, it was not to be taken as indicating a speculative doctrine of the decrees or deterministic view of God, but only as identifying the Reformed doctrine as not merely anthropological and soteriological, but primarily theological in significance. Underlying this theological understanding of the decree as ultimately to the glory of God, Bavinck recognized also a fundamentally religious motive, not a philosophical or metaphysical one.[12]

Nor, indeed, was such a conclusion about placement of the doctrine drawn in the era of Reformed orthodoxy: the Reformed thinkers saw little difference between Calvin and Beza on the point—and Arminius (in marked contrast to modern discussion) viewed Beza and Calvin as two ugly peas out of the same pod.[13] Attention to placement

---

praedestinationis, the Bolsec Controversy, and the Origins of Reformed Orthodoxy," in *Protestant Scholasticism: Essays in Reassessment*, ed. Carl R. Trueman and R. Scott Clark (Carlisle, U.K.: Paternoster, 1999), pp. 33–61.

11. Hans Emil Weber, *Reformation, Orthodoxie und Rationalismus*, 2 vols. in 3 (Gütersloh: C. Bertelsmann, 1937–1951; repr., Darmstadt: Wissenschaftliche Buchgesellschaft, 1966), I/1, pp. 240–48; cf. I/2, pp. 80–93. See the discussion of the problematic nature of Weber's thesis in general in Muller, *PRRD*, I, 2.6 (B.1–2).

12. Herman Bavinck, *Gereformeerde Dogmatiek*, 4th ed., 4 vols. (Kampen: Kok, 1928), vol. 2, pp. 321–22; cf. idem, *Reformed Dogmatics*, ed. John Bolt, trans. John Vriend, 4 vols. (Grand Rapids: Baker Academic, 2003–2008), vol. 2, pp. 360–61.

13. Cf. Jacobus Arminius, *Amica cum Francisco Iunio de praedestinatione per literas habita collatio*, translated as *Friendly Conference of James Arminius…with Mr. Francis Junius about Predestination*, in *The Works of James Arminius*, trans. James Nichols and William Nichols, 3 vols. (London, 1825, 1828, 1875; repr., Grand Rapids: Baker, 1986), vol. 3, pp. 27, 28, 32–33, 76–77, 214. This datum, by the way, ought to be profoundly embarrassing to R. T. Kendall's thesis, inasmuch as it depends for its success both on the validity of Arminius' theological perceptions and on Kendall's own assumption of the rift between Calvin and Beza; see R. T. Kendall, *Calvin and English Calvinism to 1649* (Oxford: Oxford University Press, 1979), pp. 13–17, 19, 31–32,

of the doctrine is characteristic of the twentieth-century writers who have tended to make a major distinction between the thought of Calvin and the thought of Beza. In other words, structure as indicative of meaning is far more a twentieth-century issue than a problem noted in previous eras.

Second, perhaps even more remarkable than the former issue, the claim, as stated by quite a number of twentieth-century writers (e.g., Brunner, Charles McCoy, J. B. Torrance, Armstrong, and Alister McGrath), is advanced as though it were simply obvious to all.[14] Given the absence of cogent argument and documentation of the point, this view of Calvin's and Beza's relationship to the later ordering of doctrine is open to question—as, indeed, is this understanding of the placement of predestination in the theology of Reformed orthodoxy in general. Neither the rift between Calvin and Beza nor the theological significance of differing placements of the doctrine of predestination were perceptions held either by the seventeenth-century Reformed orthodox or by Arminius—nor, indeed, were these perceptions held by the nineteenth-century proponents of the central dogma theory. Third, the historical context—notably, the rise of the late Renaissance models of education, the limitations placed on the use of reason in theology, the identification of the *principia* of theology and fundamental articles of the faith as other than the decrees or predestination, the use of the *locus* method with its exegetical basis, and the underlying concern for forms of pedagogy that belonged to the era—points in a rather different

---

34, 62. Also see idem, "The Puritan Modification of Calvin's Theology," in *John Calvin: His Influence in the Western World*, ed. W. Stanford Reid (Grand Rapids: Zondervan, 1982), pp. 197–214, for a shorter version of Kendall's thesis.

14. See Brunner, *Christian Doctrine of God*, p. 345; McCoy, "Johannes Cocceius," pp. 354, 364–69; James B. Torrance, "Strengths and Weaknesses of the Westminster Theology," in *The Westminster Confession in the Church Today*, ed. Alasdair Heron (Edinburgh: Saint Andrew, 1982), pp. 40–53; idem, "Calvin and Puritanism in England and Scotland—Some Basic Concepts in the Development of 'Federal Theology,'" in *Calvinus Reformator* (Potchefstroom: Potchefstroom University for Christian Higher Education, 1982), pp. 264–77; Armstrong, *Calvinism and the Amyraut Heresy*, pp. 31–40; Alister E. McGrath, *Reformation Thought: An Introduction*, 4th ed. (Chichester: Wiley-Blackwell, 2012), pp. 199–200; Charles Partee, *The Theology of John Calvin* (Louisville: Westminster John Knox, 2008), pp. 243–44.

direction than the modern dogmatic explanation.[15] And finally, as we will argue below, when one tries to establish the claim by examining actual documents, it simply evaporates.

Karl Barth's Examination of the Location of Predestination
The idea that the placement of the doctrine of predestination within a theological system has massive implications for the meaning of the doctrine and the logic of the system itself has a history—significantly, a history that begins after the close of the era of orthodoxy. Tracing out the origins and development of that contention is beyond the bounds of the present study. Nonetheless, it is fairly obvious that the discussion of the various placements of predestination as having an influence on the meaning of the doctrine was not part of debates of the early modern era. It did not matter to the Reformed theologians of that time where Arminians or Lutherans placed the doctrine in their theologies; rather, the issue concerned how they defined the doctrine. Nor was it part of the Arminian or Lutheran polemic against the Reformed that Reformed writers located the doctrine in relation to the doctrine of God or placed it elsewhere in their theologies. Rather, this kind of critique is characteristic of those modern writers who have argued shifts in the systematic implications of the doctrine in the early modern era and who have attempted to argue the rise of a predestinarian central dogma in the era of orthodoxy. In the midst of this modern, largely nineteenth- and twentieth-century critique, the argumentation offered by Karl Barth has had an enormous influence—inasmuch as Barth identified some six placements of the doctrine in relation to the other *loci* of theological system, each placement having its own theological significance.

Barth's own comments on the significance of the placement of the doctrine must be juxtaposed with his denial that Beza and other later Calvinists ever constructed a predestinarian system.[16] It is in fact one of the more interesting ironies of twentieth-century theological historiography that Barth, whose insistence on the centrality of Christ to

---

15. Cf. Muller, *PRRD*, I, 9.1 (A–B); II, 7.5; also note Muller, *After Calvin*, pp. 105–21.

16. Karl Barth, *Church Dogmatics*, ed. G. W. Bromiley and T. F. Torrance, 4 vols. (Edinburgh: T&T Clark, 1956–1975), II/2, pp. 78–79 (hereinafter cited as *CD*).

the understanding and formulation of all Christian doctrine (including the doctrine of predestination) played such a large role in the reinterpretation of the theology of the Reformers as "Christocentric," did not accept these generalizations about the placement of predestination and the role of Beza in the development of Reformed orthodoxy. Thus, in his excursus on the first of the six placements of predestination—namely, the placement of predestination after the doctrine of God and prior to the doctrine of creation—Barth notes that this is the more typical arrangement of the order of doctrines in Reformed orthodox dogmatics. Barth indicates that this is the pattern of the *Irish Articles of Religion* (1615) and of the *Westminster Confession* (1647), and it is found in the theological systems of Polanus, Wollebius, Wendelin, Heinrich Alting, Heidanus, Burman, Turretin, Mastricht, and van Til.[17] It is also the pattern followed in some catechetical works of the era of orthodoxy[18] and in various major theological systems not noted by Barth.[19]

This apparently majority pattern is the basis for the "modern" claim that predestination is the "central dogma" of Reformed theology. To the contrary, however, Barth declares that

---

17. Barth, *CD*, II/2, p. 77.

18. Thus, e.g., Thomas Cartwright, *Christian Religion, Substantially, Methodicallie, Plainlie, and Profitablie Treatised* (London: Felix Kingston, 1611), p. 16; Samuel Crook, *The guide unto true blessednesse* (London: John Pindley, 1613), pp. 10–11; John Boughton, *God and man. Or, a treatise catechisticall wherein the saving knowledge of God and man is plainely, and breifely declared* (London: Samuel Man, 1623), pp. 25–31; John Ball, *A Short Treatise: Contayning all the Principall Grounds of Christian Religion* (London: William Welby, 1629), pp. 56–58; Richard Mather, *A catechisme, or, The grounds and principles of Christian religion set forth by way of question and answer* (London: John Rothwell, n.d.), pp. 16–17.

19. Thus, e.g., Lucas Trelcatius Jr., *Scholastica et methodica locorum communium s. theologiae institutio, didactice & elenctice in epitome explicata: in qua, veritas locorum communium, definitionis cuiusque, loci per causas suas analysi asseritur: contraria vero argumenta, imprimis Bellarmini, generalium solutionum appendice refutantur* (London: John Bill, 1604), lib. II; Johannes Hoornbeeck, *Institutiones theologicae ex optimis auctoribus concinnatae* (Leiden: Franciscus Moyardus, 1658), § iv; Johannes Braunius, *Doctrina foederum, sive systema theologiae didacticae & elencticae; perspicua atque facile methodo*, 2nd ed. (Amsterdam: Abraham van Somern, 1691), I/II.ix (pp. 144–59); Johann Heinrich Heidegger, *Corpus theologiae christianae…adeoque sit plenissimum theologiae didacticae, elenchticae, moralis et historicae systema*, 2 vols. (Zurich: David Gessner, 1700), locus v; Eberhard Heinrich Stosch, *Institutiones theologiae dogmaticae in usum praelectionum suarum conscripsit* (Frankfurt: Carolus Gottlieb Strauss, 1779), I.iii.

there can be no historical justification for taking the concept of "central dogma" to mean that the doctrine of predestination was for the older Reformed theologians a kind of speculative key—a basic tenet from which they could deduce all other dogmas. Not even the famous schema of T. Beza was intended in such a sense. Its aim was rather (rightly or wrongly) to show the systematic interconnection of all other dogmas with that of predestination in the then popular graphic fashion. There was no question of making the latter doctrine a derivative principle for all the rest.[20]

Not only does Barth deny the central dogma thesis of Schweizer and Heppe, he goes the extra mile of concluding that "if we read [the Reformed scholastics'] expositions connectedly we are more likely to get the impression that, from the standpoint of its systematic range and importance, they gave to the doctrine too little consideration rather than too much."[21] The difference between his own theology and that of the older orthodoxy on this particular point, Barth notes, is that "with these theologians, so far as I can see, the doctrine of election was never regarded or treated as an integral part of the doctrine of God,"[22] but, instead, discussed following the *locus de Deo*. (Of course, as we will note below, there was a tradition of including predestination as an integral part of the *locus de Deo*—evident in Alexander of Hales, Thomas Aquinas, and in the early modern era, several of the Reformed.)

Barth does have an objection, however, to this formulation—and a reason not to follow it precisely in his own theology. The problem is that it begins with the notion of a general decree that establishes God's relationship with the world and then subsumes under it a special decree of God's election in which the relationship of humanity to Jesus Christ is established. Barth would reverse the order and understand the general relationship of God to the world in the light of the special relationship founded in Christ. And he laments what he believes to be the omission of any significant consideration on the part of the older orthodoxy of the *ad intra* activity of the Trinity according to which election may be understood as belonging to the "concrete

---

20. Barth, *CD*, II/2, pp. 77–78.
21. Barth, *CD*, II/2, p. 78.
22. Barth, *CD*, II/2, pp. 78–79.

life of the very being of God."[23] It is interesting that Barth objects not only to the *a posteriori* model followed by most of the Reformed confessions, but also to the *a priori* pattern followed by the majority of the Reformed dogmaticians, on the ground that it is not, so to speak, "high" enough, and he would replace it with his own form of christologically defined supralapsarianism. In accordance with his own rejection of natural theology and, moreover, of an independent, namely, nonchristological view of creation and providence, Barth proposes a christological supralapsarianism that overrules any sense of a general decree of creation and providence prior to God's willing of redemption in Christ.

As a second model, which he views as farther from his own approach than the typical Reformed orthodox pattern, Barth notes Zwingli's *Fidei ratio* (1530) and the *Consensus Bremensis* (1595)—he has found no orthodox Reformed writers to include here, but he offers two Lutheran theologians, Leonhard Hutter and Johann Gerhard. Zwingli, at least by his ordering of the *Fidei ratio*, understands election as "the crown and completion of the doctrine of providence," all of which had been preceded and framed by an exposition of the doctrines of God, Trinity, and Christ. Gerhard similarly offers the sequence of God, Christ, providence, and predestination.[24] (What Barth does not note is that this order in Gerhard both identifies a typically Lutheran inclusion of the doctrine of Christ in the Trinitarian discussion and at the same time echoes the rather traditional understanding of predestination as *pars providentiae*.) Hutter provides a variant, according to Barth, which also points toward one of the other patterns of organization: he inserts the topics of sin, law, the gospel, and justification between creation and predestination. Barth notes how this sequence does have the effect of highlighting the relationship of predestination both to God and to creation, but he sees the model as less useful than the first inasmuch as it subsumed predestination under providence and, in his view, thereby makes "ineffective" the "precedence given to Christology."[25]

---

23. Barth, *CD*, II/2, pp. 78, 79. Note that this latter conclusion of Barth's can be disputed historically: see Richard A. Muller, *Christ and the Decree* (Grand Rapids: Baker Academic, 2008), pp. 10, 94, 113–15, 149–68, 181.

24. Barth, *CD*, II/2, p. 80.

25. Barth, *CD*, II/2, pp. 80–81.

Beyond these two arrangements of the topic, Barth noted four others, all of which have in common the fact that they discuss predestination not in relation to God or creation but much further on in the sequence of doctrines, after sin, as "in some sort the key" to the doctrine of reconciliation. The first of these placements of the doctrine that Barth notes is its location in the doctrine of the church. This approach Barth also finds in Zwingli's *Fidei ratio* and it appears in the 1536 edition of Calvin's *Institutes*—although election is also mentioned in connection with faith in the 1536 edition. Barth views this ecclesiological placement as fundamentally biblical and highly to be recommended, although he prefers a model that placed election with the electing God, prior to the identification of the elect people.[26] Barth does not note that this placement carried over into the era of orthodoxy as evidenced by Ursinus' catechetical lectures and by the later sets of lectures and sermons on the Heidelberg Catechism that maintained Ursinus' model for adding *loci* to the catechetical discussions. The ecclesiological association of the doctrine is also evident in its insertion into the argument of Zanchi's *De ecclesia* and in Daneau's *Compendium sacrae theologiae*, and in works by such authors as Perkins, Ames, Yates, Martinius, and Witsius—all of whom discuss the doctrine of election and reprobation under the topic of the church in their expositions of the creed or in catechetical models based on the creedal model,[27] despite the placement of the doctrine elsewhere in

---

26. Barth, *CD*, II/2, pp. 81–83.

27. Lambert Daneau, *Compendium sacrae theologiae seu erotemata theologica, in quibus totius verae theologiae christianae summa breviter comprehense est* (Montpellier: Giletus, 1595), V.v–vi; William Perkins, *An Exposition of the Symbole*, in *The Workes of…Mr. William Perkins*, 3 vols. (Cambridge: John Legat, 1612–1619), vol. 1; William Ames, *Christianae catecheseos sciagraphia: ubi sub s. scripturae textu apposito, singulae Dominicae catech. reformatae breviter, solide, docte & perspicue enodantur, & suis documentis, usibus, & quaestionibus illustrantur* (Franeker: Berhard Berentsma, 1635); in translation, *The Substance of Christian Religion: or, A plaine and easie Draught of the Christian Catechisme, in LII lectures, on chosen texts of Scripture, for each Lords-day of the year, Learnedly and Perspicuously Illustrated with Doctrines, Reasons, and Uses* (London: T. Mabb for Thomas Davies, 1659), pp. 143–44; John Yates, *A Modell of Divinitie, Catechetically Composed. Wherein is delivered the matter and methode of religion, according to the Creed, tenne Commandements, Lords Prayer, and the Sacraments*, 2nd ed., enlarged (London: John Legatt, 1623), pp. 257–59; Matthias Martinius, *Christiana et catholica fides: quam symbolum apostolicum vocamus, perpetuis quaestionibus & responsionibus*

the theological systems of these same authors. Indeed, this is a fairly standard placement of the doctrine in catechetical works.[28]

As a final set of three models of theology, Barth notes various placements of predestination, all of which share with his third option the removal of predestination from the doctrine of God but which also relate the doctrine to soteriology, or as he calls it in his somewhat Ritschlian fashion, the doctrine of reconciliation. The first of these (the fourth in the full series) places predestination immediately following Christology, which Barth identifies as the pattern in Calvin's 1537 catechism, the *Loci communes* of Peter Martyr Vermigli, and the *De oeconomia foederum* of Herman Witsius.[29] Barth does not mention Beza's *Confessio*, which incorporated predestination into its christological *locus*. (In the case of Vermigli's *Loci*, this can be regarded as a rationalization or clarification of Calvin's 1559 outline by Vermigli's editor, Robert Masson, setting predestination at the head of an *ordo salutis*. Witsius, too, in his *De oeconomia foederum* regards

---

diligenter explicata & in III libros distincta (Bremen: Thomas Villeranus, 1618), III.2 (pp. 579–87); Herman Witsius, *Exercitationes sacrae in symbolum quod Apostolorum dicitur. Et in Orationem dominicam*, 3rd ed. (Amsterdam: Joannem Wolters, 1697); in translation, *Sacred Dissertations on what is commonly called the Apostles' Creed*, trans. D. Fraser, 2 vols. (Edinburgh: A. Fullarton; Glasgow: Kull, Blackie, 1823).

28. Note the works of Edward Dering, *A briefe & necessary instruction verye needfull to be knowen of all householders* (London: J. Awdlwy, 1572), fol. Ci verso–Cii recto; William Wood, *A fourme of cathechising in true religion consisting in questions and answers with observations thereon* (London: Thomas Dawson, 1581), p. 82r; William Horne, *A Christian exercise, containing an easie entrance into the principles of religion and the chiefest points of our salvation in Christe* (London: Robert Waldegrave, 1585), fol. C3r; and William Hill, *The first principles of a Christian* (London: Edward Griffin, 1616), fol. B3r; and see the discussion of the arrangement of the doctrine in English catechisms in Ian Green, *The Christian's ABC: Catechisms and Catechizing in England, c. 1530–1740* (Oxford: Clarendon, 1996); and David Kranendonk, *Teaching Predestination: Elnathan Parr and Pastoral Ministry in Early Stuart England* (Grand Rapids: Reformation Heritage Books, 2011).

29. Barth, *CD*, II/2, pp. 84; cf. Peter Martyr Vermigli, *P. M. Vermilii loci communes* (London: Ioannes Kyngston, 1576; 2nd ed. (much augmented), London: Thomas Vautrollerius, 1583); in translation, *The Common Places of Peter Martyr*, trans. Anthonie Marten (London: s.n., 1583); Herman Witsius, *De oeconomia foederum Dei cum hominibus libri quattuor* (Leeuwarden: Jacob Hagenaar, 1685; Utrecht: F. Halmam and G. vande Water, 1694); in translation, *The Oeconomy of the Covenants between God and Man. Comprehending a Complete Body of Divinity*, 3 vols. (London: Edward and Charles Dilly, 1763; 2nd ed., 1775).

predestination as the anchor of the *ordo*, although what preceded the exposition was not in any way the equivalent of the typical order of a seventeenth-century body of doctrine. This is not, moreover, the only arrangement that Witsius followed.) Barth indicates that he knew of no other instances of this order of doctrine—but there is, after all, Ames' *Medulla* or *Marrow*,[30] and there is the catechetical model of Thomas Wilson, which places predestination in relation to faith.[31]

Next (fifth in the series), there is the option of placing predestination following the doctrine of sin and prior to Christology. This approach, Barth indicates, is common among the Reformed confessions—the Gallican (1559), Scots (1560), Belgic (1561), the Second Helvetic (1566), the Staffort Book (1599), and the Waldensian Confession (1655). He also places the Leiden *Synopsis purioris theologiae* and Cocceius' *Summa theologiae* in this group, and Walaeus as well, despite what Barth identifies as a "highly original and capricious" arrangement of topics. As will be noted later, Barth's comments on Cocceius and the Leiden *Synopsis* are less than accurate.

Finally (third in the subset and sixth in the full series), the doctrine of predestination can be placed at the "consummation" of the doctrine of reconciliation as "the final and decisive word." This is the placement that Calvin chose in his 1539 *Institutes* and clarified in the final edition. Barth notes this placement in the list of *loci* provided at the beginning of—but not followed by—Melanchthon's 1521 *Loci communes*, but does not recognize that this is also Melanchthon's model in the major 1543 redaction of the *Loci*. Barth also noted the model in Bucanus' *Institutiones theologicae* (1602), one of the few works of the seventeenth century to follow the model of Calvin's *Institutes*.[32] In addition to these noted by Barth, there is César Pégorier's *Exposition de la religion chrétienne* (1714) in which predestination appears, with perseverance, immediately prior to the final eschatological positions of the system.[33]

---

30. William Ames, *Medulla ss. theologiae* (Amsterdam, 1623; London: Robert Allott, 1630), I.xxv.

31. Thomas Wilson, *The Childes trade or, The beginning of the doctrine of Christ* (London: J. Bartlet, 1645), fol. A5r.

32. Barth, *CD*, II/2, pp. 84–86.

33. César Pégorier, *Exposition de la religion chrétienne en forme d'entretiens, ou' l'on*

Taken as a group, Barth argues, these last three approaches understand "election as the divine reality which controls the particular activity of salvation between God and man," a point also made by the inclusion of the doctrine in relation to the church.[34] In support of his thesis that placement of the doctrine at the beginning, middle, or end of the doctrine of reconciliation identified election as "the final word" in matters of salvation (and that, therefore, all three placements are roughly equivalent), he notes the fact that Calvin placed the doctrine at the end of the sequence in his 1559 *Institutes* but at the beginning of the doctrine of reconciliation in the *Gallican Confession* of the same year—and had, in the 1537 catechism, opted for the middle position.

By way of conclusion, Barth argues that although each of these three latter placements has its virtues and that, taken together, all three rightly indicate that election "is the last or first or central word in the whole doctrine of reconciliation," he cannot accept this *a posteriori* placement. The doctrine of reconciliation itself is "the first or last or central word in the whole Christian confession or the whole of Christian dogma."[35] Election, therefore, must take precedence over every doctrine except Christology—it is the ultimate "divine self-determination" that frames the entirety of dogmatics, indeed, the entirety of the biblical revelation.[36] These considerations lead Barth to reject Calvin's so-called *a posteriori* or soteriological placement of the doctrine and to place predestination in close relation to the doctrine of God, much as in the Reformed orthodox systems and, indeed, as in the purported model chosen by Beza in the supposed establishment of the predestinarian system of "decretal theology."

An Assessment of the Barthian Reading of Traditional Reformed Placements of Predestination

However interesting this divergence of interpretation of basic materials between Barth and various other twentieth-century writers may be, the more important issue for us here is that of the accuracy and usefulness

---

trouvera le précis de toute la theologie, avec la saine doctrien, telle que nous l'avons reçuë de nos peres (Utrecht: s.n., 1714).

34. Barth, *CD*, II/2, p. 87.

35. Barth, *CD*, II/2, pp. 87–88.

36. Barth, *CD*, II/2, pp. 89–91.

of this structural analysis of the doctrine of predestination. As a pre-liminary critique of the idea of the placement of the doctrine having a major significance in the theological formulations of the Reformers and the orthodox, we note three points. First, for all his detail, Barth did not discover the entire paradigm for the various placements of the doctrine of predestination in sixteenth- and seventeenth-century Reformed theology. In the above summary of Barth's approach, we have already seen quite a few significant examples not identified by Barth—notably the ecclesiological association and placement of the doctrine in Zanchi, Daneau, Perkins, Martinius, Witsius, and various later commentators on the Heidelberg Catechism, from Ursinus, Alsted, and Voetius to Van der Kemp and Tuinman.[37] Voetius, it should be noted, offers an infralapsarian placement in his *Syllabus problematum theologicorum*, governed in part by an organizational distinction between the doctrine of God as creator and the doctrine of God as redeemer: predestination opens the discussion of *Deus Redemptor*. Here Voetius coupled the infralapsarian placement with a supralapsarian definition.[38] A supralapsarian definition without any indication of systematic order is found in his *Selectae disputationes*,[39] and an infralapsarian placement and an indeterminate definition in

---

37. Carolus Tuinman, *De Toevlucht en Sterkte van het ware Christendom in Leven en Sterven, aangewezen in Vyf en Vyftig Predikaatsien over den Heidelbergischen Catechismus* (Amsterdam: Adriaan Wor, 1739), in Lord's Day 21 (qq. 54–56), pp. 376–78. Bernardus Smytegelt is a bit of an exception. He does not offer a section on predestination in his *Des Christens eenige troost in leven en sterven of verklaringe van de Heidelbergschen Catechismus in LII Predicatien* (Den Haag: Ottho en Pieter van Thol, 1742; reissued, Utrecht: Den Hertog, 1981), but briefly defines election and reprobation in discussing Lord's Day 7 (qq. 20–23), namely, as the foundation of salvation given the fall of humanity in Adam (p. 92). Another variant is found in Lambertus De Ronde, *A System Containing the Principles of the Christian Religion, suitable to the Heidelberg Catechism; by plain Questions and Answers* (New York: H. Gaine, 1763), where the eternal decree is noted in the exposition of q. 26, but related to its execution in creation and providence, not to the doctrine of predestination (p. 49), with election being introduced only in the discussion of the church, q. 54 (p. 91).

38. Gisbertus Voetius, *Syllabus problematum theologicorum: quae pro re nata proponi aut perstringi solent in privatis publicisque disputationum, examinum, collationum, consultationum exercitiis*, 2 parts (Utrecht: Aegidius Romanus, 1643), part 2, fol. Hh1r.

39. Gisbertus Voetius, *Selectarum disputationum theologicarum*, 5 vols. (Utrecht: Joannes à Waesberge; Antonius Smytegelt, 1648–1669), pars V, *De selectis quibusdam problematis*, pars III, §15 (p. 602).

his *Catechisatie*.[40] Voetius also understood the two views, supra- and infralapsarian, to be confessionally compatible,[41] which surely accounts for the absence of the distinction from his catechism.

It can also be noted that Barth's paradigm does not exhaust the possibilities for placement of the doctrine of predestination and, as a result, does not cover all of the options for systematic ordering followed in the early modern era. As already noted, Beza incorporated predestination into the Christology of his *Confessio*, a variant of placements into soteriology that Barth seems to have missed. There is also what is probably a *sui generis* catechetical model adopted by John Godolphin that begins with the Trinity, presents the sacraments and prayer, then the articles of the creed and the Decalogue, and finally comes to the topics "Of Gods Love to Man, of Election, Creation, Redemption, Vocation," the rest of the order of salvation, and related issues.[42] The English catechist Edward Elton discussed the doctrine, at the very end of his exposition of doctrine, in connection with his eschatology,[43] while his contemporary John Frewen discussed predestination in relation to assurance, following his exposition of the sacraments.[44] There is also one work, John Edwards' *Theologia Reformata*, in which the

---

40. Gisbertus Voetius, *Catechesatie over den Heidelbergschen Catechismus*, ed. Abraham Kuyper, from the 1662 Poudroyen edition, 2 vols. (Rotterdam: Huge, 1891), vol. 1, pp. 544, 552 (unnumbered section following q. 54, on the church): "Wat is de verkiesinge? Het besluyt Godes, daer mede hy van alle eeuwigheyt heeft besloten sekere menschen ter saligheyt door sijn genade te brengen…. Wat is de verwerpinge? Dat besluyt Godts, daer mede Godt van alle eeuwigheyt besloten heeft sekere menschen tot de saligheyt ende genade niet te brengen, maer om hare sonden rechteerdighlick te verdoemen." N.B., Voetius does add a brief discussion of the general decree of God prior to q. 26, on creation (vol. 1, pp. 309–12), but only to note that it establishes all things, not to introduce election and reprobation.

41. Voetius, *Selectae disputationes*, pars I, *De iure et iustitia Dei* (pp. 356–57).

42. John Godolphin, *The Holy Arbor, Containing a Body of Divinity: or Sum and Substance of Christian Religion collected from many orthodox laborers in the Lords vineyard, for the benefit and delight of such as thirst after righteousness vvherein also are fully resolved the questions of whatsoever points of moment have been, or are, now controverted in divinity: together with a large and full alphabetical table of such matters as are therein contained* (London: John Field for Edmund Paxton, 1651), p. 311.

43. Edward Elton, *A forme of catechizing set downe by questions and answers* (London: Edward Griffin, 1616), fol. G7r.

44. John Frewen, *Certaine choise grounds, and principles of our Christian religion* (London: Roger Pott, 1621), pp. 317–26.

decrees are discussed first and foremost, followed by the doctrines of free choice, grace and conversion, the extent of redemption in Christ, and perseverance,[45] which are followed in a second volume by faith and justification[46]—all prior to the creedal exposition in which Edwards presents his doctrine of God and creation.[47]

Within the models that Barth notes, moreover, there are doctrinal relationships that he omits, some of which may be offered as explanations of the order taken by a particular work, a point that we will take up shortly. In addition, there are significant placements of the doctrine—notably in the list of divine attributes located in the doctrine of the essence or nature of God—that he misses entirely (yet another point to be discussed below). Nor does Barth distinguish between actual placements of a *locus* on predestination into a document and allusions to the doctrine at certain points in a theological system—as in the case of the contrast between Calvin's 1537 catechism (in which we have an actual *locus* on predestination between faith and justification)[48] and his catechisms of 1542 and following (in which we find a reference or allusion to predestination in the context of the church and another in the discussion of prayer and no topical elaboration of the doctrine whatsoever).[49]

---

45. John Edwards, *Veritas redux. Evangelical truths restored. Being the first part of the theological treatises, which are to compose a large Body of Christian divinity* (London: for Jonathan Robinson, John Lawrence, and John Wyat, 1707).

46. John Edwards, *The Doctrine of Faith and Justification Set in a True Light. In Three Parts Being the Second Part of the Theological Treatises, Which Are to Compose a Large Body of Christian Divinity* (London: for Jonathan Robinson, John Lawrence, and John Wyat, 1708).

47. John Edwards, *Theologia Reformata: or, the Body and Substance of the Christian Religion, comprised in distinct discourses or treatises upon the Apostles Creed, the Lord's Prayer, and the Ten Commandments*, 2 vols. (London: John Lawrence et al., 1713); and idem, *Theologia reformata, or, Discourses on those graces and duties which are purely evangelical: and not contained in the moral law, and on the helps, motives, and advantages of performing them, being an entire treatise in four parts, and if added to the two former volumes, makes a compleat body of divinity* (London: T. Cox, 1726).

48. John Calvin, *Le Catéchisme français de Calvin, publiée en 1537, reimprimé pour la première fois*, ed. Albert Rilliet and Théophile Dufour (Geneva: H. Georg, 1878), pp. 33–36.

49. John Calvin, *Catechism*, in *Selected Works of John Calvin: Tracts and Letters*, ed. Henry Beveridge and Jules Bonnet, 7 vols. (Grand Rapids: Baker, 1983), vol. 2, pp. 50, 76–77; and in John Calvin, *Opera quae supersunt omnia*, ed. G. Baum et al., 59 vols.

Second, it is at least of interest that in his own discussion of these different models, Barth noted some doublets: thus he discussed Zwingli's *Fidei ratio* in two places—as discussing predestination in relation to God, providence, and creation and then noting the doctrine again in the context of the church. We might add that the doctrine of election returns toward the end of the document when, after an extended discussion of the sacraments, Zwingli turns to discuss the preaching of the Word. Thus, there are three references to predestination or election in the *Fidei ratio*, and there are varied locations of both discussion and reference in Calvin's catechisms, confessions, and *Institutes* and (if we look far enough) in the works of seventeenth-century Reformed writers like Witsius. Given that the doctrine of predestination or election is similarly referenced in various places in the theological documents of the era, and is placed variously by the same theologians in different works of their own, we may question whether these different locations of the doctrine were intended to offer substantively different nuances of meaning. They may simply be the result of differing confessional or pedagogical contexts or the several traditionary relationships. Indeed, given some of the fairly standard placements of the doctrine (in large-scale scholastic or academic treatises following the doctrine of God; in catechetical works often in relation to the doctrine of the church), and given the different placements in works of differing genres written by the same theologian, the proper inference would be that placement reflects the genre of the work rather and an attempt to illuminate a particular dogmatic relationship.

Third, Barth offers no evidence that the various placements reflect anything more than the relationships with other doctrines that are inherent in the Reformed definition of predestination. Nor does he provide evidence to show that any particular placement indicates relationships other than those implied by the definition of the doctrine. Accordingly, when the doctrine is placed in relation to the doctrine of God and prior to creation, its definition in that place does not lose relationship to Christology, to the various doctrines concerned with reconciliation, or to the church. Even so, when the doctrine of

---

(Brunswick: Schwetschke, 1863–1900) (hereinafter cited as *CO*), vol. 6, col. 39–40, 95–98.

predestination is placed either following creation and providence or in the context of the *ordo salutis* or of the church, it is still concerned with an eternal decree, before the foundation of the world, according to which some human beings are chosen by God to be the elect, apart from any foreseen merit or belief. The series of associations noted by Barth as indicated by the placement of the doctrine are in fact associations inherent in the definition itself, no matter what the placement. In fact, Barth's own concluding discussion, in which he argues that the nature of the doctrine itself indicates that it is the first, the last, and the central "word" in the doctrine of reconciliation and, therefore, also in dogmatics as a whole, points in the direction of this conclusion concerning the historical materials rather than Barth's own.

The Location of the Doctrine of Predestination in Older Reformed Theologies

The Placement of Predestination by Calvin and Beza and Some of Their Contemporaries

Calvin offered his readers no explicit explanation for the placement of predestination in any of the editions of his *Institutes*. He did, however, leave us a series of clues to organization that bear directly on the question of placement of the doctrine and its significance. First, he did not raise issues like those noted by Dowey in his brief comparison of Calvin's *Institutes* with a generalized picture of later Calvinism: Dowey contrasts Calvin's *ordo cognoscendi* with a later *ordo essendi*—a cognitive or epistemological order and an essential or ontic order.[50] As far as I can tell, neither Calvin nor later Reformed theologians use such language in describing the shape or structure of their more systematic works. Calvin specifically identifies the need to establish an *ordo recte docendi*, an order of right or correct teaching.[51] His primary concern in shaping the *Institutes*—as perhaps one ought to infer from its title, namely an "Instruction in the Christian religion"—was neither

---

50. Cf. Dowey, *Knowledge of God*, pp. 218, 241.

51. John Calvin, *Institutio christianae religionis, in libros quatuor nunc primum digesta, certisque distincta capitibus, ad aptissimam methodum: aucta etiam tam magna accessione ut propemodum opus novum haberi possit* (Geneva: Robertus Stephanus, 1559), I.i.3; and note the translation, John Calvin, *Institutes of the Christian Religion*, 2 vols., ed. John T. McNeill, trans. Ford Lewis Battles (Philadelphia: Westminster, 1960).

epistemological nor ontological, but pedagogical. In other words, the primary implication of the order and placement of doctrines in the *Institutes* is not to convey a theological point other than that conveyed by the exposition of the topic itself, but rather to allow the topic to be understood in its scope and detail.

A close look at the development of Calvin's *Institutes* indicates that Calvin first added the doctrine of predestination to his work in 1539, perhaps because he was at that time completing his commentary on Romans, and predestination was one of the doctrinal *loci* that had arisen out of the work on the commentary. According to Calvin's approach to exegesis, predestination would not be included as a formal *locus* in the commentary, but instead added to his "*disputationes*" in the *Institutes*. In 1539, Calvin wrote a chapter on providence and predestination and placed it eighth in order after the chapters on faith and the creed (ch. 4), repentance (ch. 5), justification (ch. 6), and the relation of the Old and New Testaments (ch. 7), and before the chapter on prayer (ch. 9).[52] As I have argued elsewhere, the topics added in 1539 and the order in which they appear reflect Melanchthon's rhetorical analysis of the topics or *loci* in the epistle to the Romans.[53]

In all of the editions prior to 1559, the chapter on providence and predestination remained in roughly the same place. In 1559, as the chapters on the creed were separated out to become the anchors of the new four-book organization of the *Institutes*, and the chapter on the relation of the Old and New Testaments was moved forward out of its original location after justification and into the chapters leading up to Christology, not predestination but providence was moved. Calvin retained virtually the original location of predestination (he reversed its order with the chapter on prayer) and moved providence into relation with his doctrine of God.[54] There was, in other words, no significant

---

52. John Calvin, *Institutio christianae religionis nunc vere demum suo titulo respondens* (Strasbourg: Rihel, 1539).

53. Cf. Richard A. Muller, *The Unaccommodated Calvin: Studies in the Foundation of a Theological Tradition* (New York: Oxford University Press, 2000), pp. 29–30, 95, 102–8, 118–39; with idem, "*Ordo docendi*: Melanchthon and the Organization of Calvin's *Institutes*, 1536–1543," in *Melanchthon in Europe: His Work and Influence beyond Wittenberg*, ed. Karin Maag (Grand Rapids: Baker, 1999), pp. 123–24.

54. Cf. Muller, *Unaccommodated Calvin*, pp. 135–36.

editorial movement of predestination in Calvin's *Institutes*, just as there was no significant alteration of the definition and its implications. There was, however, an editorial movement of providence from what became book 3 to what became book 1 of the *Institutes*.[55] Far from making the causal patterning of the *Institutes* less rigorous, Calvin had in fact intensified it by retaining predestination as the causal focus of book 3 and creating a causal focus in book 1 with the doctrine of providence. There was, therefore, no conscious movement of the doctrine of predestination *away from* the doctrine of God. What is more, the chapter on predestination in Calvin's 1539 *Institutes* and his treatise *Concerning the Eternal Predestination of God* both draw out the connection between providence and predestination, a connection that is certainly not broken by the mere shifting of the placement of the topics.[56]

Barth also missed the close relationship between Calvin's arrangement of the *Institutes* and Melanchthon's modeling of the several editions of his *Loci communes*. This historical datum is also of considerable significance to the question given the development of synergistic tendencies in Melanchthon's views on predestination, grace, and free choice. Barth noted the *a posteriori* or soteriological placement of the doctrine in the list of topics given by Melanchthon in his 1521 *Loci communes* and its similarity to the pattern of Calvin's 1539 *Institutes*. In 1521, although he did not elaborate on the topic of predestination, Melanchthon was fully monergistic in his soteriology—and, of course, Calvin's 1539 reflection of Melanchthon's order did offer a radically monergistic conception of predestination and election.[57] For the present discussion, it is significant that, as Melanchthon moved away from Calvin on the subjects of predestination, grace, and free choice toward a synergistic understanding of those topics, he did not substantially

---

55. Contra Armstrong, *Calvinism and the Amyraut Heresy*, pp. 161–62; and Hall, "Calvin Against the Calvinists," p. 24. Hall in particular is utterly confused as to the text-history of the *Institutes*.

56. Cf. Calvin, *Institutio* (1539), cap. 8; with idem, *De aeterna Dei praedestinatione*, in *CO* 8, col. 249–366; in translation, *Concerning the Eternal Predestination of God*, trans. J. K. S. Reid (London: James Clarke, 1961).

57. Calvin, *Institutio* (1539), cap. 8; cf. Muller, *Unaccommodated Calvin*, pp. 120–26.

alter the placement of his doctrine of predestination: witness the 1543 *Loci communes*.[58] The result is that Melanchthon's 1543 *Loci communes* and Calvin's 1559 *Institutes* retain certain structural similarities, particularly those resting on the Pauline order of topics early on argued by Melanchthon, but their definitions widely diverge. Placement of the doctrine, in both of these cases, has little bearing on the content of the *locus*. The reason for placement is the approximation of the order of Romans for the sake of the right or proper teaching of the topics.[59]

Among the early Lutheran writers, Erasmus Sarcerius also wrote a *loci communes* and, in his ordering of the doctrines, developed as early as 1538, he moved from the doctrine of God and Trinity to offer two *loci*, the first on predestination and the second on the problem of contingency, before coming to his doctrine of creation.[60] As to predestination, Sarcerius understood it as the decree by which God brings about "all things according to the counsel of his will," not, however, by "simple necessity...but by the process and course of nature ordained by God."[61] In the case of the predestination of human beings to salvation, Sarcerius identifies this process or course as conditional: all who receive God's word will be the "children of God, whom God elects."[62] The *locus* on contingency, immediately following, underlines Sarcerius' point that the divine ordination of all things does not impose "simple necessity" but establishes contingency.[63] Placement of the doctrine clearly does not indicate determinism or imply a particular definition—rather, in Sarcerius' approach, it simply reflects an ordering of theology that accords with the priority of the divine counsel over the creation and ordering of all things. At very least, Sarcerius'

----

58. Philip Melanchthon, *Loci communes* (1543), cap. xiv, in *Opera quae supersunt omnia*, ed. C. G. Bretschreider, 28 vols. (Brunswick: Schwetschke, 1834–1860), vol. 21, col. 912–16. (Melanchthon's *Opera* are hereinafter cited as *CR*.)

59. See the discussion in Muller, *Unaccommodated Calvin*, pp. 127–30.

60. Erasmus Sarcerius, *Loci aliquot communes et theologici* (1538), [v–vi], fol. 11r–18r; in translation, *Comon places of Scripture: orderly and after a compendious forme of teachyige, set forth with no litle labour, to the great profyte and helpe of all suche studentes in gods worde as have not yet had longe exercyse in the same*, trans. Richard Taverner (London: John Bydell, 1538; other editions, 1553, 1577), cap. v–vi (pp. 16r–23v).

61. Sarcerius, *Loci aliquot communes et theologici*, [v], fol. 11r.

62. Sarcerius, *Loci aliquot communes et theologici*, [v], fol. 11v.

63. Sarcerius, *Loci aliquot communes et theologici*, [vi], fol. 15v–16r.

placement and definitions ought to give pause to those who view Beza as the restorer of the doctrine to the *a priori* placement customarily given it or who understand the placement as a characteristic of later Reformed predestinarianism.

Among Calvin's contemporaries, Musculus and Hyperius also produced full sets of *loci communes*. Musculus, standing in some relation to the approach of Calvin and Melanchthon, placed predestination into the soteriological series of doctrines after discussion of the gospel, the Scriptures, ministry of the Word, and faith, and immediately before repentance, justification, and good works. Musculus also offered some explanation of his decision to place a discussion of election and reprobation after faith. Faith, he notes, as indicated in the discussion of that doctrine, is not found in all people, but only in the elect, inasmuch as "it depends on the free election of the divine will." For this reason, the discussion of faith leads to consideration of predestination. This approach, Musculus comments, is "not unsuitable to the proper disposition of the topics [*recta locorum dispositionis*]"—not as though election follows faith or as though one becomes elect on the basis of belief, but that "after consideration of faith, it is no more unusual to approach election than after examining a river to return to the study of its source."[64] And, of course, Musculus' definition of the doctrine observes the eternity of the decree and the fact of election "before the foundation of the world."[65] Like Calvin, Musculus has an interest in the proper order of teaching or the proper arrangement of the *loci*, not in imparting a new meaning to the doctrine.

Hyperius offers a more traditional model, and he does so clearly because he has older dogmatic models in mind as the basis for his Protestant theological *Methodus*—notably those of John of Damascus, Peter Lombard, and various later *Sentence* commentators. He discusses predestination because it is one of the topics identified in Holy Scripture, and mirroring the approaches of Alexander of Hales and Thomas Aquinas, he places it among the attributes of God, as he indicates,

---

64. Wolfgang Musculus, *Loci communes sacrae theologicae* (Basel: Ioannes Hervagius, 1563), cap. 24 (p. 404).

65. Musculus, *Loci communes*, cap. 24 (p. 406).

because it so well "illustrates the glory, mercy, and justice of God."[66] Still, in his exposition of the doctrine, Hyperius emphasizes that election is in Christ and is an act of God's grace, the foundation of our faith, and the "antecedent cause of our integrity"—indicating virtually all of the relationships of predestination with other doctrines.[67] And although his ordering of doctrines is different from Calvin's, his purpose in establishing the arrangement is precisely the same: to identify a *methodus* or way through the topics that offers a suitable "order" or "way of teaching" (*docendi via*).[68]

Beza did not explain the different placements of the doctrine of predestination in his various works. Like Calvin, he did leave several models for arranging the topics of theology and, also like Calvin, made comments concerning the right order of topics for teaching the doctrine. Beza wrote some four presentations of Christian doctrine: his *Confession de la foy chrestienne* (1558), the *Autre brieve confession de la foi* (1561), the *Quaestionum et responsionum christianarum libellus* (1570–1576), and the *Petit catéchisme* (1575). There is also the famous *Tabula praedestinationis* (1555/1570), but inasmuch as it is a tract on predestination and not by any stretch of the imagination a body (or even an outline) of Christian doctrine, it does not bear at all on the question of the "placement" of the doctrine in a theological system.[69] None of these works, moreover, is a full-scale "dogmatics" elaborated to the detail either of Calvin's *Institutes* or of a later system like Polanus' *Syntagma theologiae*. This seemingly minor datum raises the rather significant question of which document Brunner was speaking of when he claimed that Beza placed predestination "at the beginning of his Dogmatics."[70] The value of the claim is just a bit offset by the fact that Beza never wrote a "Dogmatics" at the beginning of which he might have placed the doctrine of predestination—or, indeed, any other doctrine! Nor did he place the doctrine of predestination at the beginning of any treatise the subject of which was multiple doctrines. As is the

---

66. Andreas Hyperius, *Methodus theologiae, sive praecipuorum Christianae religionis locorum communium, libri tres* (Basel: Ioannes Oporinus, 1567), p. 182.

67. Hyperius, *Methodus theologiae*, pp. 186, 189.

68. Hyperius, *Methodus theologiae*, p. 1.

69. Cf. Muller, "Use and Abuse," pp. 34–35; idem, *Christ and the Decree*, pp. 79–83.

70. Brunner, *Christian Doctrine of God*, p. 345.

case with most of his slippery remarks concerning the history of Christian doctrine, Brunner offers no documentation for his claims. Similarly, Hall's claim that Beza echoed Aquinas' placement and thereby reintroduced a speculative determinism is nullified by the fact that Aquinas' theology was not a speculative determinism and, moreover, that Aquinas did not move from the doctrine of God to the doctrine of providence and then to the doctrine of predestination. Rather, Aquinas treated both providence and predestination within the doctrine of God as predicates of God and then went on to conclude the doctrine of God with a series of other attributes and the doctrine of the Trinity. Beza never produced anything remotely reminiscent of Aquinas' pattern of organization—and, in any case, Hall's description of the order and the problem does not resemble either Aquinas' teaching or Beza's.[71]

Beza's *Confession de la foy* offers what is perhaps a unique approach to the location of predestination: he adopts a christological placement—not, as in the Gallican or Belgic Confessions, between the doctrine of sin and Christology, nor, as in Bullinger's slightly more nuanced approach in the *Second Helvetic Confession*, following the problem of human free choice and before Christology, and not, as in the systems of Vermigli-Masson and Ames, after Christology and before the order of salvation. Beza places the doctrine of predestination into Christology itself after his basic statement of the identity of the person of Christ and prior to his discussion of human nature, the necessity of the Mediator, and Christ's saving work.[72] This arrangement is, as far as I know, unique—found also only in the *Confessio Hungarica* (1562), which was modeled on Beza's work.[73] Beza's emphasis in his shorter confession is, similarly, Christ's work of satisfaction, but here he offers no doctrine of predestination at all.

---

71. Cf. the discussion of Beza's several arrangements of the topics of theology in Muller, *Christ and the Decree*, pp. 83–85, 89, 95.

72. Theodore Beza, *Confession de la foy chrestienne, contenant la confirmation d'icelle, et la refutation des superstitions contraires* (Geneva: Conrad Badius, 1559; 2nd ed., 1561); also, *Confessio christianae fidei* (Geneva, 1560; London, 1575), III.v–vi.

73. Viz., *Compendium doctrinae christianae, quam omnes Pastores et Ministri ecclesiarum Dei in tota Ungaria et Transsylvania, quae incorruptum Iesu Christi Evangelium amplexae sunt, docent ac profitentur*, in E. F. K. Müller, ed., *Die Bekenntnisschriften der reformierten Kirche. In authentischen Texten mit geschichtlicher Einleitung und Register* (Leipzig: Deichert, 1903), pp. 376–449.

Beza's *Quaestionum et responsionum christianarum libellus* (1570–1576) begins with a brief discussion of God, moves on to discuss Scripture as the Word of God, then discusses the Trinity, Christ, Christ's benefits and their application, faith, justification, sanctification, providence, and predestination. Then the second volume continues with the church, sacraments, prayer, and Christian hope. Here, too, we lack the purported Bezan predestinarian arrangement: predestination is, literally, at the opposite end of the book from the doctrine of God, which in fact reflects Calvin's 1539 placement in the *Institutes*.[74] Then there is the famous *Tabula praedestinationis*, in which Beza sets forth in a diagram the order of the causes of salvation and damnation. The work is a brief tract, not a theological system, and although the diagram identified predestination as an eternal decree in God, the text attached to the diagram indicates that the order of teaching ought to follow a "Pauline" pattern and begin with sin and the law and move through grace and faith to the topic of predestination.[75] There simply is no work of Beza that sets forth an order of discussion or teaching in which predestination stands in relation to the doctrine of God. In fact, Beza's argument in the *Tabula* is a clear reflection of the Pauline method adopted by the *Institutes*. Of course, Beza places predestination in the doctrine of God in the diagram, just as he defines it in his text—in accord with Calvin—as an eternal decree. But the definition, whether given in words or in diagrammatic form, is not reflected by the placement of the doctrine in the order of teaching.[76]

A word is in order here also concerning Vermigli's *Loci communes*. Barth identifies the placement of predestination in this work as a soteriological placement, virtually identical with the placement in Calvin's 1537 catechism and related in spirit to the placement of

---

74. Theodore Beza, *Quaestionum et responsionum christianarum libellus, in quo praecipua Christianae religionis capita* κατ᾽ ἐπιτωμήν *proponuntur* (Geneva: Jean Crespin, 1570); and *Quaestionum et responsionum christianarum libellus pars altera, quae est de sacramentis* (Geneva: Eustathius Vignon, 1576).

75. Theodore Beza, *Summa totius christianismi, sive descriptio & distributio causarum salutis electorum & exitii reproborum, ex sacris literis collecta* [*Tabula praedestinationis*] (Geneva, 1555), in *Tractationes theologicae*, 3 vols. (Geneva: Eustathius Vignon, 1570–1582), vol. 1, pp. 170–205.

76. Cf. Muller, "Use and Abuse," pp. 33–61.

the doctrine in the 1559 *Institutes*. There is no reason to dissent from this analysis, but it does need to be augmented and refined from the historical data: Vermigli's *Loci communes* was, after all, not the compilation of Vermigli, but of Robert Masson, after Vermigli's death. The order of the work was based, intentionally, on that of Calvin's 1559 *Institutes*—thus the resemblance in order and arrangement of topics. The shifting of predestination from the end of the *ordo salutis* to the beginning was, therefore, a conscious departure from Calvin's arrangement and probably, in the mind of Masson, a clearer and better order.[77] This means, in the first place, that we are not exactly dealing here with an utter alternative model but one that actually grew out of the other and assumed some of its logic as a ground of revision. Second, and more importantly, this editorial history also indicates that there is no necessary relationship at all between the definition of predestination (which is Vermigli's) and the placement of the doctrine (which is Masson's).

Predestination in the Theological Systems of the Reformed Orthodox:
An Analysis of the Placements

Although the majority of academic or scholastic theologies written in the era of orthodoxy did discuss predestination under the rubric of the eternal decree, immediately following the doctrine of God and prior to the doctrine of creation,[78] contrary to Barth's sense of the problem of beginning with the notion of a general decree that establishes God's relationship with the world and then moving on to a special decree of God's election in which the relationship of humanity to Jesus Christ is established, this order offers a fair amount of variety of design in and of itself. We can only examine a sampling of these theologies. Polanus and Wollebius, both noted in Barth's discussion, adhere to the model that he presents, moving from the general decree to the special decree. Alsted (who is not cited by Barth) also follows out Barth's description

---

77. See Vermigli, *Loci communes* (1583), III.i; and note the infralapsarian definition, ibid., III.i.10.

78. Samuel Maresius, *Collegium theologicum sive systema breve universae theologiae comprehensum octodecim disputationibus* (Groningen: Joannes Nicolaus, 1645, 1649), locus iv.

in one of his theological compendia, but Mastricht (who is cited by Barth) and Turretin do not.

In both his *Definitiones theologicae* and the *Loci theologici* found in his *Encyclopaedia*, Alsted moves from a discussion of the "decrees of God in general" to the "decree of providence" as a general decree establishing all things, and he then discusses the "decree of predestination," consisting in election and reprobation. Alsted's doctrine, although indicating a double decree and placed thus prior to creation, is consistently infralapsarian, even defining reprobation as a decree to "leave" the nonelect in the fallen mass of humanity to be damned for their own sins.[79] Alsted also returns to the providential governance of the world after he has discussed creation.[80] In his separately published *Loci commmunes theologici*, however, Alsted postponed discussion of predestination until after his doctrines of Christ and the order of salvation, placing it immediately prior to his doctrines of the resurrection and the church.[81]

Mastricht and Turretin, by way of contrast, move directly from chapters "On the actions and decrees of God" to discuss predestination, election, and reprobation. They follow this with the doctrine of creation and come to providence only after they have discussed the creation of angels and men—so that in their theological models, the relation of predestination to providence is not as broadly emphasized as that of the part to the whole as it is by Alsted.[82] Nor should it be omitted that Mastricht and Turretin differed over the issue of supra- and infralapsarian definitions of the doctrine: whereas both chose the prior or supralapsarian placement, Mastricht argued the compatibility of the supra- and infralapsarian definitions, given that God's ordination

---

79. Cf. Johann Heinrich Alsted, *Definitiones theologicae secundum ordinem locorum communium traditae* (Hanau: Eifridus, 1631), cap. v–vii. The pattern is identical in Alsted's *Synopsis Theologiae Exhibens Oeconomiam singulorum locorum communium theologicorum* (Hanau: Conrad Eifrid, 1627), xv; and the *Loci theologici* found in his *Encyclopaedia septem tomis divisis*, 7 parts in 2 tomes (Herborn: Corvinus, 1630), tome II, p. 352.

80. Alsted, *Definitiones theologicae*, cap. ix.

81. Alsted, *Loci communes theologici perpetuis similitudinibus illustrati* (Frankfurt: Eifrid, 1630), xviii.

82. Petrus van Mastricht, *Theoretico-practica theologia*, 2 vols. (Amsterdam: Henricus & Theodorus Boom, 1682–1687), III.i–iv, x.

of humanity assumed a movement from possibility to actuality in which the objects of divine decreeing or ordination are, first, possible human beings capable of falling and, second, actual human beings having fallen. Turretin, by way of contrast, chose the supralapsarian placement and then argued strenuously for the infralapsarian definition.[83]

What is more, in Alsted's and Turretin's definitions, as in Aquinas' view, the identification of providence as the general and predestination the special aspect of God's decree (even the identification found primarily among the medievals of predestination as a "part" of providence) never means, as is sometimes claimed, that predestination is subordinated to providence. Even when predestination is placed after providence, it remains the higher and more ultimate will of God, with "actual providence" (the execution of the general decree) providing the temporal context for the execution of the special decree. Providence governs the temporal life and leads human beings toward the goal resident within their created nature, whereas predestination draws them to their eternal goal, beyond the gifts of their created nature.[84] This recognition of the more ultimate end of predestination, moreover, stands in direct relation to the connection established by Calvin between the two doctrines in the 1539, 1543, and 1550 editions of the *Institutes* and the treatise *Concerning the Eternal Predestination of God* (where the doctrines are juxtaposed)—leading to the conclusion, once again,

---

83. Cf. Mastricht, *Theoretico-practica theologia*, III.ii.12–13; with Turretin, *Institutio theologiae elencticae*, 3 vols. (Geneva: Samuel de Tournes, 1679–1685), IV.xviii.4–5, 21–23; and note Barth's analysis of Mastricht's approach, *CD*, II/2, pp. 132–33. In the following discussion, the terms "supra-" and "infralapsarian" are used as typically defined in the seventeenth century, "supralapsarian" indicating an understanding of the human objects of creation as "above" or prior to the fall in the order of the eternal decree, *creabilis et labilis* or *creatus et labilis*; "infralapsarian" indicating an understanding of the objects of election as "below" the fall in the order of the eternal decree, *creatus et labilis*. Given that the terms "supra-" and "infralapsarian" did not become current and the issues raised by the terms were not debated before the very end of the sixteenth century, there remains an element of anachronism in the discussion. Still, the application of the terms to various definitions of predestination serves to distinguish between what can be called a supra- or infralapsarian placement of the doctrine in a work of theology, either before or after the discussion of the fall, and a supra- or infralapsarian *definition* of the eternal decree regardless of where it is discussed.

84. Thomas Aquinas, *Summa theologiae*, Ia, q. 23, art 1.

of a continuity of definition and meaning even when the question of placement is resolved differently.[85]

François Wendel was entirely mistaken in his interpretation of the following comment in book 1 of Calvin's *Institutes*: "It would be untimely to introduce here the question concerning the secret predestination of God, because we are not considering what might or might not happen, but what the nature of man truly was."[86] Wendel understood this as indicating that raising the question of predestination "in relation to the doctrine of God was inopportune" and that such an ordering of doctrine ought to be avoided. Calvin, however, is not here commenting about the order of his topics or, indeed, about the doctrine of God, but about Adam's responsibility for the fall, and he is simply ruling out discussion of predestination as not directly relevant to his argument in this particular chapter of the *Institutes*.[87] Calvin's arrangement of topics puts predestination, as executed, into the context of the divinely governed providential order without in any way altering the fact that he understood the decree as an eternal divine willing.[88]

Among the many Reformed thinkers who adopted this placement of the doctrine after the *locus de Deo* and before the *locus* on creation, Johannes d'Outrein provided a brief explanation of the logic of the placement and ordering. Given that God is always "active" (*werksaam*), d'Outrein comments, a proper discussion of God begins with the being and name of God and then passes on to consider the divine "ways and works" (*wegen en werken*).[89] Inasmuch, moreover, as God is

---

85. Contra the conclusion in François Wendel, *Calvin: Origins and Development of His Religious Thought*, trans. Philip Mairet (New York: Harper & Row, 1963), p. 268; cf. the discussion in Muller, *Christ and the Decree*, pp. 23–24.

86. Calvin, *Institutes*, I.xv.8.

87. Contra Wendel, *Calvin*, p. 268.

88. Calvin, *Institutes*, III.xxi.5.

89. Johannes d'Outrein, *Korte schets der godlyke waarheden, soo als die in haare natuurlyke order te samen geschakelt zyn* (Amsterdam: Jacobus Borstius, 1700; 14th printing, 1726), p. 96; in translation, *A short scheme of divine truths: wherein is given a general idea of divinity* (London: J. Darby, 1705), p. 76. Note that d'Outrein's reference to the being and name of God, "het Wesen en den naame Gods," probably references his entire discussion of God, which proceeds from being and perfections to Trinity, and concludes with the divine name, thus including both perfections and Trinity under the category of the divine "being" as other Reformed writers had done in consideration of the divine "nature"; cf. the discussion in Richard A. Muller, "Unity and Distinction:

eternally active, the discussion of God's works rightly begins with the eternal decree.[90]

Although a majority of the Reformed orthodox did not discuss the doctrine of predestination as an integral part of the *locus de Deo*, several of the more important Reformed theologians of the eras of Reformation and orthodoxy, such as Hyperius, Zanchi, Junius, Maccovius, and Wishart, did discuss the decree among the divine attributes.[91] This is, moreover, a rather distinctive placement that appears to have been entirely missed by Barth. These writers, in other words, did not juxtapose the doctrine of predestination and the doctrine of God by moving through the discussion of the divine essence and attributes to the doctrine of the Trinity and then, following the Trinity, offering a *locus* on the decrees. Rather, they included predestination within the doctrine of God itself, among the divine attributes.

Examination of this placement of the doctrine and of its systematic relationships demonstrates three things. First, since only three of the five writers who followed this pattern—namely, Junius, Maccovius, and Wishart—were supralapsarian,[92] placement of the decree among the divine attributes is not in itself indicative of a supralapsarian doctrine of predestination: Hyperius and Zanchi were infralapsarian.[93]

The Nature of God in the Theology of Lucas Trelcatius, Jr.," in *Reformation & Renaissance Review*, 10/3 (2008 [2010]), pp. 315–41.

90. D'Outrein, *Korte schets*, p. 96.

91. In the cases of Zanchi and Maccovius, this is not the only association or placement of the decree. We have already noted Zanchi's ecclesiological discussion of the doctrine—and there is the infralapsarian placement of predestination in between the doctrines of creation and providence in Johannes Maccovius, *Distinctiones et regulae theologicae ac philosophicae*, ed. Nicholas Arnold (Oxford: Henry Hall, 1656), cap. vi–vii.

92. Franciscus Junius, *Theses theologicae Leydenses*, x.10; xi.2–3, in idem, *Opuscula theologica selecta*, ed. Abraham Kuyper (Amsterdam: F. Muller, 1882); Johannes Maccovius, *Loci communes theologici* (Amsterdam: Ludovicus & Daniel Elzevir, 1658), xxv (pp. 205, 208–10); William Wishart, *Theologia; or, Discourses of God, delivered in CXX Sermons*, 2 vols. (Edinburgh: John Moncur, 1716), discourse 18 (vol. 2, pp. 570–73, 599–601, 606–8).

93. Hyperius, *Methodus theologiae*, pp. 182–86; Girolamo Zanchi, *De natura Dei*, in idem, *Operum theologicorum D. Hieronymi Zanchii*, 10 vols. in 9 (Geneva: Samuel Crispin, 1617–1619), vol. 2, col. 485; cf. the similar definitions in idem, *De praedestinatione sanctorum*, in *Operum theologicorum*, vol. 8, col. 307; idem, *De ecclesia*, in *Operum theologicorum*, vol. 7/2, col. 65; also Zanchi, *De religione christiana fides* (Neustadt:

Thus, second, what might be called a radically supralapsarian place-ment of predestination in relation to the doctrine of God did not result either in a highly speculative theological model or in a *supralapsarian definition* of the doctrine. Instead, third, it represents the Protestant orthodox use of medieval systematic models like those found in the *Summa theologica* of Alexander of Hales or the *Summa theologiae* of Thomas Aquinas, both of which place the doctrine of predestination in relation to the divine attributes or predicates inasmuch as predestina-tion must be predicated of God.[94]

We noted, previously, the one early orthodox writer who mod-eled his theology largely on the pattern of Calvin's 1559 *Institutes*. Gulielmus Bucanus arrives at the doctrine of predestination in his thirty-sixth *locus*, after the order of salvation (faith, repentance, jus-tification, and related issues), Christian liberty, and prayer, just prior to his discussion of the last things,[95] the location identified by Barth as expressing the "consummation" of the doctrine of reconcilia-tion in its "final and decisive word." What is remarkable here is that Bucanus accepts this so-called *a posteriori* placement but then begins his discussion with a set of definitions that distinguish providence and predestination despite his earlier discussion of providence in the four-teenth *locus*. He then sets out the divine knowledge or foreknowledge and predestination, indicating that predestination can refer either to the eternal purpose or decree of God or to the divine disposition of rational creatures toward their ends in election and reprobation—a model that presents the decree or predestination as the initial divine intention.[96] Bucanus' definition of the decree itself, moreover, in con-trast to his placement of the doctrine, has a supralapsarian accent, although his subsequent definition of election and its objects is infra-lapsarian.[97] We note the contrast with several of his contemporaries:

Matthaus Harnisch, [1588]), III.iii; and note the discussion in Muller, *Christ and the Decree*, pp. 112, 116.

94. Cf. Alexander of Hales, *Summa theologica*, ed. B. Klumper, 4 vols. (Quaracchi: Collegium S. Bonaventurae, 1924–1948), Lib. I, inq. 1, tr. 5, q. 4, tit. 1–5 (vol. 1, pp. 315–59); with Aquinas, *Summa theol.*, Ia, q. 23.

95. Gulielmus Bucanus, *Body of Divinity, or: Institutions of Christian Religion*, trans. R. Hill (London: Daniel Pakeman, 1659), xxxvi (pp. 445–73).

96. Bucanus, *Institutions*, xxxvi (pp. 445–48).

97. Bucanus, *Institutions*, xxxvi (pp. 452, 457).

Polanus, Wollebius, and Alsted all adopt the "supralapsarian" placement of the doctrine but argue a distinctly infralapsarian definition.[98] The Leiden *Synopsis*, which, to be precise, sets forth a series of the fall, sin, free choice, the law, idolatry, oaths, the Sabbath, the gospel, and the Old and New Testaments prior to coming to predestination and then Christology, also argues an infralapsarian definition, but not precisely in the order indicated by Barth.[99]

As Van Asselt has observed, aspects of the doctrine of predestination are discussed in various places in Cocceius' *Summa theologiae*. Cocceius comes to the discussion of the decree first in his fifth *locus*, after the doctrine of the Trinity and prior to creation. Then, in the fourteenth *locus*, after providence and sin, prior to the introduction of the temporal economy of salvation, Cocceius again takes up the discussion, returning to it in the eighteenth *locus* in relation to the election or adoption of Israel. Cocceius' stated intention in thus dispersing the topic is not, as Barth hypothesized, to forge a path from the problem of sin to the work of redemption in Christ, but to show that the eternal decree or counsel of God is the cause of all things, governs both good and evil, and is related to both grace and judgment.[100] His basic definitions are infralapsarian.[101]

The location of the doctrine of the decrees, conjoined with a discussion of predestination, after creation, sin, and providence and prior to the doctrines of Christ and salvation, also appears in the high orthodox theology of Benedict Pictet—and, what is more, with a fairly clear explanation of the reason for the pattern.[102] Had Barth

---

98. Thus, Amandus Polanus von Polansdorf, *Partitiones theologiae christianae*, pars I–II (Basel: Conradus Waldkirch, 1590–1596), I.vi (p. 11); Johannes Wollebius, *Compendium theologiae christianae* (Basel: J. Genath, 1626; Oxford: Henry Hall, 1657), I.iv.2.3, and canon vi; Alsted, *Definitiones theologicae*, cap. v–vii.

99. *Synopsis purioris theologiae, disputationibus quinquaginta duabus comprehensa ac conscripta per Johannem Polyandrum, Andream Rivetum, Antonium Walaeum, Antonium Thysium* (Leiden, 1625; 6th ed., Leiden: Donner, 1881), xxiv.

100. Willem J. van Asselt, *The Federal Theology of Johannes Cocceius (1603–1669)*, trans. Raymond A. Blacketer (Leiden: Brill, 2001), pp. 201–3; cf. Johannes Cocceius, *Summa theologiae ex Scriptura repetita*, in *Opera omnia theologica, exegetica, didactica, polemica, philologica*, 10 vols. (Amsterdam: P. and J. Blaev, 1701–1706), vol. 7, *loci* V, XIV, XVIII.

101. Cocceius, *Summa theologiae*, XVIII.xxxiii.1.

102. Benedict Pictet, *Theologia christiana, ex puris s.s. literarum fontibus hausta*

encountered Pictet's *Theologia christiana*, he would have had the choice, given his paradigm, of identifying Pictet's approach as similar to that of the Gallican and Belgic Confessions—placing predestination as the "first word" in the doctrine of reconciliation—or, in view of Pictet's movement from providence to predestination, understanding predestination, as he had in the case of Zwingli's *Fidei ratio*, as "the crown and completion of the doctrine of providence." But Pictet clearly has something else in mind in his ordering of the materials, despite his genuine reflection of the confessional order. For Pictet had discussed the decrees of God in a general *locus* immediately following his doctrine of God—the supralapsarian placement—and had, there, offered a detailed and pointedly infralapsarian description of the order of the decrees.[103] He then inserted his discussion of the subtopics of his analysis of the decrees not in the general *locus* on the decrees but in separate discussions at the point in the system where the execution of the decree in the temporal order becomes relevant. Thus, a *locus* on the decree to permit the fall of angels and human beings (including the discussion of the actual fall and sin) intervenes between creation and providence,[104] while providence follows creation and, indeed, follows the fall, in order that the issue of providence and evil can be addressed.[105] So also does the doctrine of predestination follow creation and fall, and indeed, providence, not because it is "the crown and completion of the doctrine of providence" or, indeed, because it is the "first word" in the doctrine of reconciliation, but because the object of the decree is humanity resident in the created and providentially governed order of the world and fallen into sin.[106] The governing issue

---

(Geneva: Cramer and Perachon, 1696), VII.i–viii; cf. the similar arrangement in Nicholaus Gürtler, *Synopsis theologiae reformatae* (Marburg: Müller, 1731), I.vii and II.i (pp. 44–50, 99–114); note also the separation of discussion of predestination from the decrees and placement of the doctrine of predestination after the fall and prior to Christology in Samuel Willard, *A Compleat Body of Divinity in Two Hundred and Fifty Expository Lectures on the Assembly's Shorter Catechism* (Boston: B. Green and S. Kneeland, 1726), q. 20, sermons 70–79 (pp. 246–88), where predestination is understood as the divine foundation of the restitution of humanity.

103. Pictet, *Theologia christiana*, III.i–iii.
104. Pictet, *Theologia christiana*, V.i–x.
105. Pictet, *Theologia christiana*, VI, with cap. v–vi on providence and sin.
106. Pictet, *Theologia christiana*, VII.i.

in placement, for Pictet, is the right identification of the object of the decree as created and fallen humanity—but this is, of course, a doctrinal definition that he shared with numerous Reformed theologians who chose to discuss predestination in a different place in their systems.

There is also the rather unique case of John Edwards' five-volume theological project, *Veritas redux*, *Faith and Justification*, and the three-volume *Theologia Reformata*. The first volume of the five, *Veritas redux*, surveys "God's Eternal Decrees," "The Liberty of Man's Will," "Grace and Conversion," "The Extent and Efficacy of Christ's Redemption," and "Perseverance in Grace"—namely, the five topics in debate between the Reformed and the Arminians. The second volume presents the doctrines of faith and justification. Only in the third volume does Edwards come to his exposition of the creed and, there, the doctrines of the Trinity, divine attributes, and providence. His intention in beginning with the decrees and moving on to the other soteriological points as a first step in theology was not to deduce anything from the decrees or to advocate a supralapsarian position—Edwards was infralapsarian—but rather because he would "have occasion to mention these Doctrines thro' the whole Course of Divinity, because they naturally mix themselves with most of the Theological Heads" and as doctrines pertaining to the "Foundation" of the faith are "requisite to be known, in order to the right understanding and apprehending of the whole Christian Religion."[107] The placement, in other words, was largely pedagogical and, given Edwards' involvement in the controversies of the era, somewhat polemical or apologetic. A right understanding of the decrees, Edwards argued, would lead to a right understanding of other doctrines, with the decrees serving as a kind of "Ground-work of all Theology" while, conversely, a misunderstanding would lead to errors difficult or "impossible to rectifie."[108]

Placement versus Definition: An Evaluation

From the perspective of the various definitions of predestination offered by the Reformed theologians of the sixteenth and seventeenth centuries, it becomes immediately clear that the placement of the

---

107. Edwards, *Veritas redux*, p. vii.
108. Edwards, *Veritas redux*, pp. xv–xvi.

doctrine does not, shall we say, predetermine its meaning. Thus, the location of the doctrine of predestination "above" creation and fall and in some relation to the doctrine of God—a nominally supralapsarian *placement*—does not necessarily correspond, in the theological systems themselves, with a supralapsarian *definition*. Indeed, definition quite frequently did not absolutely govern the placement of the doctrine. Zanchi, for example, discussed predestination among the divine attributes in his treatise *De natura Dei*, but he also took note of the doctrine in his *De ecclesia*. In both instances the definition indicates a divine election of some out of the fallen and condemned mass of humanity, a classic infralapsarian definition.[109] The apparent reason for his discussion of predestination among the divine attributes was Zanchi's reception and use of medieval theology: following the logic of Alexander of Hales' and Thomas Aquinas' *Summas*, he asked the question "whether predestination can be predicated of God" and, given his positive answer, placed the decrees with the other divine predicates.

A similar logic is evident in Maccovius' *Loci communes theologici*, where the decree is also discussed among the divine attributes—albeit Maccovius does define the doctrine in a primarily supralapsarian manner as well as give it a supralapsarian placement. But Maccovius' definition also raises an interesting issue with regard to the whole question of supra- and infralapsarianism. For, unlike those who engaged in heated debate over the definitions (for example, Twisse and Turretin), Maccovius noted that God can and does understand the objects of his decree as "*homo condendus, conditus, permittendus in lapsum, & lapsus,*" conjoining and potentially reconciling the supra and infra perspectives.[110] Several later writers, notably Mastricht, Gill, Hill, and Brown of Haddington, also viewed the supra and infra definitions

---

109. Zanchi, *De praedestinatione sanctorum*, in *Operum theologicorum*, vol. 8, col. 305–7; *De natura Dei*, in *Operum theologicorum*, vol. 2, col. 481, 485; *De ecclesia*, in *Operum theologicorum*, 7/2, col. 65; contra Otto Gründler, *Die Gotteslehre Girolami Zanchis und ihre Bedeutung für seine Lehre von der Prädestination* (Neukirchen: Neukirchener, 1965), p. 112.

110. Maccovius, *Loci communes*, xxv (p. 209).

as reconcilable even as they adopted a supralapsarian placement of the doctrine in their theologies.[111]

It is important to note here, against any and all assumptions concerning the theologically determinative nature of the placement of the doctrine, that the so-called *a priori* placement, in relation to the doctrine of God and prior to creation, stands in absolutely no relationship to the individual theologians' choice of a supralapsarian or an infralapsarian definition of the doctrine. This despite the persistence on the part of some modern writers to declare any notion of a decree of predestination prior to the event of creation to be supralapsarian: at one of Calvin's most thoroughly infralapsarian moments, McNeill identified his views as supralapsarian solely on this mistaken ground, and Gründler, equally mistakenly, made Zanchi out to be supralapsarian on the basis of his placement of the doctrine in the *De natura Dei*.[112] We are struck by the fact that the supralapsarian definition offered by Beza never led him to a supralapsarian placement of the doctrine in any of his works on the subject, that a supralapsarian like Perkins would place the doctrine in his ecclesiology, and, conversely, that infralapsarians like Zanchi, Alsted, and Turretin chose a supralapsarian placement of the doctrine in their disputations and systems. The infralapsarian Yates, like Perkins and Alsted, chose an ecclesiological placement in his creedal-catechetical *Modell of Divinitie*.[113]

Then we have the example of several theologians who, even in the era of orthodoxy, offered different placements of the doctrine in different works, albeit without alteration of the content of the doctrine. We have registered this point in some detail already in the case of Beza, and it can be extended to Zanchi, Perkins (if his *Golden Chaine*

---

111. Mastricht, *Theoretico-practica theologia*, III.ii.12–13; John Gill, *A Complete Body of Doctrinal and Practical Divinity*, 3 vols. (London: W. Winterbotham, 1796), II.ii (vol. 1, pp. 264–65); George Hill, *Heads of Lectures*, IV.vii (St. Andrews: at the University Press, 1796), p. 79; John Brown of Haddington, *A Compendious View of Natural and Revealed Religion. In seven books*, 2nd ed., rev. (Edinburgh: Murray and Cochrane, 1796), II.ii (p. 151).

112. Cf. McNeill's note 5 to Calvin, *Institutes*, II.xii.5; with Gründler, *Die Gotteslehre*, p. 112.

113. Yates, *Modell of Divinitie*, pp. 257–59.

is viewed as establishing a systematic order),[114] Alsted, Martinius,[115] Ames, Maccovius, Voetius, and Witsius as well. Perkins' definitions and arrangements of doctrine, in particular, are instructive. His more extended definitions are clearly supralapsarian in and of themselves, and he clearly understood creation and fall as means decreed by God to the ends of election and reprobation. Still, he chose the genre-determined ecclesiological placement of the doctrine in his *Exposition of the Creede*. By contrast, in his presentation of the order of the causes of salvation and damnation, the *Golden Chaine*, where one might expect the entire doctrine of predestination to be placed in relation to the doctrine of God, Perkins presented the decree itself and a very general definition of predestination after his doctrine of God and before his comments on creation, but he reserved his discussion of election for a location between his doctrine of the fall and sin and his christological exposition, in a chapter entitled "Of Election and of Iesus Christ the foundation thereof."[116] What is more, his definition of election at that point is left indeterminate on the identification of its human objects relative to the fall. As for reprobation, Perkins leaves his discussion to the end of the treatise, after the work of salvation had been presented and again refrains from an identification of the human objects of the decree in relation to the fall.[117]

Of interest here also is the supralapsarian Maccovius, who, as we have seen, placed peredestination among the divine attributes in his *Loci communes*. But in his manual of theological and philosophical distinctions and rules, Maccovius placed predestination after the *locus* on creation and prior to providence, without, however, any substantive alteration of his definition.[118] What makes Maccovius even more interesting on the point is his identification of the object of predestination: considered *in intentione Dei*, the object of predestination is

---

114. Of course, it is not a system: see Richard A. Muller, "Perkins' *A Golden Chaine*: Predestinarian System or Schematized *Ordo Salutis*?" in *Sixteenth Century Journal*, 9/1 (1978), pp. 69–81.

115. Cf. Matthias Martinius, *Disputationes theologicae ad summulam s. theologiae enarrandam publice habitarum, decas prima* (Bremen: Johann Wessel, 1611), IX (p. 145ff.), with idem, *Christiana et catholica fides*, III.2.

116. William Perkins, *A Golden Chaine*, xv, in *Workes*, vol. 1, p. 24.

117. Perkins, *A Golden Chaine*, lii, in *Workes*, vol. 1, p. 105.

118. Maccovius, *Distinctiones*, vii.

homo creabilis, man as creatable or as possibility for creation, namely, as idea or exemplar in the mind of God, which is one of the options for supralapsarian definition. Considered according to the end or goal of the decree, however, which is to say not *in intentione* but *in executione*, the object of the divine willing is "*homo condendus, conditus, permittendus in lapsum, lapsus.*" Depending on which question one asked to determine the placement of the doctrine, *de intentione* or *de executione*, placement would vary and the definition would remain the same.

When, therefore, theologians of the era of orthodoxy placed the doctrine of predestination in relation to the doctrine of God in their more or less systematic works, but referenced it in other places, notably under ecclesiology in their creedal and catechetical theologies (all the while maintaining consistent definition, whether infra- or supralapsarian), it becomes highly improbable that placement of the doctrine was in any way conjoined to variations in content and meaning. Rather, in different literary genres belonging to the work of the theologian, differing didactic issues relate to the placement of the doctrine in terms of one or more of the relationships that it would carry with it in any case. These differing placements by the same theologian also stand in the way of the theory of the predestinarian system as presented by Emil Brunner, Basil Hall, and others, in which the so-called movement of predestination into relation with the doctrine of God signals a major doctrinal claim. Thus the rigid, logic-chopping scholastics to whom the model is attributed would appear to have been quite lax in the application of their own logic.

The many instances of the placement of the doctrine in ecclesiology, found most typically in creedal expositions, catechisms, and in lectures or sermons on the Heidelberg Catechism, deserve special note. In the first place, these examples are not separable—given that the ecclesiological placement in the catechism is in fact the creedal model. Historically, moreover, Calvin's *Catechism* of 1545 and Ursinus' lectures on the Heidelberg Catechism may have also inspired the ecclesiological placement of the doctrine in expositions of the creed by Perkins and Witsius. Arguably, particularly in later commentaries on the Heidelberg Catechism, this ecclesiological location of predestination was not the result of major theological analysis of the problem of placement on the part of seventeenth-century authors but merely the maintenance of the tradition of locating the doctrine in this place.

Perhaps even more importantly, those few theologians of the sixteenth and seventeenth centuries who actually do explain issues of placement and order of teaching—notably Calvin, Hyperius, Musculus, Beza, and Pictet—do not offer explanations that resemble the arguments about implications of placement found in Barth, Brunner, Dowey, and Hall. In Calvin's *Institutes*, the issue was not to highlight a noetic over against an ontic model, but to establish, as Calvin himself indicated, a pedagogically suitable model. Beza, as we have seen, distinguished between the diagrammatic placement of predestination as first in the order of causes of salvation and the order to be used for teaching the doctrine, in which he followed fairly precisely Calvin's 1539 Pauline ordering. Similarly, Pictet chose to follow out the model established by his infralapsarian ordering of the decrees, so that, one may again say, pedagogically, his system followed an outline that resembled the patterning of its own definition such that the decree to bring about a particular series of events is discussed prior to the discussion of those events.

This pedagogical concern, as the dominant issue in determining the order of a theology and the relative placement of individual topics, reflects, moreover, the *locus* method followed by nearly all of the Reformed writers of the eras of the Reformation and orthodoxy: the formulation of a theological system or body of doctrine consisted, first, in the identification (on the basis of exegesis and traditionary norms) of a series of *loci communes theologici*, commonplaces or standard topics and, second, in the establishment of a suitable *methodus* or path through the topics for the sake of teaching the whole in a suitable manner.[119] Indeed, as a historically contextual counter-hypothesis to the notion of profound theological implications associated with the placement of predestination, we can offer a pedagogical explanation: namely, the forward or *a priori* placement in its several variants corresponds, for the most part, with the highly developed and detailed academic model, identified by the Protestant orthodox as "scholastic" in its method; the

---

119. See the further discussion and bibliography in Muller, *After Calvin*, pp. 49–51, 57–60.

ecclesiological placement of the doctrine corresponds with the forms of catechetical theology; and the placement in the several variants of the "Pauline order" belongs, typically, to a middle category of "positive theology," such as might be taken by a confession of faith or a basic teaching manual. In the cases of Calvin's *Institutio* and Bucanus' *Institutiones*, this middle category between catechetical and scholastic/academic is surely identified in the title, *institutio* or "fundamental instruction"—as also in the case of Bucanus' work by the use of a question and answer format.[120] All of these categories or models were noted by the Protestant orthodox as basic forms of their teaching. The emphasis on pedagogy reflects the concerns of the Renaissance rhetoric and logic at the historical root of the *locus* method itself.[121]

This pedagogical or genre-determined explanation of the placement of doctrines is not, moreover, to be taken rigidly. We have already noted the wide variety of placements of predestination in larger theological works of a more or less scholastic character. It is also worth noting that expositions of the creed and catechisms of the era do not invariably discuss predestination or always locate it in the doctrine of the church. A large number of identifiably Reformed catechisms omit discussion of the doctrine entirely,[122] while a few others note the doctrine in some relation to the doctrine of God,[123] and others note the doctrine of election in relation to the doctrine of the church.[124]

The various placements of the doctrine indicate decisions to teach the doctrine according to differing patterns rather than decisions to impart different meanings to the doctrine. Nor is it the case that placement results in a new or different doctrinal emphasis, inasmuch as the various placements themselves represent different relationships and associations already present within the definitions of predestination

---

120. Cf. the discussion of *institutio* in Muller, *Unaccommodated Calvin*, pp. 104–8, 142–43, 149.

121. On which, see Muller, *PRRD*, I, 1.1 (B.2); 1.2 (B.3); 2.3 (B.2–3); 4.1 (A, B.2); 9.4.

122. E.g., Calvin, *Catechism* (1545), in *CO* 6, col. 1–160 (*Selected Works*, vol. 2, pp. 33–94); cf. Kranendonk, *Teaching Predestination*, pp. 112–14, 118–21.

123. E.g., Ball, *Short Treatise*, pp. 56–58; Crook, *Guide unto true blessednesse*, pp. 10–11; Boughton, *God and man*, pp. 25–31; cf. Kranendonk, *Teaching Predestination*, p. 108.

124. Note the list in Kranendonk, *Teaching Predestination*, p. 108.

and related doctrines rather than new associations created by the placement—and none of the various placements press one or another of the associations between predestination and other doctrines to the exclusion of other doctrinal relationships. In other words, the placements do, in fact, indicate genuine understandings of doctrinal relationships, but it is not the placement that creates the relationships. Nor does the placement argue a particular relationship to be determinative of the meaning of the doctrine beyond what has been already established by the definition.

What is more, in most of the theologians and theological systems noted, the basis for a particular placement of the doctrine (given that placement does not affect the definition) is most likely a pedagogical or traditionary choice rather than a dogmatic claim. The majority of seventeenth-century writers, including those who agreed with Pictet on the ordering of the decrees, still placed predestination after the doctrine of God and before creation, taking both a pedagogically motivated and a traditionary approach. We should not assume on the part of any of these writers that the placement of predestination was arrived at after a great amount of meditation on the theological implications of order and arrangement. The same is true for those later writers who continue the tradition of alluding to or reciting the doctrine of predestination as a part of the exposition of the creedal doctrine of the church. They followed, in other words, the path of least resistance and simply accepted the standard form of dogmatic or catechetical system that they had inherited and then, without any great worry about the order defining their doctrines for them, proceeded to define each doctrine, including that of predestination, within its own *locus* and in its traditional relationships and associations, as modified by their confessional adherence and personal proclivities.

These historical evidences lead us to the rather inevitable historiographical conclusion that nearly all of the extant discussions of the "placement of predestination" in the Reformed theologies of the sixteenth and seventeenth centuries have been fundamentally misguided. They have consistently confused placement with definition. Frequently they have inferred a supralapsarian definition from a placement of the doctrine prior to the fall, and they have also made the mistake of assuming that a soteriological or *a posteriori* placement of the doctrine implies a "softening" of the rigors of predestination even though such placement has little or no discernible effect on the definition. Contra Dowey, who claimed that Calvin's placement of the doctrine "never sees the believer…as in direct connection with the precreation decrees,"[125] one might conclude that, if placement were an issue, Calvin's placement had precisely the opposite implication. For in the *Institutes*, Calvin's definition of what Dowey calls "precreation decrees" is placed into the context of the Christian life, whereas in the typical Reformed orthodox model, the "precreation decrees" are discussed in advance of any direct reflection on the life of the believer, in the place implied by their basic definition, namely, before creation. In fact, neither Calvin nor the later orthodox understand the decree itself in "direct connection" with the believer, given that election is not an immediate or unmediated act of God but is always understood as being executed by way of secondary causes.

What is even more precarious in these formulations is that they take the supralapsarian or precreation placement of the doctrine as emblematic of a speculative and deductive model, when the most that can be said of this placement is that it presents the doctrine at the point in the system at which God wills the decree, namely, in God's eternity, prior to the foundation of the world. The assumption that God wills the decree in eternity (however one defines the relationship between the decree and its human objects) is no more and no less than the assumption of the entire church (including various "semi-Pelagians" and Arminians) since the writing of Ephesians 1:4. Contra Brunner and those who follow his thesis, the placement of the doctrine of predestination in relation to God is hardly speculative—at least no more speculative than the implication of the first chapter of the epistle to the Ephesians. With regard to Barth's argumentation, it is clear that the various placements of the doctrine of predestination in sixteenth- and seventeenth-century Reformed theologies do illustrate the different doctrinal relationships that are to be established between the notion of divine decrees and the other topics in Reformed theology, but it is equally clear that these relationships, latent in the

---

125. Dowey, *Knowledge of God*, p. 186.

doctrine and its basic definition, obtain in virtually all cases of its statement whatever its placement in the outline of a theological system.

In short, the placement of the doctrine of predestination in the Reformed theologies of the sixteenth and seventeenth centuries was, primarily, a matter of genre. Given, moreover, the various placements of the doctrine found throughout the era, there is no evidence for the claim characteristic of an earlier scholarship that there was a shift in doctrinal implication signaled by a shift in the placement of the doctrine in the generations after Calvin. There is certainly no evidence to uphold the claim that there was a movement from *a posteriori* to *a priori* placement, as there is no evidence for the claim that *a posteriori* placement evidenced a soteriological or christological emphasis and *a priori* placement a metaphysical interest. These explanations amount to the imposition of what Quentin Skinner has called a "mythology of coherence" on the materials of the past.[126] And, frankly, it is a mythology the roots of which do not go back before the twentieth century. The placement of the doctrine in any given theological treatise was not an indication of the author's intention to highlight a particular doctrinal relationship or give a particular cast or emphasis to his theology. Rather, it was, with few exceptions, an indication of the specific genre and purpose of the document—indeed, an indication of which traditional genre had been selected by the author as a vehicle for the statement of his theology.

------

126. Quentin Skinner, "Meaning and Understanding in the History of Ideas," in *History and Theory*, 8 (1969), pp. 3–53.

CHAPTER 3

Calvin on Predestination: A Developmental and Bibliographical Essay

The doctrine with which Calvin's name is most frequently associated, the doctrine of predestination,[1] stands quite firmly in the tradition of Augustinian formulation. Further, the doctrine should not be viewed, as has been claimed, either as the central theme of his theology as a whole or as his central soteriological doctrine and therefore primary polemical concern.[2] Whereas it is certainly incorrect to identify Calvin (any more than his Protestant opposite, Arminius) as the proponent of a single doctrine—or, indeed, to claim that Calvin formulated an entire theological system by a process of logical deduction from the divine decrees—it is most certainly the case that this inherited element of Augustinian theology was an issue close to the heart of Calvin's theology and piety and that it stood as one of the several doctrinal topics

---

1. Among the significant monographs are Max Scheibe, *Calvins Prädestination-slehre: ein Beitrag zur Würdigung der Eigenart seiner Theologie und Religiosität* (Halle: M. Niemeyer, 1897); Paul Jacobs, *Prädestination und Verantwortlichkeit bei Calvin* (Neukirchen: Buchhandlung des Erziehungsvereins, 1937); Hans Otten, *Calvins theologische Anschauung von der Prädestination* (Munich: Chr. Kaiser, 1938); Fred H. Klooster, *Calvin's Doctrine of Predestination*, 2nd rev. ed. (Grand Rapids: Baker, 1977); David Neeld Wiley, "Calvin's Doctrine of Predestination: His Principal Soteriological and Polemical Doctrine" (PhD diss., Duke University, 1971); Harald Rimbach, *Gnade und Erkenntnis in Calvins Prädestinationslehre: Calvin im Vergleich mit Pighius, Beza und Melanchthon* (New York: Peter Lang, 1996).

2. As in Wiley, "Calvin's Doctrine"; note Charles Partee, "Calvin's Central Dogma Again," in *Sixteenth Century Journal*, 18/2 (1987), pp. 191–200, where the author sets aside the notion of predestination as central dogma but still looks (quite in vain!) for a motif around which Calvin's thought coheres.

so essential to Calvin's thought that he spared no pains to defend it against any and all adversaries.

Given, moreover, the largely nontechnical character of Calvin's expositions, his doctrine is easily misconstrued. It is characteristic of many nineteenth-century and early twentieth-century comments on Calvin and "Calvinism" to identify predestination as the central principle or central dogma of his theology,[3] a claim that remains current in much popular literature. By contrast, it is quite typical of later twentieth-century discussions of the doctrine, written in the wake of the Christomonism of the neoorthodox theologians, to claim that Calvin's formulations, in rather stark contrast to the formulations of other, particularly later, Reformed writers, are Christocentric—even that the key to understanding Calvin's teaching is that it is Christocentric.[4] Perhaps the most extreme misrepresentation of Calvin's teaching on predestination is the claim that, in his *Institutes*, Calvin taught that "God elects to salvation those whom he foresees will be true believers" and "asserts that God foresees who will believe and elects or condemns as a function of this," effectively reading Calvin as the clear predecessor of Arminius.[5] This despite Arminius' own very clear assessment to the contrary! It is also the case that the majority of these dogmatic presentations of Calvin's teaching focus primarily on the *Institutes*, with little

---

3. E.g., Alexander Schweizer, *Die Glaubenslehre der evangelisch-reformirten Kirche dargestellt und aus den Quellen belegt*, 2 vols. (Zurich: Orell, Füssli, 1844–1847); idem, *Die protestantischen Centraldogmen in ihrer Entwicklung innerhalb der reformierten Kirche*, 2 vols. (Zurich: Orell, Füssli, 1854–1856); William Hastie, *The Theology of the Reformed Church in Its Fundamental Principles* (Edinburgh: T&T Clark, 1904).

4. Cf., e.g., Charles Partee, *The Theology of John Calvin* (Louisville: Westminster/ John Knox, 2008), pp. 240–42; and note the critique of Christocentrism in Richard A. Muller, "A Note on 'Christocentrism' and the Imprudent Use of Such Terminology," in *Westminster Theological Journal*, 68 (2006), pp. 253–60.

5. Irena Backus and Philip Benedict, introduction to *Calvin and His Influence 1509–2009*, ed. I. Backus and P. Benedict (New York: Oxford University Press, 2011), p. 13. Elsewhere, Backus argues that "Calvin argued in different works and at different periods either that God elected some men to be saved but no one actually to be damned or that God had emitted a decree predetermining some to salvation and others to damnation." Irena Backus, *Leibniz: Protestant Theologian* (New York: Oxford University Press, 2016), p. 68. The first of these characterizations is simply incorrect; the second confuses damnation and reprobation (a distinction that, admittedly, is not always clear in Calvin's writings).

attention to the development of Calvin's thought in other works, some of which were written after the final edition of the *Institutes*.

It would require a very large monograph on Calvin's understanding of predestination to examine all of the materials on predestination scattered throughout Calvin's writings—not to mention sorting through all of the secondary literature—and attempt to present yet another reading of his doctrine. It does become clear, however, from an examination of the course of Calvin's writings in which predestination was referenced, formulated, or defended, that further examination is called for in the light of the breadth of Calvin's approaches and their varied contexts and genres. What an essay like the following can provide, therefore, is a sense of the path taken by Calvin in his various writings on the subject of predestination and, therefore, also a path toward a more nuanced interpretation of his thought. From a purely bibliographical perspective, without pretending to note every text relevant to the discussion of Calvin's views, this essay offers references to major places of interest in Calvin's original texts and their locations in the *Opera Calvini*,[6] as well as noting extant translations.[7]

First Formulations, 1536–1540

Calvin first noted the topic of predestination very briefly in his 1536 *Institutes*, in his discussion of the fourth portion of the creed, "I believe in the Holy Catholic Church."[8] The church, he wrote,

> is also holy, because as many as have been chosen by God's eternal providence to be adopted as members of the church—all these

---

6. John Calvin, *Opera quae supersunt omnia*, ed. G. Baum et al., 59 vols. (Brunswick: Schwetschke, 1863–1900), hereinafter cited as *CO*.

7. I have also consulted *Commentaries of John Calvin*, 46 vols. (Edinburgh: Calvin Translation Society, 1844–1855), hereinafter abbreviated *CTS*, followed by the name of the book and the volume, as applicable, e.g., *CTS Genesis*, vol. 1. Note also that the verse numbers in *CO* sometimes differ from those in *CTS*: the *CO* verse numbers are indicated first, the *CTS* verse numbers second, in square brackets. For further bibliographical information, readers should see Wulfert de Greef, *The Writings of John Calvin: An Introductory Guide*, trans. Lyle D. Bierma, 2nd ed. (Louisville: Westminster John Knox, 2008).

8. Arguably, the different placements of the doctrine in Calvin's various works has more to do with his sense of the genre of the work and its pedagogical order; see chapter 2, "The Placement of Predestination in Reformed Theology," in the present volume.

> are made holy by the Lord…. Consequently, the Lord, when he calls his own, justified and glorifies his own, is declaring nothing but his eternal election, by which he had destined them to this end before they were born. Therefore no one will ever enter into the glory of the Heavenly Kingdom, who has not been called in this manner, and justified, seeing that without any exception, the Lord in this manner sets forth and manifests his election in all men whom He has chosen.[9]

The catechetical location of the doctrine in relation to the church fore-shadows the theme of corporate in relation to individual election that would become prominent in later commentaries. Calvin's language is of interest inasmuch as it is exceedingly sparse and nontechnical, referring to "eternal providence" rather than to predestination and noting only the positive aspect of the divine choice, namely, election. The linking of the two topics is, certainly, a reflection of the traditional understanding of predestination as "a part of providence [*pars providentiae*]."[10] In addition, the linking of predestination and providence here points toward the form of a new chapter added in 1539, "On the Predestination and Providence of God," although the passing reference to the subject in the 1536 text in no way prepares the reader for the highly developed discussion of 1539.

The appearance of this particular discussion in the *Institutes* of 1539, like the broader recasting of the entire work, directs our attention to the progress of Calvin's life and thought in the intervening years. Crucial to an understanding of this development is the catechism, entitled *Catechismus, sive christianae religionis institutio* (Catechism, or an instruction in the Christian religion), published by Calvin for use in Geneva in 1537 (the French text) and 1538 (the Latin text).[11] The

---

9. John Calvin, *Christianae religionis institutio, totam fere pietatis summam, et quicquid est in doctrina salutis cognitu necessarium, complectens: omnibus pietatis studiosis lectu dignissimum opus, ac recens editum* (Basel: Platter & Lasius, 1536), pp. 87–88; in *CO* 1, col. 1–252, here, col. 73; in translation, *Institutes of the Christian Religion: 1536 Edition*, trans. Ford Lewis Battles, rev. ed. (Grand Rapids: Eerdmans, 1986), pp. 58–59.

10. The point is ably defended by Paul Helm, "Calvin, the 'Two Issues,' and the Structure of the *Institutes*," in *Calvin Theological Journal*, 42/2 (2007), pp. 341–48.

11. John Calvin, *Catechismus, sive christianae religionis institutio, communibus renatae nuper in Evangelio Genevensis Ecclesiae suffragiis recepta* (Basel: Robertus Winter, 1538); also in *CO* 5, col. 313–62; and note John Calvin, *Le Catéchisme français de*

title of the work clearly reflects the first edition of the *Institutes*, while the topics here discussed by Calvin for the first time point toward the revision of the *Institutes* in 1539.[12] Indeed, Calvin's earliest writing in which predestination appeared as a separate topic was not the major discussion added to the *Institutes* in 1539 but the brief chapter included in his 1537–1538 catechism, where Calvin set the doctrine into the context of the chapters on faith and justification.[13]

This development of 1537 and 1538 was followed shortly by the extended new chapter on predestination and providence in the 1539 *Institutes* and by the commentary on Romans (1540),[14] in which Calvin dealt with predestination exegetically in his comments on chapters eight and nine. This development followed so quickly, indeed, that the writing of the documents must be understood as an interrelated effort in which Calvin's meditation on the text of Romans, the method to be followed in a commentary, and the related methods of basic catechesis and of further ministerial instruction led both to a model for theological argumentation not evidenced in the first edition of the *Institutes* and to an overall pattern of working that would occupy Calvin for the remainder of his career.[15] If it is correct, as has been suggested, that Calvin's commentary on Romans was based on lectures that he gave in Geneva between 1536 and 1538, there was a priority of the exegetical work over the doctrinal expansion in the *Institutes*.[16]

Calvin, publiée en 1537, reimprimé pour la première fois, ed. Albert Rilliet and Théophile Dufour (Geneva: H. Georg, 1878). A reproduction of the 1538 Latin text, with translation, is found in *Catechism or Institution of the Christian Religion*, trans. Ford Lewis Battles (Pittsburgh: Pittsburgh Theological Seminary, 1972; rev. 1976).

12. See the discussion of the document in Richard A. Muller, *The Unaccommodated Calvin: Studies in the Foundation of a Theological Tradition* (New York: Oxford University Press, 2000), pp. 103–5, 119–23.

13. Calvin, *Catéchisme français*, xiii; idem, *Catechismus, sive christianae religionis institutio*, xiii.

14. John Calvin, *Institutio christianae religionis nunc vere demum suo titulo respondens* (Strasbourg: Wendelin Rihel, 1539); and idem, *Commentarii in epistolam Pauli ad Romanos* (Strasbourg: Wendelin Rihel, 1540), in *CO* 49, col. 1–292. N.B. the text of the 1539 *Institutes* in *CO* 1 is a composite of the 1539–1554 editions.

15. See the discussion of the document in Muller, *Unaccommodated Calvin*, pp. 27–31.

16. See T. H. L. Parker, *Calvin's New Testament Commentaries*, 2nd ed. (Louisville: Westminster/John Knox, 1993), p. 15.

These exegetical efforts not only provided Calvin with a foundation for the more dogmatic or topical statements of the doctrine that can be found in the *Institutes* from 1539 onward and in his various treatises on the subject, they also served as points of reference in the ensuing debates. Calvin's larger method or pattern of working followed both an exegetical and a topical track: the editorial strata of the *Institutes* bear witness, in added text and added citations, to the commentaries and sometimes the sermons that Calvin produced prior to each new edition of the *Institutes*. It appears to have been his pattern of working to add short biblical citations and comments to the topical discussions in the *Institutes*, often for the sake of directing the reader toward the exposition in the commentary. He frequently refrains from duplicating the detail of the commentary in the *Institutes* or treatise. Thus, the citations of texts in his debates of predestination ought to lead to the reader's juxtaposition of treatise (or *Institutes*) and commentary for the sake of identifying the whole of Calvin's argument on the point. In the specific cases of Romans 8:28–30; 9:1–33; and Ephesians 1:1–12, the use of the Pauline texts in the polemical treatises is quite lacking in exegetical elaboration—and the commentaries appear to be presupposed in a radical sense.

The point that Calvin's exegetical work must be read and, indeed, chronologically coordinated with the editions of the *Institutes*, if the development and content of his theology are to be understood, is nowhere more clearly illustrated than by his doctrine of predestination. Only in 1539, as he worked through the doctrine exegetically in his commentary on Romans, did Calvin introduce an extended discussion of predestination, conjoined to the doctrine of providence, into the *Institutes*. Indeed, in terms of the model proposed in the preface to the *Institutes*, Calvin offered, in 1539, the dogmatic disputation or theological *locus* on predestination that, had he followed the Bucerian or Bullingerian pattern of exegesis, he would have placed into the commentary after the verse-by-verse analysis of Romans 9, without its related doctrine of providence. The commentary and the topical discussion in the *Institutes* must be read together,[17] and Calvin's departure from the methods of his immediate predecessors in the exposition

---

17. Cf. the discussion in Muller, *Unaccommodated Calvin*, pp. 140–58.

of Romans—Bucer, Melanchthon, and Bullinger—should not be allowed to obscure their influence on his interpretation of the text.[18]

The 1539 *Institutes* must be recognized as establishing the basic form of Calvin's doctrine (with augmentation and some adjustment in editions of 1543–1557) that would be identified with his theological position for most of his career and that he would defend in his major controversies on the topic of predestination, namely, his controversies with Albert Pighius, Jerome Bolsec, and Sebastian Castellio.[19] It is important to recognize—contrary to many scholars' comments on this issue—the integral relationship between predestination and providence that belongs not only to the editions of the *Institutes* from 1539 to 1550, but also to Calvin's *De aeterna Dei praedestinatione* (1552). The doctrine of predestination that Calvin defended against his three major adversaries was a doctrine of predestination as a special act of divine providence, and therefore intimately coordinated with God's general providential care of the world. Nor would this view be contradicted or disrupted by the formal separation of the topics in the *Institutes* of 1559. That this model of explicit connection between predestination and providence, as well as the so-called *a posteriori* placement of both doctrines, remained influential after 1559 is documented by the organization of Theodore Beza's detailed catechetical synopsis of theology, published in 1570, in which Beza echoed the 1539–1550 ordering of the *Institutes* by presenting providence and predestination together in a unified topic placed in *a posteriori* relation to the doctrines concerning Christ, faith, justification, and sanctification.[20]

---

18. Note, for example, Joel Edward Kok, "The Influence of Martin Bucer on Calvin's Interpretation of Romans: A Comparative Case Study" (PhD diss., Duke University, 1993); idem, "Heinrich Bullinger's Exegetical Method: The Model for Calvin?," in *Biblical Interpretation in the Era of the Reformation: Essays Presented to David C. Steinmetz in Honor of His Sixtieth Birthday*, ed. Richard A. Muller and John L. Thompson (Grand Rapids: Eerdmans, 1996), pp. 241–54.

19. Cf. the comments on Calvin's 1539 *Institutes* in Muller, *Unaccommodated Calvin*, pp. 118–19; and on the subsequent adjustments of the text, 1543–1557, in ibid., pp. 131–33.

20. Theodore Beza, *Quaestionum et responsionum christianarum libellus, in quo praecipua Christianae religionis capita* κατ᾽ ἐπιτωμήν *proponuntur* (Geneva: Jean Crespin, 1570), but reversing the order, with providence first (pp. 92–115) and predestination following (pp. 115–31).

A Second Stage: Polemics and Positive Statement, 1540–1559

Calvin's next referencing of predestination is probably found in the catechism, written in 1541 and thought to have been published in 1542. The earliest surviving edition dates from 1545.[21] Calvin's presentation of the doctrine here is notable for its brevity and pastoral quality and its focus solely on the election of believers. Calvin placed his statement of the doctrine under the creedal topic of the church understood as "the gathering of the faithful ordained and elected by God to life eternal" and as the "fruit" or "effect" of Christ's death.[22] This catechetical placement echoes the creedal pattern of the 1536 *Institutes* rather than the ordering of either the 1537–38 catechisms or the 1539 *Institutes*. This *locus* of the doctrine remained crucial for Calvin not so much in his doctrinal statements as in his approach to election as corporate and particular in his commentaries.

The lengthy expositions of the doctrines of free choice and predestination in Calvin's 1539 *Institutes* generated a major response from the Roman Catholic theologian Albert Pighius.[23] Calvin's response appeared in two parts, separated by almost a decade, the first part standing as a direct response to Pighius' treatise, focused on the issue of free choice, the second as being a more general treatise on predestination, brought forth by the controversy with Bolsec, but nonetheless addressed primarily to the more careful and convincing arguments of Pighius. In the first treatise, Calvin's defense of "the orthodox doctrine of the bondage and liberation of human choice,"[24] he followed the

---

21. John Calvin, *Le Catechisme de Geneve: c'est à dire le formulaire d'instruire les enfans en la Chrestienté, fait en maniere de dialogue, où le ministre interrogue, et l'enfant respond* (Geneva: Jean Girard, 1545); *CO* 6, col. 1–134; translation in *Selected Works of John Calvin: Tracts and Letters*, trans. Henry Beveridge and Jules Bonnet, 7 vols. (Grand Rapids: Baker, 1983), vol. 2, pp. 33–94.

22. Calvin, *Catechisme de Geneve*, p. 34 (*CO* 6, col. 39–40).

23. Albert Pighius, *De Libera hominis arbitrio & divina gratia libri decem* (Cologne: Melchior Novesianus, 1542); and see A. N. S. Lane, "Albert Pighius's Controversial Work on Original Sin," in *Reformation & Renaissance Review*, 4 (2000), pp. 29–61, for an account of Pighius' work and a further bibliography.

24. John Calvin, *Defensio sanae et orthodoxae doctrinae de servitute et liberatione humani arbitrii adv. calumnias A. Pighii Campensis* (Geneva: Jean Girard, 1543), in *CO* 6, 225–404; translated as *The Bondage and Liberation of the Will: A Defence of the Orthodox Doctrine of Human Choice against Pighius*, ed. A. N. S. Lane, trans. G. I. Davies (Grand Rapids: Baker, 1996); and see the studies of L. F. Schulze, *Calvin's*

order of Pighius' treatise, which itself followed the order of argument in the 1539 *Institutes*. Much of Calvin's text is devoted to a refutation of Pighius' patristic argumentation, largely for the purpose of demonstrating the patristic rootage of Calvin's own doctrine and, therefore, also its catholicity. At the heart of the disagreement with Pighius is Calvin's assumption that the fallen will is not free to will either good or evil, but is bound in sin.

Given the controversy with Pighius, it was hardly fortuitous that Calvin's Romans commentary saw the publication of an excerpted French version in 1543,[25] a printing in French in 1545 solely of the "Argument" or summary prefaced to the commentary,[26] and a complete translation in 1550.[27] In none of these printings, however, was there a significant alteration or development of doctrinal statement except by way of condensation in the 1543 text.

After Calvin's 1543 treatise against Pighius, perhaps the most striking development in Calvin's thought on predestination is the careful parsing of the causality of predestination in his 1548 commentary on Ephesians, where the decree is described according to its first, formal, material, and final causes. Calvin indicates that three causes of salvation are immediately stated in Ephesians 1:5–6, "Having predestinated

---

Reply to Pighius (Potchefstroom: Pro Rege, 1971); idem, "Calvin's Reply to Pighius—a Micro and a Macro View," in *Calvinus Ecclesiae Genevensis Custos*, ed. W. H. Neuser (Bern: Peter Lang, 1984), pp. 171–85; and Anthony N. S. Lane, "Did Calvin Believe in Free Will?" in *Vox Evangelica*, 12 (1981), pp. 79–80; idem, "Calvin and the Fathers in *Bondage and Liberation of the Will*," in *Calvinus Sincerioris Religionis Vindex*, ed. W. H. Neuser and B. G. Armstrong (Kirksville, Mo.: Sixteenth Century Journal, 1997), pp. 67–96; idem, "The Influence upon Calvin of His Debate with Pighius," in *Auctoritas Patrum II. Neue Beiträge zur Rezeption der Kirchenväter im 15. und 16. Jahrhundert*, ed. Leif Grane, Alfred Schindler, and Markus Wriedt (Mainz: Philipp von Zaberenm, 1998), pp. 125–39; and André Pinard, "Le débat sur la grâce et le libre arbitre: La 'Response aux calomnies d'Albert Pighius'—contexte et synthèse théologique," in *La Revue Farel*, 4 (2009), pp. 37–67; idem, "Libre arbitre ou liberté de la grâce? La notion de grâce irrésistible dans la 'Response aux calomnies d'Albert Pighius', par Jean Calvin," in *La Revue réformée*, 63/4 (2012), pp. 47–72.

25. John Calvin, *Exposition sur l'Epistre de sainct Paul aux Romains, extraicte des Commentaires de M. J. Calvin* (Geneva: Jean Girard, 1543).

26. John Calvin, *Argument et sommaire de l'Epistre sainct Paul aux Romains, pour donner intelligence à toute l'Epistre en peu de parolles* (Geneva: Jean Girard, 1545).

27. See Parker, *Calvin's New Testament Commentaries*, pp. 206–7, on all three of these texts.

us unto the adoption of children by Jesus Christ to himself, according to the good pleasure of his will, to the praise of his glorious grace"— "Jesus Christ," the material cause; "the good pleasure of his will," the efficient cause; and "the praise of his glorious grace," the final cause. Verse 8 supplies the formal cause, the preaching of the gospel.[28] Calvin would offer further clarification of issues of causality against Pighius in 1552,[29] and the 1559 *Institutes* would add reference to Ephesians 1:5 for the "highest cause" of predestination,[30] albeit in neither case with the precision of the commentary on Ephesians.

In 1550, Calvin published a "little book [*libellus*]" on predestination and providence. The book offers nothing new; it is simply an independent printing of chapter fourteen of Calvin's *Institutes*.[31] The printing does indicate, however, the continued importance of the doctrine as an issue in debate—important enough for the printer to extract the chapter and publish it separately.

Bolsec and Beyond, 1551–1555

Jerome (or Hieronymus) Bolsec was a former Carmelite monk of Paris who set aside his vows and fled to Ferrara in 1545 for protection under the rule of its rather freethinking duchess.[32] He there married and began to practice medicine. He subsequently displeased the duchess and was forced out of Ferrara. In 1550, he arrived at Geneva, set up his medical practice, and began to express theological opinions on the doctrine of predestination at considerable variance with those of

---

28. John Calvin, *Commentarii, in quatuor Pauli Epistolas: ad Galatas, ad Ephesios, ad Philippenses, ad Colossenses* (Geneva: Jean Girard, 1548), 1:5–8; idem, *Commentarius in Epistolam Pauli ad Ephesios*, in *CO* 51, col. 137–240, here col. 148–50 (*CTS Ephesians*, pp. 200–203).

29. E.g., John Calvin, *De aeterna Dei praedestinatione qua in salutem alios ex hominibus elegit, alios suo exitio reliquit: item de providentia qua res humanas gubernat, Consensus pastorum Genevensis Ecclesiae a Jo. Calvino expositus* (Geneva: Jean Crispin, 1552), in *CO* 8, 249–366, here col. 312.

30. Calvin, *Institutio* (1559), III.xxii.2.

31. John Calvin, *De praedestinatione & providentia Dei, libellus* (Geneva: Conrad Badius, 1550).

32. On Bolsec, see Gary W. Jenkins, *Calvin's Tormentors: Understanding the Conflicts that Shaped the Reformer* (Grand Rapids: Baker Academic, 2018), pp. 109–24; also note Philip C. Holtrop, *The Bolsec Controversy on Predestination, from 1551–1555*, 2 parts (Lewiston, N.Y.: Edwin Mellen, 1993).

Calvin. Calvin's God, he said, was hypocritical and more vile than Satan. When summoned before the Venerable Company of Pastors on March 8, 1551, and instructed in doctrine by Calvin, he remained unconvinced.[33] Called before the consistory after further remarks on the subject, he stated his own teaching in opposition to that of Calvin. He confessed that God had elected some to salvation, but that he allowed no decree of reprobation. He also maintained that grace was offered equally to all people and that the reason why some are saved and others damned lay entirely in the human faculty of free choice. There may be, as some have argued, parallels between Bolsec's argument and Bullinger's, albeit without Bullinger's clearly identifiable monergism or his occasional indication of double predestination.[34] Bolsec's claim of an equal offer of grace to all, Calvin argued, was utterly inconsistent with any genuine concept of election. Shortly thereafter, on October 16, 1551, at the Friday theological *Congrégation* in Geneva, Bolsec vociferously protested against the doctrine of predestination presented in the sermon, arguing that it was fatalism, like that of Lorenzo Valla, and that it made God into a "senseless tyrant." He was immediately detained for having caused a disturbance.

Calvin's next uttered—but only later published—thoughts on the doctrine of predestination are found in his *Congrégation* on eternal election, delivered in response to Bolsec on December 18, 1551, but only published in 1562.[35] The *Congrégation* marked Calvin's final word

---

33. Documentation of Bolsec can be found in *Registres de la Compagnie des Pasteurs de Genève au temps de Calvin*, ed. R. M. Kingdon and J.-F. Bergier, 2 vols. (Geneva: Droz, 1962–1964), vol. 1, pp. 80–131, most of which, in turn, is translated in *The Register of the Company of Pastors of Geneva in the Time of Calvin*, ed. and trans. Philip E. Hughes (Grand Rapids: Eerdmans, 1966), pp. 137–86. The materials from the *Registres*, together with other documents from the civil side of the process, are found in *Actes du Procès intenté par Calvin et les autres ministres de Genève a Jérome Bolsec de Paris*, in *CO* 8, col. 144–248.

34. On Bullinger, see Cornelis P. Venema, *Heinrich Bullinger and the Doctrine of Predestination: Author of "the Other Reformed Tradition"?* (Grand Rapids: Baker Academic, 2002).

35. John Calvin, *Congrégation faite en l'eglise de Genève par M. Iean Calvin; en laquelle la matiere de l'election eternelle de Dieu fut sommairement et clairement par luy deduite et ratifiée d'un commun accord par ses freres ministres* (Geneva: Vincent Bres, 1562), in *CO* 8, col. 89–138. The *Congrégation* has been translated as *Calvinism by Calvin; being the Substance of Discourses delivered by Calvin and the other Ministers of Geneva on*

in response to the issues raised rather ineptly by Bolsec, and Calvin delivered it orally, referencing Bolsec as an agitator without mentioning his name. The argumentation of the *Congrégation* is largely based on the Pauline Epistles, with collateral reference to the Gospel of John, Isaiah, Ezekiel, and Jeremiah, with a concluding reference to Job. Calvin's major polemical works on predestination, written at the time of the controversy, do not directly address Bolsec at all. Bolsec was tried before the consistory and subsequently before the civil authorities, who sought doctrinal advice from the other Swiss Protestant cities and reformers.[36] He was found doctrinally deficient and as having promulgated "evil views" and was expelled from Geneva.[37]

Calvin's *Concerning the Eternal Predestination of God* (1552), alternatively titled the *Consensus Genevensis*, was his second response to Pighius, that also included polemics against the more recent anti-Protestant writing of Georgius Siculus (or George of Sicily).[38] The treatise dealt with predestination and providence, reflecting the doctrinal association already established in the 1539 *Institutes*.[39] The treatise, in

---

the Doctrines of Grace, trans. R. Govett (London: James Nisbet, 1840). On the document, see Erik De Boer, "The 'Consensus Genevensis' Revisited: The Genesis of the Genevan Consensus on Divine Election in 1551," in *Ad Fontes: Teologiese, historiese en wetenskap-filosofiese studies binne reformatoriese kader, Festschrift vir Ludie F. Schulze*, ed. Victor E. D'Assonville and E. A. de Boer (Bloemfontein: Redaksiekantoor van die Universiteit van die Vrystaat, 2004), pp. 51–77.

36. Note Cornelis P. Venema, "Heinrich Bullinger's Correspondence on Calvin's Doctrine of Predestination, 1551–1553," in *Sixteenth Century Journal*, 17/4 (Winter 1986), pp. 435–50.

37. *Actes du Procès*, #LXI, in *CO* 8, col. 245.

38. Georgius Siculus, *Epistola di Giorgio Siculo servo fidele di Jesu Christo alli Cittadini di Riva in Trento conta il mendatio di Francesco Spiera, & falsa dottrina di Protestanti* (Bologna: Anselmo Giccarello, 1550).

39. Calvin, *De aeterna Dei praedestinatione*, in *CO* 8, col. 249–366; translated as, *Concerning the Eternal Predestination of God*, trans. J. K. S. Reid (London: James Clarke, 1961). It is also translated as *A Treatise on the Eternal Predestination of God*, in *Calvin's Calvinism: Treatises on the Eternal Predestination of God and the Secret Providence of God*, trans. Henry Cole, 2 vols. in 1, continuous pagination (London: Wertheim and Macintosh, 1856–1857), pp. 13–186, 223–56. Cole removed the concluding section of the *Treatise on the Eternal Predestination of God* (here pp. 223–56), where Calvin turned to a discussion of providence, in order to use it as an "Introduction by John Calvin" to the treatise *On the Secret Providence of God*, found in the second part of his translation, with only a brief note (p. 13) to explain the dislocation of the text. Pages 187–206 insert one of Calvin's 1557 treatises against Castellio between the separated

its form as the *Consensus Genevensis*, served also as a resolution to the Bolsec controversy, although it does not so much as mention Bolsec's charges. The oblique comment in Calvin's prefatory remarks concerning a troublesome person is clearly a reference to Bolsec. As the title of this treatise indicates, it was signed by the pastors of Geneva. The signatures of the pastors indicate their willingness to support Calvin's teaching as normative for Geneva during the controversy with Bolsec but do not indicate major confessional status for the document: the *Consensus* was not received beyond Geneva and, indeed, received a strenuous rebuke from Bullinger for some of its language. The work was also translated into French.[40] It offers an analysis of the doctrine's biblical basis and its rootage in Augustine, including a significant clarification of Calvin's objections to notions of divine "permission," namely, not as denials of divine permissive willing but as denials that permission can be separated from will and that anything occurs apart from or beyond the divine will.

In addition to Calvin's published works dealing with predestination, there also exists a set of brief "Articles on Predestination" found in manuscript form in Geneva.[41] J. K. S. Reid, in the introduction to his translation, argues on grounds of their "uncompromising…tone" that these articles must be of a "comparatively late date."[42] While there is nothing about the articles that would prohibit a late dating, their content is theologically unremarkable, and there is also nothing in the articles that cannot be correlated with passages in the 1539 *Institutes*. Calvin's doctrine and definitions of predestination changed so little over the course of his life, moreover, that if one chooses to identify the eleven articles as "uncompromising," then Calvin's doctrine in general ought to be called "uncompromising" as well. Reid's argument is, therefore, baseless. The date of the document is indeterminate unless further information is brought forward. There is, however, one

---

sections of the *Treatise on the Eternal Predestination of God*, where the section on providence originally appeared.

40. John Calvin, *De la prédestination éternelle de Dieu, par laquelle les uns sont éleuz à salut, les autres laissez en leur condemnation* (Geneva: s.n., 1552).

41. John Calvin, *Articuli de praedestinatione*, in *CO* 9, col. 713–14.

42. J. K. S. Reid, ed., *Calvin: Theological Treatises* (Philadelphia: Westminster, 1954), p. 178.

interesting possibility for positioning the document in Calvin's life and work, namely, at the time of the Bolsec controversy (1551–1552), given the focus of the controversy on articles or aphorisms defining the doctrine of predestination and the number of such documents written by Calvin's associates at the time. As would be clear in various of Calvin's later debates, the absence of a specific document refuting Bolsec probably points to Calvin's practice of handing off late phases of debate to Beza: there are reasons to understand Beza's *Summa totius christianismi* (1555), also known as the *Tabula praedestinatonis*, as a concluding salvo in the Bolsec controversy.[43]

Following on the Bolsec controversy, Calvin turned to a series of exegetical and homiletical efforts, several of which had a direct bearing on the development of his thought on the divine decrees, predestination, and providence: the commentary on Acts (1552–1554),[44] the commentary on the Gospel of John (1553), and the sermons on Job (1554). The Acts commentary, moreover, was preceded directly by a series of sermons on the book (1548–1552) and can be regarded as the natural conclusion to the thought process begun in the sermons.[45] In his commentary on Acts, Calvin drew on Peter's sermon in Acts 3 to argue the covenantal nature of the church as fulfillment of the promise made to Abraham that all nations would be blessed in Abraham's "seed," namely in Christ. He further connected covenant with election by arguing the apostolic founding of the church to be illustrative of the general election that constitutes the church and the special election of some to salvation: grace is shown to be the first cause of salvation and, although God's "common election is not effectual in all," the church

---

43. Cf. Richard A. Muller, "The Use and Abuse of a Document: Beza's *Tabula praedestinationis*, the Bolsec Controversy, and the Origins of Reformed Orthodoxy," in *Protestant Scholasticism: Essays in Reassessment*, ed. Carl R. Trueman and R. Scott Clark (Carlisle, U.K.: Paternoster, 1999), pp. 33–61.

44. John Calvin, *Commentariorum Ioannis Caluini In Acta Apostolorum, Liber I* (Geneva: Jean Crespin, 1552) and *Commentariorum Ioannis Caluini In Acta Apostolorum, Liber Posterior* (Geneva: Jean Crespin, 1554); in translation, *Commentary on the Acts of the Apostles*, trans. Henry Beveridge, 2 vols. (Edinburgh: Calvin Translation Society, 1844).

45. See Richard A. Muller, "Foreknowledge and the Divine Counsel in Calvin's Exegesis of Acts 2:23 and 4:28," in *Teaching Reformation: Essays in Honor of Timothy J. Wengert*, ed. Luka Ilić and Martin J. Lohrmann (Minneapolis: Fortress, 2021), 122–42.

serves as "an open gate for the special elect."[46] The minister, by preaching the gospel in the church, serves as an instrument of God's electing grace—and, indeed, is God's "elect instrument."[47] The commentary then identifies, as would the *Institutes*, a general or corporate election of the church as the covenant people, the special election of individuals to ministry, and the special election of individuals to salvation.[48]

The commentary on John, written at the same time as the commentary on Acts, most probably provided Calvin with the opportunity to create a subtopical discussion of Christ as the author of election that found its way into the 1559 *Institutes*.[49] *Institutes* III.xxii.7, a section entirely new in the 1559 edition, contains seven citations from the Gospel of John—6:37 (with v. 39); 6:44; 17:9; 13:18; 15:19; 10:28; and 17:12. There are also allusions, without citation, to John 6:70 and 17:6.[50] The section rests entirely on Johannine texts. Calvin identifies the elect as given to Christ by the Father but also, citing John 13:18, as chosen by Christ Himself: Christ is the Mediator, but He also "claims for himself, in common with the Father, the right to choose."[51]

Several issues developed in Calvin's sermons on Job arguably have roots in issues raised for Calvin during the Bolsec controversy itself and presented in summary form in his *Congrégation* of 1552. Toward the end of the *Congrégation*, Calvin declaimed against the popish doctrine of two wills in God, "one ordained and the other absolute," arguing that there is only one divine will bringing about what God has ordained.[52] This one divine will is utterly just and the source of all equity and justice. Accordngly, even when the reason that evils occur in the world is not evident, Christians must believe that nothing occurs apart from the divine will. Job provides an example of the proper understanding of this mystery: he recognizes the incomprehensibility of God and in his misery confesses the justice and equity of God's

---

46. Calvin, *Commentariorum in Acta* (1552), 3:25, citing Rom. 11:23 (*CTS Acts*, vol. 1, p. 159); cf. ibid., 2:47; 6:5; 13:17, 33 (*CTS Acts*, vol. 1, pp. 134, 237, 518, 533).

47. Calvin, *Commentariorum in Acta* (1552), 9:15 (*CTS Acts*, vol. 1, p. 380).

48. Cf. Calvin, *Institutio* (1559), III.xxi.5–7.

49. See further, Muller, *Unaccommodated Calvin*, p. 151.

50. Note that the Battles edition identifies two allusions and also references Gal. 1:16 and Eph. 3:7, neither of which is noted in Calvin's original.

51. Calvin, *Institutes*, III.xxii.7.

52. Calvin, *Congrégation*, in *CO* 8, col. 115.

judgments.[53] The Job sermons are replete with references to the ultimate justice of God, the incomprehensibility of His judgments, and warnings against blasphemously misconstruing the goodness of God or questioning the nature of His electing will.[54]

These works appeared at the time that Calvin was engaged in shifting his exegetical interests from the New Testament to the Old Testament: he had published the commentary on Genesis in 1554 and had finished his work on the New Testament with the *Harmony of the Evangelists* (1555). These commentaries evidence further thought on predestination that identify the movement of Calvin's thought after the Bolsec controversy. The Genesis commentary includes some important reflections on aspects of the doctrine, including discussion of divine permission and will in relation to the fall of Adam,[55] and once again the issue of various kinds of election—general, special, and individual—that would be factored into the new material in the 1559 *Institutes*.[56]

Exegesis and Polemics, 1556–1558

Arguably, the next major development in Calvin's thought on predestination was the editorial expansion of his commentary on Romans in 1556—a development that took place after the encounter with Bolsec and just prior to Calvin's responses to Sebastian Castellio. Calvin did not typically return to works that he had written in order to make major emendations and augmentations of the text for new editions. He did, of course, edit and augment the *Institutes* throughout his career, but this editorial labor was an effort that he projected already in the *Epistola ad Lectorem* of his 1539 Latin *Institutes* and in the *Argument du Livre* of the 1541 French translation. In both places, he identified the *Institutes* as the place in which he chose to develop his doctrinal

---

53. Calvin, *Congrégation*, in *CO* 8, col. 116–17.

54. John Calvin, *Sermons de M. Jean Calvin sur le livre de Job. Recueillis fidelement de sa bouche selon qu'il les preschoit* (Geneva: s.n., 1563), in *CO* 33–35; translated as *Sermons of Maister Iohn Calvin, upon the Booke of Iob*, trans. Arthur Golding (London: George Bishop, 1574).

55. John Calvin, *In primum Mosis librum, qui Genesis vulgo dicitur, commentarius* (Geneva: Stephanus, 1554), 3:1, in *CO* 23, col. 55–56 (*CTS Genesis*, vol. 1, pp. 144–45).

56. E.g., Calvin, *In primum Mosis librum*, 6:1; 11:10; 25:23–24, in *CO* 23, col. 112, 168, 349–52 (*CTS Genesis*, vol. 1, pp. 239, 333; vol. 2, pp. 44–48).

loci and disputations.[57] Among Calvin's commentaries, the one major revision and augmentation was that of the commentary on the Pauline Epistles, which saw a second edition of all of the previously published commentaries on Pauline Epistles in 1551 and a third in 1556.[58] Of particular interest here is that the portion of Romans 9 in which the topic of predestination is found received major reworking in the 1556 edition. Noteworthy are the additions to the commentary on verses 3 and 4 of the chapter, where Calvin expands on the place of the Jews in God's covenant, remarking that their breach of the covenant "had not rendered void the faithfulness of God; for he had not only reserved for himself some remnant seed from the whole multitude, but had as yet continued, according to their hereditary right, the name of a Church among them."[59] There is a special election within the corporate—a point that would recur throughout Calvin's commentaries on the Old Testament as well as in the 1559 *Institutes*.

The theme of a general corporate election of Israel and a particular election of individual Israelites is prominent in Calvin's sermons on Deuteronomy (1556–1557).[60] It is also present in Calvin's commentary on Hosea (1557), where he contrasts the casting aside of Israel as a "lost people" at the same time that God remains "faithful to the promise" and His election remains firm, albeit twofold—a general election presented in the covenant and a special election of those chosen to salvation from within the covenant people.[61] Calvin also references the theme of corporate election in his commentary on the Psalms.[62]

---

57. On the *Argument* in the 1541 edition, see Richard A. Muller, "Calvin's 'Argument du livre' (1541): An Erratum to the McNeill and Battles *Institutes*," in *Sixteenth Century Journal*, 29/1 (1998), pp. 35–38.

58. See Parker, *Calvin's New Testament Commentaries*, pp. 36–59.

59. John Calvin, *In omnes Pauli Apostoli epistolas atque etiam in epistolam ad Hebraeos…commentarii* (Geneva: Stephanus, 1556), Rom. 9:4, p. 80 (*CTS Romans*, p. 339).

60. John Calvin, *Sermons sur le Deuteronome*, in *CO* 27, col. 45–46; and cf. Anthony Hoekema, "The Covenant of Grace in Calvin's Teaching," in *Calvin Theological Journal*, 2 (1967), pp. 133–61, here pp. 150–52.

61. John Calvin, *In Hoseam prophetam Io. Calvini praelectiones* (Geneva: Conrad Badius, 1557), 12:3, in *CO* 42, col. 454; cf. ibid., 1:10; 11:8, in *CO* 42, col. 216–17, 444–46 (*CTS Hosea*, pp. 418–19; cf. pp. 64, 404–6).

62. John Calvin, *In librum Psalmorum Iohannis Calvini Commentarius* (Geneva: Stephanus, 1557), Ps. 24:1; 65:5 [65:4]; 118:1–4, 25, in *CO* 31, col. 243, 605–6; *CO*

The Psalms commentary, moreover, given its focus on David, adds an emphasis on the election of an individual to a particular office, often indicating the connection between election and covenant.[63] The presence of these themes in the commentaries of 1556–1557 is of interest given that the 1559 augmentation of the chapters on predestination in the *Institutes* would include entirely new sections on the corporate election of Israel in relation to the covenant and on the election of individual Israelites to salvation.[64]

Calvin's writings from 1557 and 1558 that specifically focus on predestination consist of three tracts against Sebastian Castellio and a collection of sermons on election and reprobation. Castellio had been Calvin's colleague early on in Strasbourg and had come to Geneva with Calvin in 1541 to teach languages in the Collège de Rive. Castellio differed with Calvin over the Song of Songs (he viewed it as purely a love poem) and over Christ's descent into hell. After being refused ordination by the Company of Pastors, Castellio left Geneva for Basel and there under a pseudonym published a treatise countering Calvin's justification of the execution of Servetus, and shortly thereafter, an attack on Calvin's doctrines of predestination and providence.[65] Whereas Beza responded to Castellio on the execution of heretics, Calvin himself wrote three tracts defending his doctrines of predestination and providence. The first appeared in 1557 as *A Brief Reply in Refutation of the Calumnies of a Certain Worthless Person*,[66] and was followed by *Responces à certaines calomnies et blasphèmes* (Responses to certain calumnies and blasphemies). The latter work is the only one of Calvin's works against Castellio in which Calvin mentions the name of his opponent. This treatise was probably first published in 1557,

---

32, col. 202–3, 210–11 (*CTS Psalms*, vol. 1, p. 401; vol. 2, pp. 455–58; vol. 3, pp. 378, 391–92).

63. E.g., Calvin, *In librum Psalmorum*, Ps. 18:51; Ps. 78, argument and v. 70; 89:4 [89:3], 20–21 [89:19–20], in *CO* 31, col. 193, 720, 745–46; *CO* 32, col. 812–13, 818–19 (*CTS Psalms*, vol. 1, p. 306; vol. 3, pp. 225, 280, 421, 432).

64. Calvin, *Institutes*, III.xxi.5–6.

65. On Castellio and his relationship to Calvin, see Jenkins, *Calvin's Tormentors*, pp. 63–76.

66. John Calvin, *Brevis responsio Io. Calvini ad diluenda nebulonis cuiusdam calumnias*, in *CO* 9, col. 257–66, translated as *A Brief Reply in Refutation of the Calumnies of a Certain Worthless Person*, in *Calvin's Calvinism*, pp. 187–206.

although no exemplar of this first edition is known to survive.[67] The third tract, *On the Secret Providence of God* (1558), in translation, is the longest of Calvin's responses to Castellio.[68] Here again, it appears that the work of producing the final major salvo against Castellio was passed on to Beza, who not only produced an even more extended treatise against Castellio, *Ad sycophantarum quorumdam calumnias*,[69] but a

---

67. John Calvin, *Responces à certaines calomnies et blasphèmes, dont quelsques malins s'efforcent de rendre de la doctrine de la prédestination de Dieu odieuse*, appended to John Calvin, *Treze sermons traitans de l'élection gratuite de Dieu en Iacob et de la réiection en Esau* (Geneva: s.n., 1562), in *CO* 58, col. 1–198, with the *Responses*, col. 199–206; translated as *An Answeare to Certaine Slaunders and Blasphemyes, wherewith certaine evill disposed persons have gone aboute to bring the doctrine of Gods everlasting Predestination into hatred*, in Calvin, *Thirteene Sermons of Maister Iohn Caluine, Entreating of the Free Election of God in Iacob, and of Reprobation in Esau. A treatise wherin euery Christian may see the excellent benefites of God towardes his Children, and his maruelous iudgements towards the reprobate*, trans. Iohn Fielde (London: Thomas Dawson for Thomas Man and Tobie Cooke, 1579), fol. 171r–176v. DeGreef, *Writings of John Calvin*, p. 165, and Reid, *Calvin: Theological Treatises*, p. 332, note the three treatises against Castellio, but presume the French *Responces* to be lost. DeGreef (p. 97, n. 77) knows of the appendix to the *Treze sermons*, but assumes that it is identical with the *Brevis responsio*. In any case, the *Responces* is a distinct work, not to be identified as the *Brevis responsio*.

68. John Calvin, *Calumniae nebulonis cuiusdam, quibus odio et invidia gravare conatus est doctrinam Ioh. Calvini de occulta Dei providentia. Ioannis Calvini ad easdem responsio*, in *CO* 9, col. 269–318, translated as *On the Secret Providence of God*, in *Calvin's Calvinism*, trans. Henry Cole, pp. 257–350; unfortunately, in Cole's translation more than half of Castellio's argument four, two portions of the text of argument seven, and the final paragraph of argument eleven are missing. *Calvin on Secret Providence*, trans. James Lillie (New York: Robert Carter, 1840), is complete. Both Cole and Lillie, moreover, altered the order of Calvin's text: whereas the 1558 edition offered Castellio's prefatory letter, followed by fourteen articles selected by Castellio from Calvin's writings, Castellio's refutations of the articles, and then Calvin's response to the entirety of Castellio's treatment, the nineteenth-century translators divided the text, so that each single article could be immediately juxtaposed with Castellio's refutation and Calvin's response. There is also a new translation: *The Secret Providence of God*, trans. Keith Goad (Wheaton, Ill.: Crossway, 2010).

69. Theodore Beza, *Ad sycophantarum quorumdam calumnias, quibus unicum salutis nostrae fundamentum, id est aeternam Dei praedestinationem evertere nititur, responsio Theodori Bezae Vezelii.* (Geneva: Conrad Badius, 1558); in translation, *An Euident Display of Popish Practises, or Patched Pelagianisme, wherein is Mightelie Cleared the Soueraigne Truth of Gods Eternall Predestination* (London: Ralph Newberie and Henry Bynnyman, 1578). Note that in Beza's *Tractationes theologicae*, 3 vols. (Geneva: Eustathius Vignon, 1570–1582), pp. 337–424, the title has been modified to read, *Ad Sebastiani Castellionis calumnias.*

lso a French translation of *On the Secret Providence of God*, augmented by his own further responses to Castellio.[70] This latter work, despite its significant juxtaposition of Calvin's argument with Beza's explanations, has not, to my knowledge, been examined in the scholarship.

Calvin also preached through the epistle to the Galatians in 1557–1558 and the epistle to the Ephesians in 1558. The sermons on Galatians contain extended references to divine election, while the sermons on Ephesians 1:4–6 and 7–10 echo his commentary on the text a decade earlier, but without the emphasis on fourfold causality. The sermons on Ephesians were published in 1562 and those on Galatians in 1563.[71] In both cases the sermons offer more extended but also less technical expositions of the doctrine than are found in the commentaries, which is important for an understanding of Calvin's sense of the practical dimensions of the doctrine and its relationship to assurance of salvation.

The Lectures on the Minor Prophets and 1559 *Institutes*

Calvin's lectures on the Minor Prophets (1559) contain a considerable number of references to predestination.[72] The theme of the corporate election of Israel, with clear application of the concept to the church, appears in the lectures on Joel, Obadiah, and Micah. Calvin works through the issue that the election of Israel and of the church is corporate but also directed salvifically to a remnant of the faithful. Election is known, then, through an outward general or indiscriminate call and an inward or special call.[73] Also prominent in the lectures on the Minor Prophets is the theme of the divine decree ordering events and

---

70. John Calvin and Theodore Beza, *Response de Jehan Calvin et Theodore de Besze, aux calomnies & argumens d'un qui s'efforce par tous moyens de renverser la doctrine de la providence secrete de Dieu* (Geneva: Conrad Badius, 1559).

71. John Calvin, *Sermons de Jean Calvin sur l'epistre S. Paul apostre aux Ephesiens* (Geneva: Jean Baptiste Pinereul, 1562); in translation, *The Sermons of M. Iohn Calvin, upon the Epistle of S. Paule too the Ephesians*, trans. Arthur Golding (London: Thomas Dawson, 1577; rev. trans., Edinburgh: Banner of Truth, 1973).

72. John Calvin, *Praelectiones in duodecim prophetas (quos vocant) minores* (Geneva: Jean Crispin, 1559), in *CO* 42–44; in translation *CTS Minor Prophets*, 5 vols.

73. Calvin, *Praelectiones in duodecim prophetas*, Joel 2:32; Obad. 17, 19; Mic. 7:14, in *CO* 42, col. 576, 579; *CO* 43, col. 196, 197–98, 422–23, 424 (*CTS Minor Prophets*, vol. 2, pp. 107, 111, 449, 452; vol. 3, pp. 390, 393).

achieving the ends willed by God through the use of angels and human instruments, including pagan nations, notably in Joel and Nahum.[74] Calvin also argues that conditional threats and seeming divine repentance are accommodations to human understanding that are in fact both expressions of an "inviolable decree,"[75] an exegetical conclusion that would reinforce Calvin's assumptions concerning the relationship of predestination and providence.

The placement of Calvin's doctrine of predestination in the third book of the 1559 *Institutes* has been the source of considerable discussion, particularly granting the tendency (albeit far from universal) of later Reformed theology to place predestination into relation with the doctrine of God, near to the beginning of the theological system—although, arguably, the placement of the doctrine in the order of theological topics had more to do with the genre of a work than with differences in understandings of the doctrine and its systematic implications.[76] We must, in particular, take issue with Wendel's comment that "in 1559 Calvin said that the question of predestination which might be raised in relation to the doctrine of God was inopportune."[77] This is simply an incorrect inference from Calvin's statement, found in his discussion of the original created integrity of human nature, to the effect that "in this integrity man by free will had the power, if he so willed, to attain eternal life. Here it would be out of place to raise the question of God's secret predestination because our subject is not what can happen or not, but what man's nature was like. Therefore Adam could have stood if he wished, seeing that he fell solely by his own will."[78] It can, surely, be inferred that Calvin did not see fit to discuss predestination between his discussion of the creation of human beings and his discussion of the fall, but only because he wanted to emphasize the freedom and responsibility belonging to human nature

---

74. Calvin, *Praelectiones in duodecim prophetas*, Joel 2:2; Nah. 1:14; 2:10, in *CO* 42, col. 535–36; *CO* 43, col. 454, 468 (*CTS Minor Prophets*, vol. 2, p. 47; vol. 3, pp. 446, 470–71).

75. Calvin, *Praelectiones in duodecim prophetas*, Joel 2:13, in *CO* 42, col. 545–46 (*CTS Minor Prophets*, vol. 2, p. 61).

76. See chapter 2, "The Placement of Predestination in Reformed Theology," in the present volume.

77. Wendel, *Calvin*, p. 268.

78. Calvin, *Institutes*, I.xv.8.

in its original created state and to discuss not God's eternal plan but human nature as such. Calvin's comment does not relate to the issue of the overarching systematic organization but rather to the issue of the nature of a particular topic in his theology. What cannot be concluded from this statement is that Calvin had a similar objection to the placement of predestination in close relation to the doctrine of God—where, incidentally, he had moved the doctrine of providence in this last edition of the *Institutes*—or that Calvin sought to sever the traditional relationship between providence and predestination. The comment refers only to the discussion of sin and the fall, not to the organization of the first book of the *Institutes* as a whole, and not to the relationship of predestination to providence.

After the *Institutes*: 1560–1563

In 1560, Calvin published French translations of both treatises against Pighius—the *Response aux calomnies d'Albert Pighius* on free choice[79] and the *Traité de la prédestination éternelle de Dieu*. The latter translation was also augmented by Calvin's *Treze sermons traitans de l'élection gratuite de Dieu en Iacob et de la réiection en Esau*, a series of thirteen sermons directed against no particular adversary that stands as a fragment of Calvin's massive series of sermons on Genesis, one of only two portions of these sermons published in the sixteenth century.[80] The sermons were also published as a separate volume in 1562.[81] Appended to this separate printing of the sermons is the *Responces à certaines calomnies et blasphèmes*, a translation of which also appears

---

79. John Calvin, *Response aux calomnies d'Albert Pighius. Contenant la defense de la saine et saincte doctrine contre le franc arbitre des papistes: par laquelle est monstré que la volonté de l'homme est naturellement serve et captive de peché: et aussi est traicté par quel moyen elle vient à estre affranchie, et mise en liberté* (Geneva: François Jaquy, Antoine Davodeau & Jacques Bourgeois, 1560).

80. John Calvin, *Traité de la prédestination éternelle de Dieu, par laquelle les uns sont éleuz à salut, les autres laissez en leur condemnation* (Geneva: Jean Crespin, 1560); cf. the discussion in DeGreef, *Writings of John Calvin*, pp. 97, 165. A critical edition of the French text is found in John Calvin, *De aeterna Dei praedestinatione / De la predestination eternelle*, in *Ioannis Calvini Scripta Ecclesiastica*, vol. 1, ed. Wilhelm Neuser and Olivier Fatio (Geneva: Droz, 1998).

81. Calvin, *Treze sermons*, in *CO* 58, col. 1–198; and note the translation, *Thirteene Sermons of Maister Iohn Caluine*.

in the sixteenth-century English edition of the sermons.[82] Although they evidence little of the technical language of theology, the sermons provide an index to aspects of Calvin's later thought on election and reprobation as both corporate and individual and as defined in relation to the election of Israel and the covenant made with Abraham. They also offer a rather unique window, via the personages of the biblical narrative, into Calvin's understanding of the way in which God accomplishes his ends in and through the often contrary acts of human beings.

There is also significant material on the doctrine of predestination in Calvin's later commentaries and lectures on Scripture—and although little that is new, much that stands as exegetical support to the final text of the *Institutes*, and some that reflects the concerns of Calvin's final polemics. Calvin's prefatory letter to the publication of his lectures on Daniel (1561) concludes on a note of assurance concerning the certainty of salvation belonging to all whose names are written in God's "book," by which the text means the eternal counsel of God: election may be hidden in the secret counsel of God, but the testimony concerning membership in the body of Christ provides assurance in this life.[83]

The theme of a twofold election, general or corporate and special or individual, that became prominent in the 1559 *Institutes* appears with some frequency in these exegetical works, now stated explicitly in terms of the election of the nation of Israel and the election either of some to salvation or of the remnant that would escape the destruction of the nation, the latter as especially illustrative of special election within the corporate. These arguments appear in Calvin's harmony

---

82. Calvin, *Responces à certaines calomnies*, in *CO* 58, col. 199–206; translated as *An Answeare to Certaine Slaunders and Blasphemyes*, in Calvin, *Thirteenne Sermons*, fol. 171r–176v.

83. John Calvin, *Praelectiones in librum prophetiarum Danielis, Joannis Budaei et Caroli Jonvillaei labore et industria exceptae* (Geneva: Jean I de Laon, 1561), sig. *7v (the dedicatory letter is not included in *CO* 40); and *Leçons de M. Jean Calvin sur le livre des propheties de Daniel. Recueillies fidelement par Jean Budé et Charles de Jonviller, ses auditeurs* (Geneva: Jean I de Laon, 1562), sig. a8r; *CTS Daniel*, vol. 1, p. lxxv.

on the "last four" books of Moses[84] and in his lectures on Jeremiah and Ezekiel.[85]

In the harmony of the last four books of Moses, moreover, Calvin argues double predestination in relation to his identification of love and reverence to God and "integrity of heart" as fruits of God's "secret election" not given to the reprobate—and also in relation to the issue of election to office, although he can also refer to the rejection of some as a passing over.[86] This election of some and passing over others is not unjust, given that God is free and under no obligation.[87] In short, all of the categories of election identified in summary form in the *Institutes* are found exegetically derived in the harmony—including the inference of reprobation from the fact of the election of some.

The commentaries transcribed from Calvin's last series of lectures, delivered between 1560 and early 1564, on Jeremiah, Lamentations, and Ezekiel, contain numerous substantive references to the doctrine of predestination, generated by the prophetic pronouncements concerning Israel's exile and its relation to covenant, assurance, and the divine calling of Israel. The Jeremiah commentary raises the issues of corporate election in relation to covenant and the call of Abraham,[88] individual election and reprobation as inferred from people's relation

---

84. John Calvin, *Mosis libri V: cum Iohannis Caluini commentariis; Genesis seorsum, reliqui quatuor in formam harmoniae digesti* (Geneva: Stephanus, 1563), in *CO* 24–25 as *Commentariorum in quinque libros Mosis*. Note that this represents a new edition of the Genesis commentary, which had been published in 1554, now published together with the harmony of the remaining books of the Pentateuch. In translation, *CTS Genesis*, 2 vols.; and *CTS Four Last Books of Moses*, 4 vols.

85. John Calvin, *Praelectiones in Librum prophetiarum Jeremiae, et Lamentationes. Joannis Budaei et Caroli Jonvillaei labore et industria exceptae* (Geneva: Jean Crespin, 1563), in *CO* 37–39; John Calvin, *In viginti prima Ezechielis prophetae capita praelectiones, Joannis Budaei et Caroli Jonvillaei labore et industria exceptae* (Geneva: François Perrin, 1565), in *CO* 40.

86. Calvin, *Commentariorum in quinque libros Mosis*, Deut. 13:3; Ex. 33:19; Num. 17:2, in *CO* 24, col. 279; *CO* 25, col. 110, 230 (*CTS Four Last Books of Moses*, vol. 1, p. 446; vol. 3, p. 381; vol. 4, p. 125).

87. Calvin, *Commentariorum in quinque libros Mosis*, Ex. 33:15, 19; Num. 23:18, in *CO* 25, col. 107–8, 110–11, 283 (*CTS Four Last Books of Moses*, vol. 3, pp. 376, 381; vol. 4, p. 212).

88. Calvin, *Praelectiones in Ieremiam prophetam*, 2:1–2; 12:14; 13:11; 46:27, in *CO* 37, col. 496–97; *CO* 38, col. 148, 158; *CO* 39, col. 303–4 (*CTS Jeremiah*, vol. 1, pp. 70–72; vol. 2, pp. 151, 168; vol. 4, pp. 603–4).

to God's covenant,[89] election as a ground of assurance,[90] and God as faithful to the remnant of Israel even in the destruction of the nation.[91] Calvin also here references the perpetual statute or decree as ordaining the course of nature,[92] as immutable and accordingly standing as a prohibition to pray that Israel not be exiled,[93] as inviolable or unalterable in its law and its provisions,[94] and as reflected in God's faithfulness to His covenant.[95]

In his comments on Lamentations, Calvin again implies the distinction between eternal decree and temporal execution when he explicitly identifies the divine thought to destroy the walls of Jerusalem with the divine decree, adding that nothing occurs apart from the divine decree and that the divine hand is hidden in the temporal ruin brought on by the Chaldeans.[96]

The commentary on Ezekiel (1565) is notable for the variety and extent of its comments on predestination. It contains reference to the secret eternal election of God as distinct from the "external state" of things known in time;[97] the gracious election of a remnant out of the fallen nation of Israel;[98] the faithfulness of divine election despite the

---

89. Calvin, *Praelectiones in Ieremiam prophetam*, 10:25; 49:8, in *CO* 38, col. 95; *CO* 39, col. 355 (*CTS Jeremiah*, vol. 2, p. 66; vol. 5, p. 68).

90. Calvin, *Praelectiones in Ieremiam prophetam*, 11:16–17, in *CO* 38, col. 120 (*CTS Jeremiah*, vol. 2, p. 106).

91. Calvin, *Praelectiones in Ieremiam prophetam*, 13:12–14; 16:19, in *CO* 38, col. 160, 162, 256 (*CTS Jeremiah*, vol. 2, pp. 171, 175, 330).

92. Calvin, *Praelectiones in Ieremiam prophetam*, 5:22, in *CO* 37, col. 632 (*CTS Jeremiah*, vol. 1, p. 296).

93. Calvin, *Praelectiones in Ieremiam prophetam*, 14:11–12, in *CO* 38, col. 187 (*CTS Jeremiah*, vol. 2, p. 217).

94. Calvin, *Praelectiones in Ieremiam prophetam*, 20:1–2; 26:4–6, 17–19; 38:1–4, 21; 46:18, 23; 47:6–7; 49:12; 50:45, in *CO* 38, col. 334, 517, 532; *CO* 39, col. 159, 174, 297, 314, 359, 437 (*CTS Jeremiah*, vol. 3, pp. 13, 314, 337; vol. 4, pp. 389, 411, 593. 617; vol. 5, pp. 74, 194).

95. Calvin, *Praelectiones in Ieremiam prophetam*, 23:2; 33:23–24, in *CO* 38, col. 403; *CO* 39, col. 74–75 (*CTS Jeremiah*, vol. 3, p. 130; vol. 4, p. 265).

96. Calvin, *Praelectiones in lamentationes Ieremiae*, 2:4, 8; 3:37–38; 4:20, in *CO* 39, col. 538, 543, 588–89, 624–25 (*CTS Lamentations*, pp. 350, 357, 428, 484).

97. Calvin, *In Ezechielis propheta*, 13:8–9, in *CO* 40, col. 280–81 (*CTS Ezekiel*, vol. 2, pp. 16–17).

98. Calvin, *In Ezechielis propheta*, 13:21, in *CO* 40, col. 296 (*CTS Ezekiel*, vol. 2, p. 39).

failures of God's people;[99] election as twofold, namely, the general election of the children of Abraham and the special election of the faithful remnant;[100] the connection between election and the covenant or promise;[101] the impenetrability or inscrutability of the eternal decree of election;[102] and the opposition of election to a notion of salvation by merit.[103] Here, too, Calvin sees the text as arguing that all things occur because of the divine decree, albeit in matters concerning the temporal order, as mediated by angelic movers—which is a point of comfort to believers: "When we tremble in doubtful circumstances, what can we do but acquiesce in this teaching? namely, that the end of everything will be according to God's decree, because nothing is carried except by his decision [*arbitrio*], and that there is no motion, no agitation under the heavens, unless he has inspired it by his angels."[104] Calvin's exposition of the wheels in Ezekiel's vision offers, moreover, evidence of his assumptions concerning the mediated nature of the divine work in the world—at the same time that the Ezekiel lectures also testify to the inviolability of the decree and therefore also to the certainty of its execution.[105] The commentary on Joshua (1564) clarifies the notion of

---

99. Calvin, *In Ezechielis propheta*, 16:1–3, in *CO* 40, col. 336 (*CTS Ezekiel*, vol. 2, p. 95).

100. Calvin, *In Ezechielis propheta*, 16:21, in *CO* 40, col. 355 (*CTS Ezekiel*, vol. 2, pp. 121–22).

101. Calvin, *In Ezechielis propheta*, 16:60; 20:13–14, in *CO* 40, col. 392–93, 487 (*CTS Ezekiel*, vol. 2, pp. 172–73, 305).

102. Calvin, *In Ezechielis propheta*, 18:25, in *CO* 40, col. 451 (*CTS Ezekiel*, vol. 2, p. 255).

103. Calvin, *In Ezechielis propheta*, 20:5–8, in *CO* 40, col. 475 (*CTS Ezekiel*, vol. 2, p. 288).

104. Calvin, *In Ezechielis propheta*, 1:21; cf. 1:4; 10:17, in *CO* 40, col. 48; cf. col. 33, 220–21 (*CTS Ezekiel*, vol. 1, p. 89; cf. pp. 67, 339). Note that the CTS translation of 1:21 mistakenly reads *arbitrio* as "permission" rather than as "decision." On the interpretation of Ezekiel's "wheels" as angelic movers, see Richard A. Muller, "Causality, Clocks, and Ezekiel's Wheels: Theodore Beza on Providence and Divine Concurrence," in idem, *Providence, Freedom, and the Will in Early Modern Reformed Theology* (Grand Rapids: Reformation Heritage Books, 2022), pp. 61–73.

105. Calvin, *In Ezechielis propheta*, 4:8, 14–15; 14:14, 15–16, in *CO* 40, col. 112, 115–16, 319, 322 (*CTS Ezekiel*, vol. 1, pp. 181, 187; vol. 2, pp. 72, 76–77).

corporate election by indicating the connection between circumcision as the sign of God's covenant with Israel and the election of Israel.[106]

Conclusion

As indicated at the outset, this essay makes no attempt to offer an analysis of the details in Calvin's developing doctrine of predestination. What it has attempted to do—and, hopefully, succeeded in doing—is to provide a preliminary guide to such an analysis. It should be clear that the development of Calvin's views needs to be examined and that the development must be traced not only through the several stages marked out by the editions of the *Institutes* and the several major treatises, but also in a number of shorter works and, more importantly, in the progress of Calvin's exegetical and interpretive work in commentaries and sermons. The commentaries and sermons often prove to be the places in which Calvin came to grips with more specific and focused issues, and they also provide a more detailed set of markers for understanding his development. This specificity is perhaps most apparent in the Old Testament commentaries and sermons. This essay has also indicated several works of Calvin belonging to this development that have been little examined, and it has also identified several collateral documents—notably Beza's annotated edition of Calvin's major work against Castellio, *On the Secret Providence of God*—that illuminate the patterns of argument and help to place Calvin's work into the context of Reformed debate in his time but that were not examined in the older scholarship.

Given the amount of attention paid to Calvin's doctrine of predestination, it is perhaps surprising that so much remains to be done both to set his doctrine into its historical context and developmental patterns and to look at the doctrine in its relation to the larger corpus of Calvin's writings. What the world does not need is yet another decontextualized dogmatic study based primarily on the two chapters found in Calvin's 1559 *Institutes*.

---

106. John Calvin, *In librum Iosue brevis commentarius* (Geneva: François Perrin, 1564), 5:6 [5:9], in *CO* 25, col. 460 (*CTS Joshua*, pp. 81–82).

CHAPTER 4

Inclusive Supralapsarianism: The Heritage of Franciscus Junius and the Leiden Theology in Early Modern Reformed Thought

Debate over the supralapsarian and infralapsarian definitions of predestination has been a staple of Reformed theological argument and definition since the Arminian controversy of the early seventeenth century.[1] Although there were various earlier ways of defining predestination among Reformed theologians of the sixteenth century, often with reference to the creation and fall of Adam and Eve, major debate over the precise identification of the object of predestination arose largely because of Arminius' identification of several Reformed views as inconsistent with one another and his proposal of an alternative ordering of the divine decrees in his *Declaration of Sentiments*, delivered before the States of Holland in 1608.[2] Understandings concerning the

---

1. For a general overview of supralapsarian and infralapsarian developments in Reformed thought, note Klaas Dijk, *De Strijd over Infra- en supralapsarisme in de Gereformeerde Kerken van Nederland* (Kampen: Kok, 1912); John V. Fesko, *Diversity within the Reformed Tradition: Supra- and Infralapsarianism in Calvin, Dort, and Westminster* (Greenville, S.C.: Reformed Academic, 2001); and Joel R. Beeke, *Debated Issues in Sovereign Predestination: Early Lutheran Predestination, Calvinian Reprobation, and Variations in Genevan Lapsarianism* (Göttingen: Vandenhoeck & Ruprecht, 2017).

2. Jacob Arminius, *Verclaringhe Iacobi Arminii…aengaende zijn ghevoelen, so van de predestinatie, als van eenige andere poincten der Christelicker Religie; daerinne men hem verdacht heeft ghemaeckt…. Wtghegheven by de weduwe van den overleden ende haere broeders* (Leiden: Thomas Basson, 1610); in Latin, *Declaratio sententiae authoris horum operum de praedestinatione, providentia Dei, libero arbitrio, gratia Dei, divinitate Filii Dei, & de iustificatione hominis coram Deo*, in *Opera theologica* (Leiden: Godefridus Basson, 1629), pp. 91–133; in English, *Declaration of Sentiments*, in *The Works of James Arminius*, trans. James Nichols and William Nichols, 3 vols. (London, 1825, 1828,

origins of the supra-infra question, and over which theologians were supralapsarian and which infralapsarian, have varied both in the early modern era and in modern scholarship. Given that the seventeenth-century debates over the doctrine were concerned with both the objects of divine willing and the logical ordering of God's eternal decree—typically by distinguishing decrees concerning election, reprobation, creation, and fall—earlier theologians like Calvin, Musculus, or Vermigli were differently identified as infra- or supralapsarian. Arminius, for one, identified Calvin as supralapsarian. Modern scholarship has continued to differ on the identification of Calvin, with various writers identifying the beginnings of Reformed supralapsarianism with Beza's rendering explicit an issue raised by various predecessors, including Vermigli and Calvin, and with Beza's purported speculative shift away from the christological emphases of earlier Reformed thought.[3]

Little has been done to examine the development of supralapsarian argumentation after Beza. With one significant exception, moreover, the scholarship has maintained a simple division of the topic between infra- and supralapsarian, based on the identification of the object of divine willing: Does God elect and reprobate human beings considered as created and fallen (infra) or as creatable possibles, prior to the willing of creation (supra)? Otto Ritschl's treatment of the issue is

---

1875; repr. Grand Rapids: Baker, 1986), vol. 1, pp. 580–732. W. Stephen Gunter, *Arminius and His Declaration of Sentiments: An Annotated Translation with Introduction and Theological Commentary* (Waco, Tex.: Baylor University Press, 2012), provides a translation of Arminius' Dutch version. Arminius' ordering of the decrees is also found in the posthumously published *Articuli nonnulli diligenti examine perpendendi, authoris de praecipuis doctrinae Christianae capitibus sententiam plenius declarantes*, in *Opera*, pp. 948–66, here p. 957; in *Works*, vol. 2, pp. 706–31, here pp. 718–19, probably from 1607.

3. Notably, Dijk, *De Strijd*, pp. 31–36; Donald M. Sinnema, "Beza's View of Predestination in Historical Perspective," in *Théodore de Bèze (1519–1605): Actes du Colloque de Genève (Septembre 2005)*, ed. Irena Backus (Geneva: Droz, 2007), pp. 219–39, here pp. 225–29; idem, "Calvin's View of Reprobation," in *Calvin for Today*, ed. Joel R. Beeke (Grand Rapids: Reformation Heritage Books, 2009), pp. 115–36, here p. 124; and implied but not stated in Beeke, *Debated Issues*, pp. 180–81. Further, Beza is said to have created a predestinarian system as opposed to the christologically focused theology of Calvin in Basil Hall, "Calvin against the Calvinists," in *John Calvin*, ed. G. Duffield (Grand Rapids: Eerdmans, 1966), pp. 19–37, here p. 27; and Alister E. McGrath, Iustitia Dei: *A History of the Christian Doctrine of Justification*, 3rd ed. (Cambridge: Cambridge University Press, 2005), pp. 265–66; similarly, idem, *Reformation Thought: An Introduction*, 4th ed. (Oxford: Blackwell, 2012), p. 203.

the exception. Ritschl recognized that Franciscus Junius (1545–1602) identified the "common object" of divine willing as the entire human race in all times and under all conditions.[4] Arguably, however, Junius' view was not intended to mediate between the supra- and infralapsarian theories as Ritschl suggests, but to formulate a view that was inclusive of all categories of divine knowing and willing. Nor did Ritschl understand the grounding of Junius' view in scholastic distinctions concerning God's eternal knowledge of possibles and actuals. Beyond this, Ritschl's account does not deal with the context of Junius' formulations in his epistolary debate with Arminius just prior to the outbreak of the Arminian controversy and, accordingly, with the radically different understandings of divine knowledge and foreknowledge at play in Junius' and Arminius' theologies.

Junius' formulations of his paradigm for understanding the divine decree or decrees were rooted—at least in view of what can be discerned from his published writings—in his university disputations on predestination and in his posthumously published debate with Arminius over the doctrine, the *Amica collatio* or *Friendly Conference*. It was, moreover, in Junius' responses in the *Amica collatio* that he was pressed to deal with Arminius' division of the Reformed into separate and, in Arminius' view, significantly divergent camps. Junius did not dispute the presence of different patterns of argumentation among the Reformed. Rather, he argued a fundamentally supralapsarian view of the divine decrees that, by looking to distinctions in divine knowledge and foreknowledge, refuted Arminius' contention of conflicting Reformed views.[5] A line of argument resting on Junius' responses, moreover, can be found in the writings of Reformed theologians throughout the seventeenth and eighteenth centuries. In what follows, I propose to examine Junius' argumentation, identify its impact on the thought of later Reformed theologians, and demonstrate both that the

---

4. Otto Ritschl, *Dogmengeschichte des Protestantismus: Grundlagen und Grundzüge der theologischen Gedanken- und Lehrbildung in den protestantischen Kirchen*, 4 vols. (Leipzig: J. C. Hinrichs, 1908–1912; Göttingen: Vandenhoeck & Ruprecht, 1926–1927), vol. 3, p. 311.

5. Carl Bangs, *Arminius: A Study in the Dutch Reformation* (Nashville: Abingdon, 1971), pp. 201–10, mistakenly claims that Junius both "draws back from a full supralapsarianism" and identifies the object of predestination as "man created."

supralapsarian position could be developed as a formulation inclusive of the infralapsarian view, in contrast to the often pointed rejection of supralapsarian views on the part of infralapsarians, and that the supralapsarian position, as formulated by Junius and those who drew on his argumentation, drew less on the logic of final causality than on a distinction in the ways of divine knowing that belonged to the scholastic argumentation of the era.

Arminius and the Problem of the Order of the Divine Decrees

The origins of Arminius' own worries over the decree and its human objects, however, were rooted in a series of developments and debates that took place in early orthodox Reformed circles after 1590. In probable chronological order, we can note the various orderings of the decree or decrees identified by William Perkins in his *Armilla aurea*, beginning with the second edition (1591);[6] the debates took place largely at Cambridge University over the teaching of Peter Baro and led to the Lambeth Articles of 1595.[7] The English debate was followed by the epistolary debate between Arminius and Junius that took place largely between 1596 and 1598.[8] Arminius then argued against the elaborate structuring of "degrees" (*gradus*) in the divine decree in Perkins' 1598 *De praedestinationis modo et ordine*.[9] Further debate boiled over during Arminius' tenure as professor of theology at Leiden (1602–1609) and

---

6. William Perkins, *Armilla aurea, id est, Theologiae descriptio mirandam seriem causarum & salutis & damnationis iuxta verbum desproponens: eius synopsin continet annexa ad finem tabula. Editio secunda. Accessit practica Th. Bezae pro consolandis afflictis conscientijs* (Cambridge: John Legatt, 1591), sig. after Aii verso, and cap. 51–53 (sig. T3r–U5v).

7. See Keith D. Stanglin, "Arminius *Avant la Lettre*': Peter Baro, Jacob Arminius, and the Bond of Predestinarian Polemic," in *Westminster Theological Journal*, 67 (2005), pp. 51–74.

8. Richard A. Muller, "Arminius's 'Conference' with Junius and the Protestant Reception of Molina's *Concordia*," in *Beyond Dordt and* De Auxiliis*: The Dynamics of Protestant and Catholic Soteriology in the Sixteenth and Seventeenth Centuries*, ed. Jordan J. Ballor, Matthew T. Gaetano, and David S. Sytsma (Leiden: Brill, 2019), pp. 103–26, here pp. 106–15.

9. William Perkins, *De praedestinationis modo et ordine: et de amplitudine gratiae divinae Christiana & perspicua disceptatio* (Cambridge: Iohn Legat, 1598); in translation, *A Treatise of the Manner and Order of Predestination, and of the Largenes of Gods Grace*, trans. Francis Cacot and Thomas Tuke (London: William Welby, 1606).

continued for a decade following his death, concluding in the Synod of Dort (1618–1619).

Identification of varied orderings of divine decrees appeared, prior to Arminius' debates, in the controversy over Baro's doctrine. Baro, as would Arminius, understood Calvin and Beza as both arguing a first decree to elect some and reprobate others, prior to creation and fall, without consideration of Christ's mediation or of the means of salvation; and a second decree that Adam should fall.[10] A second view, attributed by Baro to Augustine, Zanchi, and Georg Sohn, identified the object of predestination as created and fallen humanity.[11] The third view, which Baro argued had been taught by Augustine before the Pelagian controversy and later by Melanchthon and Hemmingsen, identified the objects of election as those eternally foreknown as believing in Christ and the objects of reprobation as those continuing in sin apart from Christ.[12]

The specific contours of Arminius' views on different formulations of the divine decrees can be traced to this early encounter with Junius, in which Arminius argued a series of distinctions and disagreements among the various Reformed definitions of predestination.[13] Arminius' distinction of Reformed views has affinities with Baro's arguments, but is clearly independent of them.

---

10. Peter Baro, *Summa trium de praedestinatione sententiarum. Cum clarissimorum theologorum, D. Iohannis Piscatoris ad eam notis: et D. Francisci Junii ad eandem disquisitione: ac denique D. Guilhelmi Whitakeri praelectione adversus universalem gratiam* (Harderwijk: Thomas Henricus, 1613), pp. 1–2; in translation, *Three Opinions Concerning Predestination*, in Arminius, *Works*, vol. 1, pp. 92–93; cf. Stanglin, "Arminius *Avant la Lettre*," p. 59.

11. Baro, *Summa*, pp. 2–3; in Arminius, *Works*, vol. 1, pp. 93–94; cf. Stanglin, "Arminius *Avant la Lettre*," pp. 60–61.

12. Baro, *Summa*, pp. 6–7; in Arminius, *Works*, vol. 1, pp. 96–97; cf. Stanglin, "Arminius *Avant la Lettre*," p. 62.

13. Jacob Arminius, *Amica cum Francisco Iunio de praedestinatione per literas habita collatio* (Leiden: Godefridus Basson, 1613); also *Amica cum Francisco Iunio de praedestinatione per literas habita collatio*, in Arminius, *Opera*, pp. 445–619; in translation, *Friendly Conference of James Arminius…with Mr. Francis Junius about Predestination*, in Arminius, *Works*, vol. 3, pp. 1–248.

Franciscus Junius: Arminius' Senior Partner in Debate

Until quite recently, Junius has been remembered primarily for the role that he played in the development of the thought of Arminius in their epistolary debate over predestination, which was left unpublished until more than a decade after Junius' death.[14] Unfortunately, even this best known of his contributions to the history of Christian thought has been little examined, and Junius' own analysis of the definition and meaning of predestination little studied, despite the insight it might provide into the beginnings of the Arminian controversy and, indeed, into the much-debated history of supra- and infralapsarians within the Reformed confessional tradition.

In his own time, Junius was regarded as a significant thinker in his own right—one of the chief architects of early Reformed orthodoxy. He had been trained in Geneva during the last phase of Calvin's work in that city, and brought an irenic form of Reformed Protestantism to the Netherlands. Junius took a pastorate in Antwerp in 1565 but was forced to flee for his life in 1566. He subsequently taught theology in Neustadt (1576–1584) and Heidelberg (1584–1592), settling finally in Leiden (1592) as professor of theology.[15] Junius' treatise *De theologia vera* and his Leiden *Theses theologicae* mark the entry into Reformed theology of the formal and preliminary analysis of theology into *theologia archetypa* and a threefold *theologia ectypa*: *theologia unionis, viatorum,* and *visionis.*[16] The *De theologia vera* alone would have guaranteed his fame: its definitions, used to frame theological prolegomena, were adopted by most of the Reformed and adapted by many

---

14. Cf. Bangs, *Arminius*, pp. 199–203, with Dijk, *De Strijd*, pp. 64–72.

15. See J. Reitsma, *Franciscus Junius: een levensbeeld uit den eersten tijd der Kerkhervorming* (Groningen: J. B. Huber, 1864), pp. 46–54, 101–7.

16. Franciscus Junius, *Libellus de theologia vera, ortu, natura, formis, partibus et modo illius* (Leiden: Plantiniana, 1594); idem, *Theses theologicae quae in inclyta academis Lugdunobatava ad exercitia publicarum disputationum, praeside D. Francisco Iunio variis temporibus a theologiae candidatis adversus oppugnantes propugnatae sunt,* in *Opera theologica Francisci Junii Biturigis sacrarum literarum professoris eximii: catalogum librorum, qui primo tomo continentur, exhibet pagina Epistolae dedicatoriae subincta / prefixa est vita auctoris, omnia cum indicibus VII acuratissimis,* 2 vols. (Heidelberg: Sanctandreana, 1608), vol. 1, fol. 1592ff. Both works are also found in Franciscus Junius, *Opuscula theologica selecta,* ed. Abraham Kuyper (Amsterdam: F. Muller, 1882); the *De theologia vera* has been translated as *On True Theology,* trans. David Noe (Grand Rapids: Reformation Heritage Books, 2014).

of the Lutheran theologians of the seventeenth century.[17] In addition to the gatherings of his disputations in his *Opera*, his later theses can be found, together with those of Lucas Trelcatius Sr. and Franciscus Gomarus, in the compilation of disputations conducted at Leiden University between 1598 and 1601.[18]

His reputation as an irenic figure, seeking the peace of the church in times of controversy, stems certainly from the major ecclesiological writings that appeared during the course of his career.[19] Junius was also recognized as a major linguist and exegete: together with the Hebraist Immanuel Tremellius he had translated the Bible into Latin from the original languages and had annotated the text.[20] He also translated the Arabic version of the Acts of the Apostles and 1 and 2 Corinthians into Latin.[21] His Hebrew grammar was widely used.[22] His annotations on Revelation were used to augment the English translations of the New Testament of the Geneva Bible,[23] and his full commentary on the Apocalypse was widely admired.[24] He also produced a series of

---

17. See Willem J. van Asselt, "The Fundamental Meaning of Theology: Archetypal and Ectypal Theology in Seventeenth-Century Reformed Thought," *Westminster Theological Journal*, 64 (2002), pp. 319–35.

18. *Compendium theologiae thesibus in Academia Lugd. Bat. ordine à … Fr. Junio, Luc. Trelcatio, et Fra. Gomaro publicè propositis, ab anno 1598 usq. ad annum 1605* (Hanau: Guilelmus Antonius, 1601).

19. Franciscus Junius, *Ecclesiastici sive de natvra et administrationibus Ecclesiae Dei, libri tres, nunc primum conscripti, atque in lucem editi* (Frankfurt: Andreas Wechelums, 1581); idem, *Eirenicum de pace ecclesiae catholicae inter christianos, quamvis diversos sententiis, religiose procuranda, colenda atque continenda, in psalmos Davidis CXXII et CXXXIII meditatio* (Leiden: Plantin, 1593).

20. *Testamentis Veteris Biblia Sacra sive libri canonici priscae Iudaeorum Ecclesiae a Deo traditi, Latini recens ex Hebraeo facti … ab Immanuele Tremellio & Francisco Iunio* (London: Henry Middleton, 1585).

21. *Acta Apostolorum et Epistolae duae S. Pauli ad corinthios ex arabica translatione latine reddita* (S.l.: s.n., 1578).

22. Franciscus Junius, *Grammatica Hebraeae linguae* (Frankfurt am Main: Andreas Wechel, 1580; Geneva: Ioannes Aubrius, 1596).

23. *The New Testament of our Lord Jesus Christ, translated out of Greeke by Theod. Beza: With briefe summaries and expositions upon the hard places by the said Author, Ioac. Camer. and P. Loseler. Villerius. Englished by L. Tomson. Together with the Annotations of Fr. Junius upon the Revelation by S. John* (London: Deputies of Christopher Barker, 1599).

24. Franciscus Junius, *Apocalypsis S. Ioannis Apostoli et Evangelistae, Methodica Analysi Argumentorum, notisque breuibus ad rerum intelligentiam et Catholicae ac*

meditations on Jonah, exegetical notes on Jude, and a major treatise analyzing the use of the Old Testament in the New.[25]

Junius came to his post at the University of Leiden as a highly recognized and widely published theologian, and while at Leiden his international reputation, which was already established, was augmented by a series of highly significant and respected works in both biblical exegesis and doctrinal theology. At the time of their epistolary debate, Arminius was a fairly recent graduate of the Academy of Geneva, a minister in Amsterdam, and virtually unknown. Arminius addressed Junius perhaps as a fellow graduate of the Genevan Academy and certainly as an eminent thinker of the day, known to be irenic in his approach to debated issues, and potentially receptive to Arminius given his relationship to Junius' colleague, the rector of the theological faculty, Johannes Kuchlinus. History has, in effect, reversed the polarity of the debate, remembering Arminius as the more renowned.

The *Amica collatio*: Text, Intention, Prefaces, and the Silence of Junius

Arminius' original letter to Junius, insofar as it can be extracted from the larger text of the *Amica collatio*, reveals Arminius' intention in writing and the initial boundaries of his comments to Junius. After his epistolary prologue, in which he sets forth his desire to discuss the issue of predestination privately with Junius, Arminius offers a short

---

Christianae Ecclesiae historiam pertinentibus (Heidelberg: Hieronymus Commelinus, 1591); also, *Apocalypse ou Revelation de S. Jean: avec une briefve et methodique exposition* (Geneva: P. de Sainct André, 1592); and, *The Apocalyps, or Revelation of S. John with a Brief Exposition*, trans. Thomas Barbar (Cambridge: John Legat, 1596).

25. Franciscus Junius, *Lectiones in Jonam prophetam ex ore Francisci Junii excerptae: in his sacrae scripturae explicandae methodus breviter et perspicuè ostenditur* (Heidelberg: Sanctandreana, 1594); idem, *In Epistolam S. Judae apostoli perbreves notae, ex lectionibus Francisci Junii Biturigis, Quibus perspicue ex Verbo Dei cum hujus epistolae, tum etiam totius Scripturae demonstratur autoritas* (Antwerp: Aegidius Radaeus, 1584; Heidelberg: Sanctandreana, 1598); idem, *Sacrorvm Parallelorvm Libri Tres: Id Est Comparatio locorum Scripturae sacrae, qui ex Testamento vetere in Novo adducuntur: summam utriusque in verbis convenientiam, in rebus consensum, in mutationibus fidem veritatemque breviter & perspicue ex fontibus Scripturae S. genuinaque linguarum Hebraeae & Graecae conformatione monstrans…Francisci Iunii Biturigis* (Heidelberg: Commelinus, 1588); also *Sacrorum parallelorum libri tres: id est comparatio locorum Scripturae sacrae, qui ex testamento vetere in Novo adducuntur*, 2nd ed. (London: G. Bishop, n.d.).

definitional introduction to the discussion (propositions i–v), in which he defines three views on predestination then currently taught among the Reformed—namely, the view of Calvin and Beza, the view of Thomas Aquinas, and the view of Augustine. Significantly, he identifies Calvin and Beza as teaching the same doctrine. He then offers a brief critique of the Calvinian and Bezan view (proposition vi). Next, he engages in a lengthy examination of the second view, identified as that of Thomas Aquinas, but clearly, from Arminius' perspective, it is the view held by Junius (propositions vii–xxi). The form taken by his examination of this view is a set of three questions (propositions vii–viii), followed by substantial responses to each question (q. 1, propositions ix–xii; q. 2, propositions xiii–xvi; q. 3, propositions xvii–xxi). Then follows another section in which Arminius offers his comparison of the first and second views (propositions xxi–xxvi). In a very brief concluding comment, Arminius notes that he will not take up the third view, that of Augustine, given that, should Junius explain the Thomist approach to Arminius' satisfaction, he could be satisfied with Augustine's doctrine as well.[26] In its initial form, Arminius' proposal to Junius rejects outright a full supralapsarian view, which Arminius associates with both Calvin and Beza, and then poses a series of questions and issues to Junius regarding the viability of what Arminius took to be Junius' thoughts on the matter. As the propositions comparing the Calvinian/Bezan view with Thomistic/Junian approach indicate, moreover, Arminius held that Junius' own teaching was so implicated in the problems of the Calvinian/Bezan view that it was not really a viable alternative.[27]

Significantly, this paradigm remains in Arminius' final address regarding these issues in the *Declaratio sententiae*, albeit with different emphases. There the supralapsarian approach he associated with Calvin and Beza is discussed and refuted at great length; the approach associated with Thomas Aquinas and Junius refuted in shorter form, but viewed as having the same problems as the Calvinian and Bezan doctrine; and the fully infralapsarian Augustinian model refuted with

---

26. *Amica collatio*, prop. xxvii, p. 609 (*Works*, vol. 3, p. 234).
27. *Amica collatio*, prop. xxi, pp. 585–86 (*Works*, vol. 3, p. 200).

far less vigor than the first two approaches.[28] Junius' own doctrine, moreover, contrary to the conclusion that has been drawn from his irenicism, was supralapsarian, but in far more nuanced form than that of Beza, indicating a significant development of understanding and scholastic distinction beyond Beza's rather brief formulations.[29]

The preface of the *Amica collatio*, attributed to "the nine orphaned children of Arminius," but actually written by Petrus Bertius,[30] no longer speaks of Calvin with the relative hesitance and lingering respect characteristic of some of Arminius' statements about the Reformer but adumbrates the view that Arminius would express of the supralapsarian doctrine of the decree in his later *Declaration of Sentiments*—namely, that "this chief doctrine, as it was put forth by Calvin, was not only foreign to all reason, but also alien to the nature of God himself, and to the sacred writings; moreover, so opposed to morals and all religion, that if anyone were to regulate his life by the tenor of that opinion, he could not by any means arrive at salvation."[31] Bertius' preface also dismisses Junius' own doctrine, arguing that it differed from that of Calvin and Beza, but contained "nearly as many absurdities" as Calvin's view.[32] One particular absurdity at the heart of Junius' response was a

---

28. Arminius, *Declaratio sententiae*, in *Opera*, pp. 110–16 (Calvin and Beza); 116–17 (Aquinas and Junius); 117 (infralapsarian); also, *Works*, vol. 1, pp. 641–45, 645–46, 648.

29. Cf. Junius, *Responsio*, in *Amica collatio*, pp. 482, 483, 512 (*Works*, pp. 50, 52–53, 139–40); with Franciscus Junius, *Theses theologicae de aeterna Dei praedestinatione: quas…sub praesidio Francisci Junii…pro viribus tuebor Samuel Bouchereau* (Leiden: Joannes Patius, 1602), x; N.B. this disputation is identical with Junius' Leyden *Theses theologicae*, x, in *Opera*, vol. 1, col. 1617–22. Correcting the statements in Richard A. Muller, *God, Creation, and Providence in the Thought of Jacob Arminius: Sources and Directions of Scholastic Protestantism in the Era of Early Orthodoxy* (Grand Rapids: Baker, 1991), p. 26; Caspar Brandt, *The Life of James Arminius, D.D.*, trans. John Guthrie (Nashville: Stevenson & Owen, 1857), p. 107 (*Historia vitae*, p. 100); and Bangs, *Arminius*, pp. 200–201.

30. On Bertius' authorship of the preface, see Muller, "Arminius's 'Conference' with Junius," pp. 109–10n32.

31. *Amica collatio*, p. 451 (*Works*, vol. 3, p. 7); cf. Arminius, *Declaration of Sentiments*, especially pp. 623–26, 631–34 (*Opera*, pp. 105–7, 110–12); and note the identification of the views of Calvin with those of Beza in the *Amica collatio*, pp. 465–66, 470, 498, 499–500, 595, et passim (*Works*, vol. 3, pp. 27, 28, 32–33, 74, 76–77, 214).

32. Cf. the prefatory epistle in *Amica collatio*, pp. 452–53 (*Works*, vol. 3, pp. 8–9); with *Amica collatio*, pp. 478–79, 508–9 (Junius), 490–91, 510 (Arminius) (*Works*, vol. 3, pp. 45–46, 63–64, 89–92).

refusal to accept Arminius' strict differentiation of supra- and infralapsarian. "Junius replied," the "children" comment, "not according to the expectation of the inquirer: since, partly by putting a common *ratio* to the object—which is almost *akatalepton*, viz., incomprehensible—partly by twisting the words of the authors, he attempted to make up one opinion out of several, contrary to their intention, each of whom maintained his own."[33] So cogent, moreover, in the view of the "children," was Arminius' response to Junius, that had Junius chosen to proceed further with the debate, he "would have been reduced to extremities, and would either have changed his opinion…or have betrayed his obstinacy, which was most foreign to his manners."[34] In other words, had the irenic and mannered Junius responded, he would have had to admit the force of Arminius' arguments against his comments.[35] So, at least, claimed Bertius, alias "the nine orphaned children of Arminius."

There is, however, another explanation of Junius' silence. Junius most probably did not receive the full text of Arminius' responses as eventually published, nor, probably, did he receive the full text of Arminius' comments on his 1593 disputation on predestination. What he most probably received was a series of brief responses to his comments, lacking the detail of the final version of Arminius' replies in the published *Amica collatio*.[36] Junius, moreover, despite the claims of the "children," had clearly found his arguments against Arminius' rather neat division of predestinarian definitions into several conflicting camps to have been conclusive. He may have already seen and responded to the similar claims against Reformed doctrine made by Peter Baro in 1595—although the date of his comments on Baro's

---

33. *Amica collatio*, p. 453 (*Works*, vol. 3, p. 9).

34. *Amica collatio*, p. 453 (*Works*, vol. 3, pp. 9–10).

35. Cf. Bangs, *Arminius*, p. 200.

36. Cf. Muller, "Arminius's 'Conference' with Junius," pp. 112–14. The theses in question are found in Arminius, *Opera*, pp. 611–19 (*Works*, vol. 3, pp. 236–48), together with Arminius' comments: *D. Francisci Junii de divina praedestinatione, ab ipso composita & sub eiusdem praesidio a Guilhelmo Coddaeo in Academia Lugdunensis Batava anno 1593, publice disputata: itemque brevicula D. Jacobi Arminii ad easdem notae*. Hereinafter cited as Junius, *De divina praedestinatione* (1593) and Arminius, *Notae*, respectively. I have not located a copy of Junius' original 1593 disputation.

Summma is uncertain.[37] He had concluded his response to Arminius' original propositions with a brief statement of the underlying agreement of the Reformed positions with Augustine and had ended the correspondence with the comment, "I have done what I could in this case, your case, my brother, with the greatest diligence and rapidity of which I am capable, since other things often interrupt me. Accept my work in good part, even if it does not answer to your expectations. May the God of peace and truth seal his salvific peace upon your soul, more and more, and graciously lead us and all those who are his in the way of truth, to his glory and the edification of his Church in Christ Jesus our Saviour. Amen."[38] Despite being very busy in his professorial duties, Junius had responded to Arminius at length and in an irenic spirit. He also recognized that Arminius might well not be satisfied with his response, but he sent it on and said "Amen" to it.

Arguably, what followed from Arminius' pen, namely, his initial brief responses, did not seem to Junius to further the debate or do justice to the arguments he had presented. He had done enough. He was, as he said, quite busy. And he saw no need for further response. There is, however, another possibility. Junius presided over two disputations on predestination subsequent to Arminius' initial rejoinders—one disputation in 1599,[39] the other in 1602.[40] Given the date of these theses, they may stand as a quiet response to Arminius' rejoinders in the penultimate text of the *Amica collatio*, which had probably been completed by 1599, if indeed Junius ever saw that text. Nor are there any indications in the published text of the *Amica collatio* (1613) that Arminius saw fit to deal with these later efforts of Junius.

Whereas the highly partisan preface to the *Amica collatio* offered by Bertius surely overstated the impact of Arminius' rebuttal on Junius

---

37. Note *Francisci Junii viri clarissimi in eandem Petri Baronis Summa trium de praedestinationis sententiarum brevis disquisitio*, in Baro, *Summa*, pp. 22–29.

38. Junius, in *Amica collatio*, pp. 609–10 (*Works*, vol. 3, p. 234).

39. Franciscus Junius, *Disputationum theologicarum repetitarum quadragesima, de divina praedestinatione…sub praesidio D. Francisci Iunii…Daniel Gorreus* (Leiden: Joannes Patius, 1599); identical with Junius' Leyden *Theses theologicae*, xi, in *Opera*, vol. 1, col. 1622–24.

40. Franciscus Junius, *Theses theologicae de aeterna Dei praedestinatione: quas… sub praesidio Francisci Junii…pro viribus tuebor Samuel Bouchereau* (Leiden: Joannes Patius, 1602).

(and certainly engaged in a bit of wishful thinking if it hoped to convince various Reformed pastors and theologians of the day that Junius' work was riddled with absurdities and misinterpretations of the views of his Reformed and predestinarian predecessors), it was quite correct that Junius argued the basic congruity of several distinct Reformed approaches to the doctrine of predestination. This argument, moreover, went to the heart of the dispute between Arminius and Junius, inasmuch as Arminius' own arguments depended in large part on the division of the Reformed approach into three divergent and incompatible positions. What is more, Arminius' identification of incompatible positions within the Reformed tradition on predestination remained central to his complaint, and it is found spelled out in detail in his final effort, the *Declaratio sententiae* of 1608. The significance of Arminius' final, elaborated replies must also not be underestimated. Whatever the reasons for Junius' lack of further response, the ultimately published form of Arminius' work served to underline several major issues intrinsic to the later debate over his theology and to the development of Reformed understandings of supra- and infralapsarianism—among them the issue of differences among the Reformed and the unwillingness, sometimes polemically expressed, of some infralapsarians to consider the supralapsarian position valid.[41]

Arminius to Junius: The Varieties and Problems of Reformed Predestinarianism

Recent scholarship has denied Arminius' direct involvement in the debate over the views of Dirk Coornhert, has argued against a reaction to Beza as the primary basis for Arminius' doctrine, and has understood his difficulties with the Reformed understandings of predestination as the product of a gradual development.[42] Arminius' initial comments to

---

41. Cf. Pierre Du Moulin, *The Anatomy of Arminianisme: or the opening of the Controversies lately handled in the Low-Countryes, Concerning the Doctrine of Providence, of Predestination, of the Death of Christ, of the Nature of Grace* (London: T. S. for Nathaniel Newbery, 1620), xiii; with Francis Turretin, *Institutio theologiae elencticae, in qua status controversiae perspicue exponitur, praecipua orthodoxorum argumenta proponuntur, & vindicantur, & fontes solutionum aperiuntur*, 3 vols. (Geneva: Samuel de Tournes, 1679–1685), IV.ix.5–8.

42. Keith D. Stanglin and Thomas H. McCall, *Jacob Arminius: Theologian of Grace* (New York: Oxford University Press, 2012), p. 29.

Junius bear out these conclusions. Thus, Arminius first notes his lack of "full persuasion" concerning the views of various "learned men" of the past on the doctrines of "predestination and reprobation," despite what he feels is an adequate training in their views. He comments to Junius on the perplexity of his situation: he cannot rightly assent to something of which he is not fully persuaded, nor can he dare to affirm the alternative view that contradicts the received opinion. Arminius goes on to say that he has actually had discussions with "some of [his] equals and with others who are in authority"—to little avail, and even with some personal injury to himself.[43] The discussions with "others," certainly with regard to the personal injury, can probably be understood as a reference to the arguments with Plancius in classis Amsterdam, an acrimonious debate fresh in Arminius' memory, with ongoing repercussions. Junius, by contrast, was by reputation a person with whom Arminius believed he could confer "without fear." Arminius based this assumption both on Junius' writings—notably the recent theses on predestination (1593) and the treatise on the fall of Adam (1595)—and on testimony of others, among them Arminius' uncle by marriage, Johannes Kuchlinus.

In his initial comments to Junius, Arminius echoes the Cambridge theologian Peter Baro, whose pattern of analysis distinguished three different approaches to predestination, all of them found among the Reformed. Arminius identifies all three as more or less objectionable to him, and associates each with famous theologians—the first with Calvin and Beza, the second with Thomas Aquinas and Junius, and the third with Augustine.[44] These three, Arminius indicates, agree "that God by an eternal and immutable decree determined to give certain men—others being passed by—life eternal and supernatural, and to afford the same men those means which are necessary and efficacious for obtaining that life."[45] Nonetheless, the three versions of the doctrine differed in their identification of the objects of the divine willing. Calvin and Beza, according to Arminius, identified the objects of the

---

43. Arminius, *Amica collatio*, in *Opera*, p. 458 (*Works*, vol. 3, pp. 16–17).

44. Cf. Baro, *Summa trium de praedestinatione sententiarum*, pp. 1–11; translated as *Three Opinions Concerning Predestination*, in Arminius, *Works*, vol. 1, pp. 92–100; on Baro's argumentation, see Stanglin, "Arminius *Avant la Lettre*," pp. 59–63.

45. Arminius, *Amica collatio*, prop. i, in *Opera*, pp. 459–60 (*Works*, vol. 3, p. 18).

decree as "men not yet created, but to be created." Aquinas, by contrast, viewed them as men "created…but considered *in puris naturalibus*… to be raised out of nature above nature" in the act of predestining and electing; "when passing by, as considered in the same nature"; and "as sunk in sins by their own fault" in the act of reprobating. Augustine, distinct from both of these views, understood the objects of predestination "as fallen in Adam, and lying in the mass of corruption and perdition…to [God] both when electing and predestinating, and when passing by and reprobating."[46] In this view, Calvin and Beza are taken to be what, in later definition, would be identified as pure or classic supralapsarians. Aquinas is still taken as a supralapsarian of a sort, but as identifying humanity in the decree as created but not fallen—and as further safeguarding the justice of God's reprobation by distinguishing between what is usually called a negative reprobation or passing over and positive reprobation, the condemnation of certain persons not yet fallen for the sins that they will commit given that they have not been included among the elect. As Junius would note, however, Arminius did not actually use the language of negative and positive reprobation and consistently reserved "reprobation" as a term for the condemnation of sin—in Junius' view, a mistake that confused Arminius' argumentation.[47] Augustine is defined as a classic infralapsarian. When pressed, Arminius included Junius in the Thomistic camp, perhaps without the clearest evidence, given Junius' supralapsarianism.[48]

Junius' Account of the Compatibility of the Supra- and Infralapsarian Positions and Arminius' Replies

Presumably, Junius did not respond as Arminius expected. Rather than either conceding to Arminius or defending one or another of the positions distinguished by Arminius, Junius argued that the various definitions cited by Arminius as standing in some tension with each other did not in fact disagree, but rather represented "different" but nonetheless compatible "regards or relations" in the "mode of

---

46. Arminius, *Amica collatio*, prop. ii, in *Opera*, p. 463 (*Works*, vol. 3, p. 24).

47. Cf. Junius, *Responsio*, prop. xix, xxiii, in Arminius, *Opera*, pp. 574, 598–99 (*Works*, vol. 3, pp. 182–83, 218–19).

48. Arminius, *Replica*, prop. ii, in *Opera*, pp. 464–65 (*Works*, vol. 3, pp. 25–26); cf. Arminius, *Notae*, thesis x, in *Opera*, p. 615 (*Works*, vol. 3, p. 242).

contemplating" the objects of election and different usages of terms within basically the same doctrinal understanding of predestination.[49] In Junius' understanding, the Thomistic and Augustinian approaches identified by Arminius did not conflict with the Calvinian/Bezan definitions, but rather "handed down in a different manner parts of the same argument in a certain respect distinct."[50] Thus, rather than taking Arminius' three views as mutually exclusive, Junius emphasized their commonality and, in his own definitions, drew on the broad paradigm for understanding the movement from possibility to actuality, arguing that the object of divine predestination was "man not yet created, created, fallen, &c., lastly man in general, however you may take him, to be the object of God's power, knowledge, will, mercy, and justice."[51]

The disagreement between Junius and Arminius concerning the three patterns of predestinarian definition indicates, if nothing else, very different approaches to the problem. Arminius' rejoinder to Junius' initial comments argues the presence of three opinions among the Reformed, namely, that there are in fact significant differences concerning the identity of the "objects" of the decree: in the first view, the objects of the decree are "not created, but to be created"; in the second, they are understood as created but as not yet fallen; in the third variant, they are discussed as created and fallen.[52] Junius had, in response to a subsequent section of Arminius' letter, indicated that in his own understanding of the decree, these three identifications of the object all belonged to the divine knowledge and, accordingly, to the decree. Elsewhere, Junius had argued the traditional distinction between the

---

49. Junius, *Responsio*, prop. vi, ix, xxi, in Arminius, *Opera*, pp. 478–79, 508–9, 586 (*Works*, vol. 3, pp. 45–46, 89, 200).

50. Junius, *Responsio*, prop. vi, in Arminius, *Opera*, pp. 478–79 (*Works*, vol. 3, p. 46).

51. Junius, *Responsio*, prop. vi, in Arminius, *Opera*, p. 482 (*Works*, vol. 3, p. 50; cf. pp. 52–53): "statuo hominem nondum conditum, conditum, lapsum, &c. denique hominem communiter, utcumque accipias, obiectum esse potentiae, scientiae, voluntatis, misericordiae, & iustitiae Dei"; cf. ibid., p. 483 (*Works*, vol. 3, p. 52): "Deus qua homines, sive nondum conditos, sive conditos, sive lapsos, ac potius simul communiter coram ipso." Also note Junius, *Theses theologicae de aeterna Dei praedestinatione*, x: "*Commune obiectum circa quod versatur*, est universum genus humanum, i. omnes & singuli homines, a Deo communiter considerari, secundum universam rationem ipsorum, & omnium temporum: nondum conditi, conditi, lapsi."

52. Arminius, *Replica*, prop. i, pp. 461–62 (*Works*, vol. 3, p. 21).

divine *scientia simplicis intelligentiae* and *scientia visionis*—namely, the knowledge of all possibles, some of which God wills freely to create, and the knowledge of all actuals as created by God. The object of this knowledge, then, is "twofold," consisting in "existents and non-existents" (*Entia, & non Entia*), a knowledge that God has of Himself and of all things beyond Himself, both "universal & particular, which are, were, or will be, whether good or evil, contingent or necessary."[53]

By implication, this is a knowledge of all possible creatable human beings and a knowledge of all actual created human beings in all of their conditions. Further, he added that failing to acknowledge that God knows the objects of His willing as not yet created, as created, and as fallen would amount to a claim that there is "something outside of common providence and special predestination" that is "not an object for God."[54] A further implication of Junius' model that will also appear in several of the subsequent inclusive approaches that we will examine is that the model removes the issue of the location of a decree to create in relation to a decree to elect and to reprobate: the willing of creation is no longer separated from the willing of the objects of predestination. In other words, by arguing against Arminius' various models of the divine decree and its logical ordering into different gradations or degrees, Junius also arguably looked toward a view of the decree significantly different from the typical opposing patterns of multiple decrees found among infralapsarians, supralapsarians, and Arminians.

Junius went on in the *Amica collatio* to explain his sense of the agreement of the three opinions of the object of predestination with specific reference to Calvin and Beza. Those advocating the first opinion, who regard the object of predestination as "to be created" do not simply or rigidly make this assumption but identify the object of predestination as all human beings "in common, according to their universal condition, and of all times," inasmuch as "in the act of predestination God contemplated the entire human condition all at once, even as there are

---

53. Junius, *Theses theologicae*, ix.4, in *Opera*, vol. 1, col. 1615. On *scientia visionis*, also note Junius, *Disputationum theologicarum tertia de essentia Dei et attributis illius... praeside...D. Francisco Juniuo...sustinebo Samuel Bouchereau* (Leiden: Ioannes Patius, 1602), xxxiii.

54. Junius, *Responsio*, prop. vi, in Arminius, *Opera*, p. 482 (*Works*, vol. 3, p. 50).

various parts in the execution of that decree."[55] Beza, for example, had stated both that when Christ is considered as Mediator, human corruption must take precedence in the order of causes, but creation and human righteousness must also be understood to precede corruption, with the result that Beza's supralapsarian model includes the other two models, namely, the objects of divine willing as created but not yet fallen and as created and fallen.[56] Even so, those who place election before the fall, identifying the objects of divine willing as created but not yet fallen, do not intend to deny the eternity of predestination, but only to insist that election and reprobation occur without reference to sin. The difference between the first and second views is not a matter of substance, but on the manner or mode of statement. Similarly, the third option, created and fallen, is merely an emphasis on another part of the full argument.[57]

Arminius agreed that the "decree of God was made from eternity, before all actual existence of any object whatever and howsoever considered," and he conceded that all three of the Reformed opinions placed no cause of election or reprobation in the individual person, but in the divine will alone.[58] He did not, however, concede the point that the three options actually cohered with one another as parts of one whole, and reiterated his claim that the three understandings of the object of predestination represented different doctrinal positions: some of the Reformed, he commented, "ascend higher than others, and extend the acts of the decree further."[59] Still, he also recognized, as Junius had implied, that the divine knowledge consists in God's knowledge of Himself, of all possibles, of all things that are to be, and of all things that come to pass by the acts of creatures. Where he differed with Junius, and already indicated his acceptance of a notion of middle knowledge, was in his assumption that God's knowledge of

---

55. Junius, *Responsio*, prop. vi, p. 478 (*Works*, vol. 3, p. 45): "certe auctores illius hominem contemplari non simpliciter & solum ante creationem, &c. Sed communiter secundum universam rationem ejus & omnium temporum   Deumque in actu praedestinationis totam simul tationem hominis contemplatum, prout varie sunt partes in exsequutione illus aeterno decreto."

56. Junius, *Responsio*, prop. vi, p. 478 (*Works*, vol. 3, p. 45).

57. Junius, *Responsio*, prop. vi, p. 479 (*Works*, vol. 3, p. 46).

58. Arminius, *Replica*, prop. vi, p. 490 (*Works*, vol. 3, p. 63).

59. Arminius, *Replica*, prop. vi, p. 490 (*Works*, vol. 3, p. 63).

futures may be posterior to a "foreseen act of the human will."[60] This entrance of *scientia media* into the debate indicates a contrast with Junius' arguments, which presumed only two kinds of eternal divine knowing, namely, the *scientia simplicis intelligentiae* of all possibles and the *scientia visionis* of all actuals as willed to exist by God, to the exclusion of a "middle knowledge" intervening between God's knowledge of possibles and His knowledge of willed actuals. Although Junius would affirm that distinction elsewhere, he did not make it explicit in his replies to Arminius.[61]

Arminius' unanswered replies to Junius also raised a series of issues not broached by Junius in his responses to Arminius' proposition but of formative importance to later argumentation. Arminius argued at some length that the very use of the terms *mercy* and *justice* by his supralapsarian opponents—represented by Calvin and Beza—was improper, given that "mercy presupposes misery" and "justice presupposes fault."[62] To claim an eternal willing of mercy and justice the object of which is creatures not only not yet created but also viewed by God as unfallen is utterly to misuse the terms. Further, Arminius argued that placing the entire cause of predestination in the freedom of God does not remove the point that the formal character (*ratio*) of the decree must correspond with the formal character (*ratio*) of its object.[63] Or, to make the point in another way, the utter freedom and absolute power of God are "circumscribed" by God's own nature and by His own antecedent acts: there are, accordingly, some acts that are not within God's power.[64]

Junius would reiterate his point concerning the objects of the decree in short form in the disputation over which he presided in 1602. There, Junius defined the object of predestination as "the universal human

---

60. Arminius, *Replica*, prop. vi, p. 491 (*Works*, vol. 3, pp. 65–66).

61. Cf. Junius, *Responsio*, prop. vi, pp. 479–80 (*Works*, vol. 3, pp. 47–48), where divine knowledge is treated but the distinction is not noted; with idem, *De attributis Dei*, ix.4, in *Opera*, vol. 1, col. 1615, where the distinction is made.

62. Arminius, *Replica*, prop. iii, p. 468 (*Works*, vol. 3, p. 30).

63. Arminius, *Replica*, prop. v, p. 476 (*Works*, vol. 3, p. 48).

64. Cf. Richard A. Muller, "God, Predestination, and the Integrity of the Created Order: A Note on Patterns in Arminius' Theology," in *Later Calvinism*, ed. W. Fred Graham (Kirksville, Mo.: Sixteenth Century Journal, 1994), pp. 431–46, here pp. 438–41.

genus," namely, all human beings whether in general or in particular, according to the "universal" *ratio* or condition of humanity—therefore human beings "in all time" and known by God as "not yet made, made, fallen [*nondum conditi, conditi, lapsi*]."[65] This must be so inasmuch as the divine knowledge, to which nothing can be added and nothing taken away, is eternal and understands all things at once.[66] Accordingly, understood from the perspective of God's eternity and the utterly present understanding of all things that belongs to God, God knows human beings as not yet created, as created, and as fallen—so that God eternally and simply knows His grace as concurring with election, knows absolutely that His grace is communicated to elect human beings and angels, and knows that after the fall His grace is conjoined with mercy. In reprobation the case is different, inasmuch as the absence of grace is not understood *simpliciter* with reference to human beings, who are also known as fallen and as not receiving mercy.[67] Reprobation, as defined in a previous and subsequent thesis, is "non-election" and therefore the non-bestowal of grace.[68] It follows infallibly upon sin and the punishment of sin on those who are destitute of the light of saving grace. Reprobation, then, strictly is a consequence not a cause of sin.[69]

Theses on the Decrees at Leiden after Junius: Arminius, Gomarus, Trelcatius, and Arminius' Response (1604–1609)

Beyond the issue of Arminius' complaint, there remains the question of the relationship between supralapsarian and infralapsarian views among the Reformed, given the infralapsarian implication of the Reformed confessions (including the Canons of Dort) and the absence of any

---

65. Junius, *Theses theologicae de aeterna Dei praedestinatione* (1602), x; also in *Opera*, vol. 1, col. 1618.

66. Junius, *Theses theologicae de aeterna Dei praedestinatione* (1602), xi; also in *Opera*, vol. 1, col. 1618.

67. Junius, *Theses theologicae de aeterna Dei praedestinatione* (1602), xv; also in *Opera*, vol. 1, col. 1618.

68. Junius, *Theses theologicae de aeterna Dei praedestinatione* (1602), v, xlxi; also in *Opera*, vol. 1, col. 1618, 1621; cf. Junius, *De divina praedestinatione* (1593), xv, in Arminius, *Opera*, p. 617 (*Works*, vol. 3, p. 245).

69. Junius, *Theses theologicae de aeterna Dei praedestinatione* (1602), liii, lv; also in *Opera*, vol. 1, col. 1622.

condemnation of supralapsarians by Reformed synods—particularly given Arminius' contention that the two positions were incompatible. The importance of Junius' answer to Arminius on this particular point of the compatibility of the supra- and infralapsarian formulations is underlined by the fairly significant series of Reformed theologians who returned to Junius' point and elaborated it in some detail. The series of elaborations began with Junius' successors, the two faculty colleagues of Arminius, Franciscus Gomarus and Lucas Trelcatius Jr. Arminius, then, contrary to what has often been alleged, did not encounter "Bezan supralapsarianism" at Leiden.[70] What he encountered was Junian supralapsarianism.

There are four further Leiden disputations of the era that take up the issue. Arminius presided over the first of these in February 1604. Two more were set by Gomarus, one in 1604 and the other in 1609. Yet another, set in 1606, was presided over by Trelcatius. When Arminius returned to the issue of predestination in his theses for Wilhelmus Bastingius' public disputation in 1604,[71] he offered nothing in the way of elaboration of the issues that he had raised in correspondence with Junius, but his definition of the objects of predestination was more than enough to set Gomarus on edge. Arminius there defined the "Object or Material" of predestination as twofold, "either divine things, or persons, to whom the communication of those things was predestined by this decree."[72] The "divine things" are the "spiritual blessings" of justification and adoption bestowed on the "persons," who, in Arminius' definition, are the "faithful" who believe in Christ. Given that the decree to bestow spiritual blessings assumes that its objects are sinners who have faith, Arminius presumes that predestination of spiritual blessings on the elect rests on divine foreknowledge of faith, perhaps with the implication of divine middle knowledge. The

---

70. Cf. Gunter, *Arminius*, p. 70.

71. Jacob Arminius, *Disputationum theologicarum trigesima, de divina praedestinatione. resp. Wilhelmus Bastingius; praeside Jac. Arminio* (Leiden: Joannes Patius, 1604); also in *Disputationes publicae*, xv, in *Opera*, pp. 283–86 (*Works*, vol. 1, pp. 226–30).

72. Jacob Arminius, *Disputationes publicae*, xv.7, in *Opera*, p. 284: "Objectum seu Materia Praedestinationis duplicem ponimus: tum res divinas, tum personas, quibus illarum communicatio est hoc decreto praedestinata"; cf. the undated disputation in *Disputationes privatae*, xl.5, in *Opera*, p. 390, where Arminius only indicates "Materia" but defines it nearly identically.

"object or material" of the decree belongs entirely to the postlapsarian temporal order. This implication of the disputation was offset somewhat by Arminius' previous thesis that predestination "is the decree of God's good pleasure in Christ…from eternity" to save those "on whom he decreed to bestow faith,"[73] but clearly not offset enough to satisfy Gomarus.

Gomarus' disputation of 1604 was set outside of the regular sequence of disputations for the decree and has been typically viewed as a response to the disputation on predestination over which Arminius had presided earlier in the year.[74] We also have Arminius' posthumously published comments on Gomarus' disputation.[75] Arminius' biographers, Caspar Brandt and Bangs, identify Gomarus' 1604 disputation as a direct response to Arminius' earlier disputation on predestination. Brandt notes that "Gomarus did not think fit to wait till a proper opportunity should be furnished him for disputing on the subject of predestination, but…so far overstepped order and his own proper turn, as to expose to public view certain theses on that self-same subject, which according to the sole custom of the Academy, and in his proper rotation, Arminius had already discussed."[76] Geeraert Brandt indicates that

73. Jacob Arminius, *Disputationes publicae*, xv.2, in *Opera*, p. 283. On Arminius' advocacy of middle knowledge, see Eef Dekker, "Was Arminius a Molinist?," in *Sixteenth Century Journal*, 27/2 (1996), pp. 337–52; also Muller, "Arminius's 'Conference' with Junius," pp. 115–16, 120–26.

74. Arminius, *Disputationum theologicarum trigesima, de divina praedestinatione* (1604); also Arminius, *Disputationes publicae*, xv, in *Opera*, pp. 283–85; and *Works*, vol. 2, pp. 226–30.

75. Franciscus Gomarus, *Theses theologicae de praedestinatione Dei Samuel Gruterus; sub praesidio Franc. Gomari* (Leiden: Joannes Patius, 1604); also in Jacob Arminius, *Examen thesium D. Francisci Gomari de praedestinatione* (Amsterdam: s.n., 1645), with Arminius' responses. Note the translation in Arminius, *Works*, vol. 3, pp. 526–658.

76. C. Brandt, *Life of James Arminius*, p. 199; cf. Bangs, *Arminius*, pp. 262–64; and Gunter, *Arminius and His Declaration of Sentiments*, p. 68, who base their accounts on Brandt. Also see the account and partial description of the theses in Jan Uytenbogaert, *De kerckelicke historie, vervatende verscheyden gedenckwaerdige saecken, inde Christenheyt voorgevallen, van het jaer vierhondert af, tot in het jaer sesthien-hondert ende negenthien, voornamentlick in dese Geunieerde provintien* (Amsterdam: s.n., 1646), pp. 323–24, who assumes that Gomarus was aware of Arminius' *Amica collatio* with Junius; and the response in Jacob Triglandius Sr., *Kerckelycke geschiedenissen begrypende de swaere en bekommerlijcke geschillen, in de Vereenigde Nederlanden voor-gevallen, met derselver bestissinge: ende aenmerckingen op de Kerckelycke historie van Johannes Wtenbogaert: uyt*

Gomarus set his theses "diametrically opposed to those of *Arminius*... partly out of zeal, and in defence of his own opinions, and partly, as it is thought, at the instigation of others."[77] Uytenbogaert's and Triglandius' accounts of the two disputations of 1604 assume that Gomarus not only disagreed with the theses then presented by Arminius, but that he was also aware of Arminius' views on the diversity of Reformed opinions ranging from the supralapsarian views of Calvin and Beza to the infralapsarian view of Georg Sohn, as expressed at length in Arminius' remarks in the *Amica collatio*.[78]

Several considerations serve to modify this account. First, the claim that Gomarus did not wait is exaggerated, given that Arminius' disputation was held in February and Gomarus' in October. It is also not the case that Gomarus violated the custom of the theological faculty in setting the disputation. This was not a disputation inserted out of order into the agreed-upon series or *repetitio*,[79] but a set of *theses theologicae* for disputation set apart from the *repetitio*, probably one of the standard *extra ordinem* practice disputations, the subject of which was at the discretion of the presider and respondent.[80] Such *extra ordinem* theses for disputation were hardly unusual nor, among them, were theses on predestination. Whereas between 1595 and 1609 there were only four disputations on predestination in the set series or repetitions (Junius, 1599; Arminius, 1604; Trelcatius, 1606; and Gomarus, 1609), there were seven *extra ordinem* disputation on the subject (Junius, 1595, 1599, 1602; Lucas Trelcatius Sr., 1597; Gomarus, 1599, 1604; and Kuchlinus, 1600)—yielding a fairly continuous series of *extra ordinem*

---

autentycke stucken getrouwelijck vergadert, ende op begeerte der Zuyd en Noort-Hollantsche Synoden uytgegeven, tot nodige onderrichtinge door Jacobum Triglandium (Leiden: Adriaen Wyngaerden, 1650), pp. 289–97.

77. Geeraert Brandt, *The History of the Reformation and Other Ecclesiastical Transactions in and about the Low Countries: from the Beginning of the Eighth Century, down to the Famous Synod of Dort*, 4 vols. (London: T. Wood, 1720–1723), vol. 2, p. 31; and further, pp. 35–36.

78. Uytenbogaert, *De kerckelicke historie*, p. 323; Triglandius, *Kerckelycke geschiedenissen*, p. 289b.

79. On various kinds of disputations, see Keith D. Stanglin, *The Missing Public Disputations of Jacobus Arminius: Introduction, Text, and Notes* (Leiden: Brill, 2010), pp. 12–19.

80. Cf. Stanglin, *Missing Disputations*, pp. 17–18.

disputations: 1595, 1597, 1599 (two), 1600, 1602, and 1604. These *extra ordinem* disputations were conducted frequently—Gomarus himself set at least three others in 1604. And finally, Gomarus' disputation—however pointedly he directed it against opponents, such as Castellio, Coornhaert, and the "Lutherans," and defended Calvin and Beza—did not explicitly mention Arminius or refer to previous disputations in the university.[81]

Unfortunately, we do not have Gomarus' introductory remarks as presider over the October 1604 disputation, which, by Caspar Brandt's account, were inflammatory and clearly directed toward Arminius.[82] Gomarus, moreover, may well have been aware of some of the more detailed arguments of Arminius against supralapsarianism. It must be taken seriously that Gomarus was acquainted with a manuscript version of a draft of the *Amica collatio* consisting in Arminius' propositions and Junius' replies, and if Uytenbogaert's account is correct, a later version including some or all of Arminius' lengthy responses to Junius.[83] We do know that Arminius took umbrage at Gomarus' introductory comments at the October 1604 disputation and understood them to be directed at him. In his then-unpublished response, Arminius would reply pointedly and in detail to Gomarus.

In the disputation, Gomarus argued that the causality and objects of predestination should be considered both as "remote" in the divine purpose and as "proximate" in the effective divine willing. In the remote divine purpose, the objects are "rational creatures indefinitely foreknown," namely, possibles; in the proximate divine willing they are

---

81. Gomarus, *Theses theologicae de praedestinatione, Corollarium*, ad fin.

82. C. Brandt, *Life of James Arminius*, p. 199.

83. Uytenbogaert, *De kerckelicke historie*, p. 323; Triglandius, *Kerckelycke geschiedenissen*, p. 289b; and cf. Muller, "Arminius's 'Conference' with Junius," pp. 110–15, on the probable history of composition. Both Uytenbogaert and Triglandius reference Arminius' appeal to Georg Sohn as a Reformed theologian of views similar to his own. Arminius references Sohn only in his reply to Junius' response to the sixth proposition, which would not have been in the initially circulated manuscript with Junius' responses. He also cited Sohn in the *Notae* on Junius' 1593 theses on predestination: see *Opera*, pp. 492, 612 (*Works*, vol. 3, pp. 66, 237). Either Gomarus has access to or at least knowledge of the contents of the unpublished manuscripts or Uytenbogaert and Triglandius wrote their accounts filling in what they knew from the posthumous publications.

actual, individual human beings.[84] At the heart of Gomarus' disputation is Arminius' identification of the objects of predestination only in the most proximate sense and foreknown as faithful, despite the earlier thesis that God bestows faith. Gomarus' raising the issues of *possibilia*, as also his identification of these possibles as *creabiles*, marks a development and clarification beyond what can be found in Junius. If, as Uytenbogaert suggested, Gomarus had access to a manuscript of the full text of the *Amica collatio*, the reason for his emphasis on divine knowledge of possibles becomes clear: it relates directly to an issue raised in Arminius' reply to Junius (in the same place as the reference to Sohn) and left unanswered given the absence of a further rejoinder from Junius.[85] Further, if Gomarus' access to the *Amica collatio* is accepted, then also some of the content of the disputation itself, notably its comments regarding possibles, could be taken as a direct response to more developed aspects of Arminius' thought than were evident in the February 1604 disputation on predestination.

Gomarus argues that the "object of predestination" is the "indefinite" or undefined possibles, known to the "indefinite foreknowledge" of God, which is to say, all rational creatures that are both savable and creatable that could either come to be or not come to be. The subject of predestination, then, is some individual persons out of all the possibles, those certain persons that according to the counsel of His will and according to His freedom, God predestines. God could, Gomarus adds, predestine and create innumerable other creatures, but according to the counsel of His will and His freedom, He has willed only a certain number.[86] Gomarus' terminology here is a distinct development beyond Junius' definitions: he has introduced the notion of a divine knowledge of pure possibles—in the case of the objects of

---

84. Gomarus, *Theses theologicae de praedestinatione*, ix.

85. Cf. Arminius, *Replica*, prop. vi, p. 491 (*Works*, vol. 3, pp. 65–66).

86. Gomarus, *Theses theologicae de praedestinatione*, x: "Obiectum enim voluntati praedestinanti ab intellectus divini praescientia indefinita (quae est rerum possibilium ac nondum definitarum, sive ea futurae sint, sive non sint, notitia) monstratum, sunt creaturae rationales servabiles & creabiles universae: subjectum vero praedestinationis sunt singulares quaedam ex iis. Ut enim Deus innumeras etiam alias & aliter destinare potuit ac creare, pro sua omnipotentia, idque voluntati objecit, pro infinita & indefinita scientia; ita certum tantum earum numerum, certasque personas, voluntatis propositio, pro sua libertate, predestinavit."

predestination, *creabiles*—which by definition are the objects of the divine simple or absolute knowledge (*scientia simplicis intelligentiae*) and of the absolute divine power (*potentia absoluta*). Gomarus does not here note these latter terms for absolute knowledge and power, but his identification of *possibilia* opens the way to their use. The knowledge of possibles and the possibles themselves are "indefinite" or indeterminate because they could come to be or not come to be: they are objects of divine knowledge prior to the utterly free act of the divine will by which some are actualized and some are not.[87]

Unfortunately, Gomarus did not set any of the disputations on divine essence and attributes in the several "repetitions" that took place in Leiden at this time (1597–1609).[88] He did do so later, in the Groningen disputations printed in the posthumous *Opera* of 1644 and 1664. There he not only identified the ultimate objects of the decree as indefinitely foreknown, he explicitly noted that this indefinite foreknowledge refers to the *scientia simplicis intelligentiae*.[89] He did, however, in a subsequent thesis of his 1604 Leiden disputation, correlate the notions of possibles with the absolute power of God: "Just as the creatable depends on the indeterminate & absolute omnipotence of God, so does what is to be created depend on that [omnipotence] determined to creation by the predestination of [God's] will."[90] The objects of predestination must precede predestination. Accordingly, the ultimate objects of predestination are "rational creatures" known to God indefinitely as possibles that are "salvable, damnable, creatable, fallible, restorable," which is to say, not "definitely" known as "to be saved or to be lost, to be created, about to fall or remain standing, or about to be restored."[91] As Gomarus presents the issue, the object of

---

87. Gomarus, *Theses theologicae de praedestinatione*, x; cf. the similar language of "indefinitely" known human beings in Gomarus' posthumous Groningen *Locorum communium theologicorum epitome* (Amsterdam: Joannes Jansson, 1653), pp. 58–59.

88. See the lists in Stanglin, *Missing Disputations*, pp. 589–96.

89. Franciscus Gomarus, *Disputationes theologicae*, x.23, 27, in *Opera theologica omnia, maximam partem posthuma*, 2 parts in 1 vol. (Amsterdam: Joannes Jansson, 1664), pt. 2, p. 27.

90. Gomarus, *Theses theologicae de praedestinatione*, xiii: "Ut enim creabile, ab indeterminata & absoluta Dei omnipotentia, sic creandum, ab es, per voluntatis praedestinationem ad creationem determinata, dependet."

91. Gomarus, *Theses theologicae de praedestinatione*, xiii: "creaturae rationales, non qua

predestination to certain ends must precede the decree concerning it, not in temporal sequence but "in the order of nature"—but since the decree establishes its object as to be what it will be, prior to the decree the object is indefinite, after it, definite. Accordingly, the object, understood as "to be saved, to be created, to fall, and to be restored" follows the decree,[92] and is known by God according to His *scientia voluntaria*, God's eternal knowledge of all that He has willed. In this order, as in the case of Junius' ordering of the objects, there is no juxtaposition of a decree to predestine with a distinct decree to create: from the outset, the willing of objects of predestination is connected with the willing to create.

In a disputation conducted under his presidency in 1606, Trelcatius repeated Junius' formula with augmentation akin to Gomarus' development of the argument in 1604. Trelcatius defined the object or *materia* of the divine decree as human beings considered *communiter*, namely, universally in all times—"therefore in every possible manner, [as] creatable, to be created, created, liable to fall, fallen, restored, etc."[93] Thus, the object of the divine decree of predestination, given the eternity and omniscience of God, is the human being in the entire range of divine knowledge, from the purely possible to the fallen condition, to eschatological glory. As in Junius' formulation, Trelcatius' version of supralapsarianism includes the infralapsarian identification of the object of the divine decree as created and fallen. Also following Junius, Trelcatius identifies the object of predestination as humanity considered universally and in all times. The range of knowing belongs to God inasmuch as God, in His eternity, knows all things, places, and times at once (*simul*).[94] Trelcatius adds, however, the categories of humanity as creatable (*creabilis*) and restored (*restauratus*), and he divides the category of created and fallible into two, yielding six understandings of the object rather than Junius' three.

---

reipsa servandae aut perdendae, creandae, lapsurae aut perstiturae, reparandae: sed quatenus potentia remota & indefinita servabiles, damnabiles, creabiles, labiles, reparabiles."

92. Gomarus, *Theses theologicae de praedestinatione*, xiii.

93. Lucas Trelcatius Jr., *Disputationum theologicarum quarto repetitarum trigesima, de aeterna Dei praedestinatione* (Leiden: Joannes Patius, 1606), vii: "Consideramus ergo quocunquemodo creabilem, creandum, creatum, labilem, lapsum, restauratum, etc."

94. Trelcatius, *Disputationum…de aeterna Dei praedestinatione*, vi.

Gomarus' second disputation on predestination, offered in 1609, indicated that the objects of predestination are, first, creatable (namely, indeterminate and subject to the absolute power of God), to be created according to the divine will, and then determined by God to their creation. Nor, Gomarus adds, is it as if these objects of divine willing are external to God and in any sense impulsive causes, as if the divine will were suspended on a condition.[95] It is significant that Gomarus has paired God's knowledge of possibles, the *scientia simplicis intelligentiae*, with the *potentia absoluta*, but has also identified the divine willing as an operative power of God, by implication, the *potentia ordinata*, which would be paired with the divine *scientia voluntaria*.

Arminius' posthumously published response to Gomarus' 1604 disputation followed out the pattern of argument that he presented in the *Amica collatio* with Junius and assumed some of the further argumentation developed in his *Examen modestum* of Perkins' treatise on the manner and order of predestination.[96] Arminius countered Gomarus by arguing that possibles indefinitely known to God as "salvable, damnable, creatable, fallible, restorable" cannot be understood as the object of predestination inasmuch as an object must exist "in the order of nature prior to the action of power occupied about the object."[97] It is not that God cannot know an object in its "bare" or "mere purity" prior to creating it, but that object cannot be qualified by any property that would result from an action upon it. Further, since an uncreated object of divine knowing is a nonexistent, a *non ens*, it is not susceptible of *passio*—namely, of change—which is, in Arminius' view, what Gomarus implied: a mere possible human being could be subject to salvation or damnation.[98] Arminius also believes his argument demonstrates the

---

95. Franciscus Gomarus, *Disputationum theologicarum quinto repetitarum trigesima quarta: de Dei praedestinatione…sub praesidio…D. Francisci Gomari* (Leiden: Joannis Patius, 1609), xlv–xlvi.

96. Jacob Arminius, *Examen modestum libellus, quem D. Gulielmus Perkinsus… edidit…de praedestinationis modo et ordine*, in *Opera*, pp. 621–777 (*Works*, vol. 3, pp. 249–484).

97. Jacob Arminius, *Examen thesium D. Francisci Gomari de praedestinatione* (Amsterdam: s.n., 1645), xiii (p. 47); in *Works*, vol. 3, pp. 526–658, here p. 565; and cf. the comments in Muller, "God, Predestination, and the Integrity of the Created Order," pp. 435–36.

98. Arminius, *Examen thesium*, xiii (pp. 47–48); *Works*, vol. 3, pp. 565–66.

priority of the decree to create and permit the fall over any decree of predestination either to salvation or to damnation: the object of predestination must exist and be in its existence savable or damnable in order for God to destine it to salvation or damnation.

That neither Junius' responses nor Gomarus' argumentation altered Arminius' perspective is clear from his *Declaratio sententiae*, where he maintained his argument for several opposing Reformed perspectives, infra- and supralapsarian. He also intensified his objections to the supralapsarian view, according to which, in his view, "God by an eternal and immutable decree has predestinated, from among men, (whom he did not consider as created, much less as being fallen), certain individuals to everlasting life, and others to eternal destruction, without any regard whatever to righteousness or sin, to obedience or disobedience, but purely of his own good pleasure, to demonstrate the glory of his justice and mercy."[99] In this view, creation, fall, and the loss of original righteousness are reduced to the means to God's end of election and reprobation. What is striking about Arminius' arguments in the *Declaratio sententiae*, however, is that they return to the original point that he made in his initial letter in the *Amica collatio*— that there is a basic division of the Reformed doctrine, supra- and infralapsarian. He neither drew on Junius' and Gomarus' arguments for what we have called an inclusive supralapsarianism, nor reprised his arguments against the predestination of mere possibles or indefinites. The *Declaratio sententiae* identified supralapsarianism as simply an identification of the objects of predestination "not as created [*non ut creatos*]," without further nuance.[100] Virtually none of the technical argumentation found in the *Amica collatio*, the *Examen modestum libellus* against Perkins, or the *Examen thesium* against Gomarus, is present in the *Declaratio sententiae*. Junius' theses of 1602 were left unanswered during Arminius' lifetime, though perhaps answered by implication in the posthumous *Examen thesium*.

---

99. Arminius, *Declaratio sententiae*, in *Opera*, p. 100 (*Works*, vol. 1, p. 614).
100. Arminius, *Declaratio sententiae*, in *Opera*, p. 100 (*Works*, vol. 1, p. 614).

The Object of the Decree according to Piscator (1614–1615) and Twisse (1646–1653)

Four works of William Twisse, one published in the year of his death (1646), the other three shortly thereafter, addressed the problem of the object of predestination with specific reference to the formulations of Junius and Johannes Piscator. The first of these works, Twisse's treatise against John Cotton, noted the issue of various Reformed understandings of the object of predestination and identified Piscator's attempt to resolve the issue as superior to Junius' formulation: "About the object of predestination, there hath bin a triple difference in opinion: some standing for *massa nondum condita*; others for *massa pura*, that is *condita* but *nondum corrupta*; others for *massa corrupta*: yet both *Junius* did endeavour: but very obscurely; and *Piscator* hath endeavoured very perspicuously to reduce them into one. If he failed therein, especially in someone particular, his failing, rightly observed and discerned, may open a way for the discovery of the entire truth."[101]

Similarly, in his treatise against Samuel Hoard and the editorial additions to Hoard's work, Twisse commented, "The difference in opinion thereabouts is usually observed to be threefold…for some conceive the object of Predestination to be man-kind as yet not created; others conceive the object to be man-kind created, but not yet corrupted. A third sort maintaine the object thereof to be man-kind both created and corrupted. Now D. *Junius* hath endeavoured to reconcile the three opinions, making place for each consideration in the object of predestination; And *Piscator* after him adventures on the like reconciliation, and hath performed it with more perspicutie and with better successe in my judgment then *Junius*."[102] Piscator, as observed

---

101. William Twisse, *A Treatise of Mr. Cottons, Clearing Certaine Doubts Concerning Predestination. Together with an Examination Thereof* (London: J. D. for Samuel Creek, 1646), p. 40. Similar language is found in William Twisse, *Vindiciae gratiae, potestatis, ac providentiae Dei hoc est, ad examen libelli Perkinsiani de praedestinatione modo et ordine, institutum a J. Arminio, responsio scholastica* (Amsterdam: Joannes Jansson, 1648), I/I.iv (p. 48, col. 1, C–D), where Twisse notes differences among the Reformed: "Agnosco Theologos nostros dissentire inter se de objecto praedestinationis constituendo: dum alii volunt esse massam conditam: alii forsitan conditam, sed nondum corruptam; alii & conditam & corruptam considerationi divinae volunt objectum fuisse decretum praedestinationis instituerit."

102. William Twisse, *The Riches of Gods Love unto the Vessells of Mercy, consistent*

by Otto Ritschl, had addressed the issue of the object of predestination in several places—although several of Ritschl's citations lead only to declarations that God has eternally willed to save particular human beings, without any further qualification.[103] Twisse clearly was not referring to these passages.

Twisse referenced Piscator fairly frequently, with specific consideration of various understandings of the object of predestination in his animadversions on the Armnius-Junius *Amica collatio* and Johannes Corvinus' defense of Arminius.[104] His source was neither the *Aphorismi* nor the 1598 *Disputatio*. Rather, Twisse referenced the definition and arguments found in the *Quaestio de objecto praedestinationis* appended

---

with his absolute hatred or reprobation of the vessells of wrath, or, An answer unto a book entituled, Gods love unto mankind…in two bookes, the first being a refutation of the said booke, as it was presented in manuscript by Mr Hord unto Sir Nath. Rich., the second being an examination of certain passages inserted into M. Hords discourse (formerly answered) by an author that conceales his name, but was supposed to be Mr Mason…whereunto are annexed two tractates of the same author in answer unto D.H. together with a vindication of D. Twisse from the exceptions of Mr John Goodwin in his Redemption Redeemed, by Henry Jeanes, 2 vols. (Oxford: L. Lichfield and H. Hall for Thomas Robinson, 1653), vol. 2, p. 10.

103. Ritschl, *Dogmengeschichte*, vol. 3, p. 312; thus Ritschl's citations of Johannes Piscator, *Aphorismi doctrinae christianae, ex Institutione Calvini excerpti: hactenus in schola Herbornensi publicé ad disputandum propositi, & deinceps (si Deus voluerit) proponendi* (Herborn: Corvinus, 1589), is not to the point. What Piscator indicates here (p. 65) is that God eternally determines what He will do with each human being, not identifying the objects of predestination of any order of decrees. Piscator's *Tractatus de divina praedestinatione* (Herborn: Corvinus, 1618), is an exposition of the *aphorismi* on predestination. So also Johannes Piscator, *Disputatio theologica de praedestinatione: ac nominatim de tribus quaestionibus hodie controversis; Videlicet I. An Deus velit singulos homines salvos fieri. Ii. An Christus pro singulis hominibus sit mortuus. Iii. An Electio pendeat à Fide praevisa. Opposita disputationi Andreae Schaafmanni Ecclesiastae Tremoniani: cui tituluum fecit, De divina, pro singulorum hominum salute, voluntate, etc.* (Herborn: Christoph Rab, 1598), theses i, xlix, (pp. 19, 34, 48–49); other passages cited by Ritschl reference conditions of salvation as before and after the fall, thesis lxxxix (pp. 70–71); and that the decree is absolute and not based on foreknowledge, thesis xcix (p. 90).

104. William Twisse, *Ad Jacobi Arminii Collationem cum Francisco Junio; & Johan. Arnoldi Corvini Defensionem sententiae Arminianae, de praedestinatione, gratia, & libero arbitrio, &c. Quam adversus Danielis Tileni Considerationem edidit, Animadversiones* (Amsterdam: Johannes Janssonius, 1649), part 1, *Ad Arminii Collationem*, p. 8, col. 2; p. 127, col. 1; p. 133, col. 2; part 2, *Ad Corvini Defensionem*, p. 17, col. 1–2; p. 18, col. 1–2; p. 29, col. 1; p. 148, col. 2–149; p. 280, col. 2. Hereinafter cited by part, as *Ad Arminii Collationem* and *Ad Corvini Defensionem*.

to Piscator's 1614 treatise on the grace of God, or the 1615 disputation on predestination, where Piscator declares that the "object of election is not each and every human being, but only certain ones and they are considered [by God] both as not yet created, and as created upright, but as capable of falling, & then also, as fallen."[105] Piscator also used the distinction between the eternal decree and its execution to define the decree as respecting all creatures considered either universally (*commune*) and indifferently or particularly as intelligent or rational—namely, angels and men—but he did not at this point connect this distinction directly with an eternal willing of the ends of not-yet-created objects.[106] Piscator also appealed to the logical point that the last in execution must be first in intention. Twisse notes in particular that Piscator had indicated the priority of the decree to glorify some human beings over the decrees to create and permit the fall.[107]

Piscator's *Quaestio de objecto praedestinationis* was preceded by a general epistle to ministers of the word of God in schools and in the churches of the Netherlands in which he objects to the "calumny" against his teaching on predestination that appeared in the dedicatory epistle prefixed to the newly published *Amica collatio* (1613) between Arminius and Junius. The author of that epistle—probably Petrus Bertius—had compared Piscator's view of God to the Roman emperor Tiberius, who was reported to have had a virgin violated in order for him subsequently to have her strangled without his breaking

---

105. Cf. Twisse, *Ad Corvini Defensionem*, p. 17: "quaeritur (inquit [Piscator]) hodie inter doctos, an objectum praedestinationis divinae sit homo consideratus ut nondum conditus: an vero ut conditus sed nondum lapsus: an denique ut lapsus"; with Johannes Piscator, *Tractatus de gratia Dei: in quo disputatur quaestio controversa, An gratia Dei salvifica sit universalis: seu, an Deus velit ut singuli homines salvi fiant.... Cui addita est ejusdem Johan. Piscatoris Refutatio calumniae atrocis...item Explicatio quaestionis de objecto praedestinatonis* (Herborn: s.n., 1614), pp. 173–74: "objectum praedestinationis esse hominum consideratum & ut nondum conditum, & ut conditum, sed adhuc integrum, & ut lapsum peccatoque corruptum"; hereinafter cited as *Quaestio de objecto praedestinationis*. Also note Johannes Piscator, *Disputatio theologica de praedestinatione* (Herborn: s.n., 1615), thesis 48: "Objectum electionis non sunt universi & singuli homines, sed soli certi: iique considerati, & nondum conditi, & ut conditi integri, sed labi potentes, & denique ut lapsi."

106. Johannes Piscator, *Hypotyposis ss. theologiae ad leges methodi qua popularis qua scholasticae delineata* (Herborn: s.n., 1611), p. 11.

107. Twisse, *Vindiciae gratiae*, p. 67, col. 1, 2.

a law against the murdering of innocents.[108] God, Piscator responded, does not mandate sin; He forbids it. And He does not punish innocents, only the guilty—and Piscator's own teaching only declared that what God does in time was also decreed from eternity.[109] The *Quaestio* appears both as a clarification on a very specific issue of Piscator's response to the calumny and, as Picaator had probably originally intended, as a continuation of his polemic against Vorstius.

Piscator began with the question of whether the object of predestination was humanity not yet created, or created but not yet fallen, or created and fallen. The question itself, Piscator observed, is mistaken and based on the false hypothesis that these three statements of the object of predestination are mutually exclusive. The statements, however, are diverse but not opposed.[110] When the term "predestination" is understood in general, as indicating both election and reprobation, rather than being taken *in specie* as the decree of election, the object of predestination must be understood as humanity not yet created, and as created and still in original integrity, and as fallen into sin and corrupt.[111] In support of this argument, Piscator had insisted in debate with Vorstius on distinguishing between the temporal order of God's work and the order established logically between ultimate and proximate ends and, similarly, on distinguishing between temporally successive moments and logically ordered "moments of nature."[112] Given the divine eternity and the nondiscursive, nontemporal nature of divine knowing, the sequence of human objects of divine predestination that are stated from a human perspective as in a temporal sequence are in fact logically ordered moments of nature in the divine intellect.

In addition to drawing on Junius and Piscator, Twisse added his own rationale for indicating that Reformed proponents of the three different identifications of the object of predestination ought not to dispute but should accept a reconciliation such as argued by Junius and Piscator. In the first place, Twisse contended, the differences were "not

---

108. Piscator, *Refutatio calumniae atrocis*, in *Tractatus de gratia Dei*, p. 164.

109. Piscator, *Refutatio calumniae atrocis*, in *Tractatus de gratia Dei*, pp. 169–70.

110. Piscator, *Quaestio de objecto praedestinationis*, p. 173.

111. Piscator, *Quaestio de objecto praedestinationis*, pp. 173–74.

112. Johannes Piscator, *Ad Conradi Vorstii, S. Theol. D. amicam collationem, etc. notae Johan. Piscatoris* (Herborn: s.n., 1613), § xxxix (p. 82).

so much in Divinitie, as in Logick and Philosophie," given that the issue being argued was the order of divine intentions, which should "be composed according to the right stating of the end intended, and of the meanes conducing to the end; it being generally confessed, that the intention of the end is before the intention of meanes conducing thereunto…. [W]hat is first in intention, the same must be last in execution."[113] The logic of the issue, then, would necessarily yield a supralapsarian conclusion but, in Twisse's view, one that would include the infralapsarian identification of the objects of predestination.

In the second place, all of the Reformed, whatever their understanding of the object of predestination, would "agree in two principall points":

> 1. That all men, before God's eternall predestination and reprobation, are considered as equall in themselves, whether as uncreated, or as created, but not corrupted, or lastly, whether created or corrupted.

> 2. That God's grace only makes the difference, choosing some to work them to faith, & repentance, & perseverance therein; while he rejecteth others, leaving them as he findes them, & permitting them to finish their dayes in sinne, whereby [the prerogative of God's sovereignty] is upheld and maintained.[114]

Given this basic agreement, when it comes to an identification of the object of the divine decree—whether it is humanity *nondum condita*, *condita*, *nondum corrupta*, or *corrupta*—Twisse raises the issue of the eternity of the decrees and therefore their "unity both in time and nature, God willing all things *uno & eodem actu*." If God is to be rightly understood first as knowing all possibles in His necessary or natural knowledge and then as willing all actual things eternally in one and the same act, then the decrees concerning various objects of predestination are not "a concatenation…by consequent after consequents" but are "*coordinata & conjuncta*."[115]

---

113. Twisse, *Riches of Gods Love*, vol. 2, p. 10.
114. Twisse, *Riches of Gods Love*, vol. 2, p. 10.
115. Twisse, *Riches of Gods Love*, vol. 2, p. 182.

Patterns of Argument among the Continental Reformed: Ames, Maccovius, Hoornbeeck, and Mastricht (1629–1699)

The Junian argument that I have tentatively identified as inclusive supralapsarianism was also perpetuated by a significant series of Continental Reformed theologians, beginning with the Franeker theologian, William Ames. Ames proposed a full schema of the divine counsel, the decrees, and predestination, in which he correlated the order of divine knowing and willing both with the issue of divine knowledge of possibles and actuals and with the two major distinctions concerning divine knowledge and divine power—namely, the distinction between the divine *scientia simplicis intelligentiae* and the divine *scientia visionis* and the distinction between the divine *potentia absoluta* and *potentia ordinata*. The divine understanding or *intellectus Dei* is simple, devoid of composition and discursiveness, unchangeable, eternal, and infinite,[116] but also essentially endued with the "idea of all things" that are "imitable in the creatures."[117] Further, "the ideas as they are considered antecedent to the Decree of divine will, represent the essence of things & only possible existence: as they are considered after the determination of divine will, they represent the same things as to be in actuality, according to their actual existence."[118] This distinction between ideas as eternally known possibles and eternally known actuals that are to be corresponds with the "distinction of the divine knowledge" into *scientia simplicis intelligentiae* and *scientia visionis*. The first, as antecedent to the divine will, is "a most perfect knowledge" of

---

116. William Ames, *Medulla ss. theologiae, ex sacris literis, earumque interpretibus, extracta, & methodicè disposita* (London: Robert Allott, 1629), iv.53–56; cf. the translation, *The Marrow of Sacred Divinity, Drawne out of the Holy Scriptures, and the Interpreters Thereof, and Brought into Method* (London: Edward Griffin, 1642).

117. Ames, *Medulla ss. theologiae*, vii.14; cf. Richard A. Muller, "Calvinist Thomism Revisited: William Ames (1576–1633) and the Divine Ideas," in *From Rome to Zurich, between Ignatius and Vermigli: Essays in Honor of John Patrick Donnelly, SJ*, ed. Kathleen M. Comerford, Gary W. Jenkins, and W. J. Torrance Kirby (Leiden: Brill, 2017), pp. 103–20.

118. Ames, *Medulla ss. theologiae*, vii.23; cf. similarly, the argument of Ames' contemporary, John Robinson, *A Defence of the Doctrine Propounded by the Synode at Dort: Against Iohn Murton and His Associates, in a Treatise Intituled; a Description of What God, &c..* (S.l.: s.n., 1624), i (p. 8). Robinson tied the issue directly to his defense of the doctrine of predestination. See the essay "Defending Dort: John Robinson and the Separatist Predestinarian Controversy" in this volume.

"all possibles" that can be brought into being by God.[119] The second, consequent only on the divine will, is an eternal knowledge of all actuals that will be, whether necessary, or free, or contingent.[120]

Thus, Ames could argue that the decree of predestination presupposed no reason or condition other than the divine will, inasmuch as it was grounded in its "order of intention" only in "that simple intelligence which is of all possibles."[121] There are, then, no qualities in created human beings that bring about God's will to elect some and reprobate others: the formal object of predestination is simply the human race, all human beings and each human being. The differences among human beings that relate to salvation and damnation are not dependent on human beings, but follow from the decree.[122] Inasmuch as the qualities that render human beings salvable and damnable are not qualities predicated of mere possibles, but are qualities consequent on the divine decree, Ames obviated Arminius' primary objection.

Accordingly, Ames could argue that "predestination necessarily presupposes neither its goal nor its object as existing, but posits that it exist: so that by the power of predestination it is ordained, that it might be."[123] Against the Remonstrant critique of supra- and infralapsarianism, Ames argued the impossibility of human beings explaining an infinite and most simple divine willing. There is but a single act of will "by which [God] simultaneously wills all that he wills,"[124] that is variously conceived by human beings. As Junius had argued, the universal or common object of predestination is the entire human race considered generally, as "not yet created" and also as "created & fallen."[125]

Johannes Maccovius' final approach to the topics of theology, the

---

119. Ames, *Medulla ss. theologiae*, vii.25.

120. Ames, *Medulla ss. theologiae*, vii.26.

121. Ames, *Medulla ss. theologiae*, xxv.11.

122. Ames, *Medulla ss. theologiae*, xxv.10.

123. Ames, *Medulla ss. theologiae*, xxv.8: "Praedestinatio enim, nec terminum, nec objectum suum necessario praesupponit ut existens, sedponit ut existat: ita ut vi praedestinationis ordinetur ut sit."

124. William Ames, *Anti-synodalia scripta, vel animadversiones in dogmatica illa, quae Remonstrantes in Synodo Dordracena exhibuerunt, & postea divulgarunt* (Amsterdam: Gulielmus Blaeuw, 1633), pp. 27–28.

125. Ames, *Anti-synodalia*, p. 28.

posthumously published *Loci communes*,[126] was an elaboration of the earlier work that he had begun in the theological disputations over which he presided beginning in the 1620s.[127] In his disputation on predestination, Maccovius offered a definition of the object of predestination distinguished into the object considered in the divine intention and considered in the execution of the divine decree: "The object of predestination is one thing considered according to its end, as it is in [divine] intention, another thing as it is in execution; according to its end, as in intention, it is the human being as possible, as they like to say in the Schools, creatable [*creabilis*]; according to the end, as in execution, the human being to be created, created, being permitted to fall, & fallen."[128] In other words, given the ways in which God knows the order that He creates, He must eternally know the objects of His willing first as purely possible and capable of being created (*scientia simplicis intelligentiae*) and as created, permitted to fall, and fallen (*scientia visionis*).[129] Maccovius adds a consideration that largely obviates Arminius' objection to the notion of the predetermination of possibles:

------

126. Johannes Maccovius, *Loci communes theologici* (Franeker: Ioannes Arcerius, 1650; Amsterdam: Ludovicus & Daniel Elzevir, 1658). On Maccovius' doctrine, see Michael D. Bell, "*Propter Potestatem Scientiam, ac Beneplacitum Dei*: The Doctrine of Predestination in the Theology of Johannes Maccovius" (PhD diss., Westminster Theological Seminary, 1986), pp. 130–68.

127. Johannes Maccovius, *Collegium theologicum miscellanearum quaestionum: Publice disputatarum in Acad. Franekerana, anno 1620 et 1621 sub praesidio Johannis Macowii* (Franeker: Uldericus Balck, 1632); and *Collegium theologicum miscellanearum quaestionum: Publice disputatarum in Academia Franekerana, anno 1622. subpraesidio Johannis Maccowii* (Franeker: Uldericus Balck, 1631); and *Thesium theologicarum per locos communes disputatarum in academia Franequerana*, 2 vols. (Franeker: Uldericus Balck, 1639–1641).

128. Maccovius, *Thesium theologicarum*, disp. xxvii.1.3 (vol. 1, pp. 225–26): "Objectum Praedestinationis aliud est ratione finis, prout est in intentione, alius prout est in executione, ratione finis, prout est in intentione, est homo possibilis factu, sicut in Scholis loqui amant, Creabilis; Ratione finis, prout est in executione, homo condendus, conditus, permittendus in lapsu, & lapsus." The same definition appears in Maccovius' *Loci communes*, xxv (pp. 208–9); also note Johannes Maccovius, *Distinctiones et regulae theologicae et philosophicae* (Franeker: Joannes Archerius, 1653), vii.4 (p. 72); and in translation, *Scholastic Discourse: Johannes Maccovius (1588–1644) on Theological and Philosophical Distinctions and Rules*, ed. Willem van Asselt, Michael D. Bell, Gert van den Brink, and Rein Ferwerda (Apeldoorn: Instituut voor Reformatieonderzoek, 2009), pp. 156–57.

129. Cf. Bell, "*Propter Potestatem*," pp. 161–62.

given that God eternally has a goal for human beings, there must be a goal with respect to "intention." Even God cannot have a goal "for nothing [*de nihilo*]." The particular person for whom God has a goal in intention is considered "as what he could become," namely, with a clear and certain goal as determined by God.[130] God, in other words, cannot will the end of manifesting His mercy and justice in fallen human beings prior to having considered human beings as creatable—as possible to be made—and, once made, capable of being permitted to fall, and subsequently as fallen.[131]

As with Junius, Lucas Trelcatius Jr., and Gomarus, Maccovius argues that God's knowledge of the created or created and fallen object of His willing is only one aspect of the divine knowing. Maccovius' argument is similar to that of Trelcatius, albeit less elaborate. Whereas Junius had identified the objects of predestination as "not yet created, or created, or fallen" (*sive nondum conditus, sive conditus, sive lapsus*), Maccovius added the prior category of *creabilis*, yielding four ways in which God eternally knows the human objects of His willing: as possibles capable of creation, as to be created (but not yet), as created and permitted to fall, and as fallen, leaving out Trelcatius' seguc into the order of salvation.

Johannes Hoornbeeck's *Institutiones theologicae* consists of sets of theses supported by quotations from various predecessors in the Reformed tradition.[132] The theses are original to Hoornbeeck, but the text of the volume is drawn from a group of Reformed predecessors, among them Calvin, Vermigli, Junius, Gomarus, Lucas Trelcatius Jr., Ames, and Maccovius.[133] Accordingly, the importance of the work lies not in any originality on Hoornbeeck's part, but in Hoornbeeck's delineation of trajectories of argument in early modern Reformed theology leading to the state of certain theological questions in his own time.

Hoornbeeck begins the chapter on divine decrees with a thesis posed in a set of distinctions, in which the immanent acts of God are distinguished into essential and personal, the essential into those that

---

130. Maccovius, *Distinctiones et regulae*, vii.4 (p. 72).

131. Maccovius, *Thesium theologicarum*, disp. xxvii.1.3 (vol. 1, p. 226).

132. Johannes Hoornbeeck, *Institutiones theologicae ex optimis auctoribus concinnatae* (Leiden: Franciscus Moyardus, 1658).

133. Hoornbeeck, *Institutiones theologicae, Praefatio*, sig. ***5r–v.

are necessary (*necessaria*) and those consisting in a judgment or deter-mination (*arbitraria*). He cites Ames as pointing out that the freedom of God in acts or operations *ad extra* is not merely concomitant with divine operations *ad intra*. Rather, the *ad intra* operations are anteced-ent and serve as the *principia* or foundations of the *ad extra*. Thus, "when God wills to act *ad extra*, he does not will by a necessity of nature, but on the basis of a prior choice: there is, then, no necessary connection between the divine nature, & those acts."[134]

Again citing Ames at length, Hoornbeeck proposes a second thesis: "God fully understands [*intelligit*] all possible things, in his omnipotence: accordingly he decrees to make whatever & whatsoever is pleasing to him: as a consequence he sees future things in his decree concerning them: in no way through some middle knowledge, ante-cedent to his decree, & on the basis of things and their conditions."[135] Arguably, Hoornbeeck chose *intellego*, "to understand," rather than another verb such as *cognosco*, in order to underline that the divine knowledge of all possibles resides in the *intellectus* or *intelligentiae Dei*, and that this knowledge of all possibles belongs to God's *scientia simplicis intelligentiae*, a point that is confirmed in a quotation from Ames. There Ames comments on the distinction between the divine *scientia simplicis intelligentiae* and *scientia visionis*, the former being a knowledge of all possibility, namely, of "each and every thing, that can be made" residing "most perfectly in the knowledge of God"; and the latter being "the knowledge of all future things that in their nature are necessary, or free, or contingent." Ames continues, "Those things that God knows by his knowledge of absolute understanding [*scien-tia simplicis intelligentiae*], he knows through his all-sufficiency: those that he knows by his knowledge of vision [*scientia visionis*], he knows

---

134. Hoornbeeck, *Institutiones theologicae*, iv.1 (p. 138): "Quoniam quod Deus vult operari ad extra, non vult ex necessitate naturae, sed electione praecedente: non est enim necessaria connexio inter naturam divinam, & istos actus."

135. Hoornbeeck, *Institutiones theologicae*, iv.1 (pp. 139–40): "Intelligit Deus res omnes possibiles, in sua ipsius omnipotentia: hinc decernit fieri quascunque & quo-modocunque sibi placitum: quas proinde futuras videt in decreto illis suo: nulla per scientiam quadam mediam, decretum suum antecedentem, & a rebus earumque con-ditionibus ortam."

through his efficiency, or from the decree of his own will."[136] Accordingly, "God decrees all things by one eternal act of will, not by several or by temporal acts."[137]

With these distinctions in place, Hoornbeeck can posit that "the object of predestination, as [understood] in general is the possible and the indefinite: thus specifically, a possible human being,"[138] which is to say, a human being known as a possibility for creation in the *scientia simplicis intelligentiae*. Here again, Hoornbeeck's initial citation is from Junius, with subsequent citations from Trelcatius, Maccovius, and Friedrich Spanheim. The citation from Spanheim references three understandings of the object of predestination and concludes by declaring them compatible and different only in their manner of teaching or addressing the issue.[139]

Petrus van Mastricht's contribution to the debate over supra- and infralapsarianism drew on a series of earlier thinkers and presented a variant form specifically intended to offer a resolution of the problem that would provide a way past the controversy between supra- and infralapsarians. He proposed, in short, the basis for the late orthodox synthesis of the two perspectives, modifying the earlier definitions of Ames,[140] Maccovius, and others. Mastricht indicated the existence of four strictly defined forms of the Reformed doctrine of predestination. These were the "rigid Supralapsarians," who identified the human objects of predestination restrictively as *creabiles & labiles*; the "rigid Infralapsarians," who identified the human objects of predestination restrictively as *creatus & lapsus*; a mediating orthodox group, the *Medii* ὀρθοδοξώτατοι, who distinguished between the human objects of predestination as *creabiles & labiles* and the same humans

---

136. In Hoornbeeck, *Institutiones theologicae*, iv.2 (p. 141): "Quae novit Deus per scientiam simplicis intelligentiae, novit ex sua omnisufficientia: quae vero novit per scientiam visionis, novit per suam efficientiam, vel ex decreto suae propriae voluntatis."

137. Hoornbeeck, *Institutiones theologicae*, iv.4 (p. 146).

138. Hoornbeeck, *Institutiones theologicae*, iv.11 (p. 155): "Obiectum praedestinationis, uti generalis est το possibile atque indefinitum: ita hic, homo possibilis."

139. Hoornbeeck, *Institutiones theologicae*, iv.11 (p. 157).

140. The influence of Ames on Mastricht should not be overestimated: see Adriaan Neele, *Petrus van Mastricht (1630–1706). Reformed Orthodoxy: Method and Piety* (Leiden: Brill, 2009), pp. 77–80; cf. Jan van Vliet, *The Rise of Reformed System: The Intellectual Heritage of William Ames* (Eugene, Ore.: Wipf & Stock, 2013), pp. 211–28.

as objects of election and reprobation, *creatus & lapsus*; and the "Universalist Reformed," who understood the objects of the decree as also redeemed and called.[141] Beyond these four, there is only the Pelagian or Pelagianizing option that views the objects of predestination as believers and unbelievers.[142]

Mastricht based his own view—an expanded version of the mediating orthodoxy—on an argument concerning the "four acts of God" belonging to the work of predestination: first, the eternal purpose (*propositum*) of manifesting the divine glory in the deliverance of mercy and justice; second, the decision to create human beings and to permit their fall in their common ancestor; third, from the created and fallen humanity to elect some in the manifestation of His mercy and reprobate others in the vindication of His justice; and fourth, the intention to prepare the means of both election and reprobation.[143] The four acts take up the issue of God's knowledge of possibles and divinely willed actuals, but also distinguish the human objects of these acts into objects of predestination in the first two acts and objects of election and reprobation in the third act.

In the first of these acts, human beings must be considered as possibles, *creabilis & labilis*, capable of being created and capable of falling. The *creabilis* comes from a line of predecessors—Trelcatius, Gomarus, and Maccovius—while the *labilis* is an addition to Mastricht's definition and may be added as an approach to the infralapsarian position. The objects of predestination, then, in the initial nontemporal act, are creatable and fallible. This argument would not, however, have satisfied Francis Turretin, who declared categorically that "a non-Entity cannot be an object of Predestination, but man [considered] purely as creatable, or fallible is a non-Entity, since [man] was brought forth from

---

141. Petrus van Mastricht, *Theoretico-practica theologia, qua, per capita theologica, pars dogmatica, elenchtica et practica, perpetua successione conjugantur*, 2 vols. (Utrecht: van de Water, Poolsum, Wagens & Paddenburg, 1715), III.ii.13. And note the translation, *Theoretical-practical theology*, trans. Todd M. Rester, ed. Joel R. Beeke, 3 vols. to date (Grand Rapids: Reformation Heritage Books, 2018–). In their preface to Mastricht, vol. 3, Rester and Beeke discuss Mastricht's "mediating lapsarian position" in detail (pp. xxvii–xxxiv).

142. Mastricht, *Theoretico-practica theol.*, III.ii.13.

143. Mastricht, *Theoretico-practica theol.*, III.ii.12.

non-being into being by creation."[144] The object of predestination, Turretin insisted, as distinct from the object of creation, must be an object "already established" in existence.[145]

In the second act, the objects of the decree are considered *creandus & lapsurus*, to be created and apt or ready to fall. Here again it is arguable that Mastricht's addition of *lapsurus* is an inclination toward the infralapsarian view, as distinct from earlier inclusive supralapsarian patterns that had only indicated either *creandus* or *condendus*. Does the addition draw an infralapsarian element, the impending future fallenness, into the divine understanding of the humanity that is to be created, or has Mastricht simply implied the issue of divine permission of the fall on which infra- and supralapsarians could agree? In either case, the objects to be created and apt or ready to fall are objects of divine predestination not yet distinguished into election and reprobation. Mastricht's approach here may be intended to deal with the strict infralapsarian argument that uncreated possibles cannot be proper objects of divine willing, although objects understood as *creandus & lapsurus* remain within the realm of divinely known possibles, not yet future actuals.

In the third act, they are considered *creatus & lapsus*, the created and fallen objects of God's election and reprobation, and in the fourth, humanity as *electus & reprobus*, elect and reprobate.[146] Thus, in the third act, Mastricht identifies human beings not generally as objects of predestination but specifically as objects of election and reprobation, sharing with infralapsarians the point that election and reprobation are directed toward the salvation of some eternally known as fallen and sinful just as reprobation is directed toward others, eternally known as fallen and sinful. The distinction between as yet uncreated and not yet fallen objects of predestination and created and fallen objects of election and reprobation also raises the possibility of arguing an

---

144. Turretin, *Institutio*, IV.ix.9.

145. Turretin, *Institutio*, IV.ix.9; cf. Du Moulin, *Anatomy*, xiii.13–15.

146. Mastricht, *Theoretico-practica theol.*, III.ii.12; cf. Ames, *Marrow*, I.xxv.19–21, 23, 31–34, 39 (where three acts are argued for election and for reprobation, with the first and the second implying, respectively, a supralapsarian and an infralapsarian object); Piscator, *Tractatus de gratia Dei*, pp. 174–76; and Maccovius, *Loci communes*, xxv (p. 209).

infralapsarian notion of a decree to create and permit the fall prior to a decree to elect and reprobate. Mastricht, however, does not state this option, but continues to identify the decrees of willing to predestine and willing to create as coordinate. Mastricht's pattern of the decree, if understood in terms of its initial definition of the object of the decree, retained a basic supralapsarian direction inasmuch as the first act, even with the addition of *labilis*, does not overcome the infralapsarian objection that God cannot predestine nonentities. On the other hand, as defined and taken by itself, the act of electing and reprobating has taken a distinctly infralapsarian direction. This infralapsarian note, insofar as it has distinguished the willing of objects of predestination from the willing of objects of election and reprobation, with the latter alone as specifically created and fallen, has reintroduced the problem of the location of creation in an order of the decree or decrees.[147]

Mastricht's terms themselves are also of interest, inasmuch as they both rest on and differ from the earliest forms of what we have identified as Junian or inclusive supralapsarianism: *nondum conditus, sive conditus, sive lapsus* (Junius); *creabilis, creandus, creatus, labilis, lapsus, restauratus* (Trelcatius); *creabilis*, and further, *indefinita servabiles, damnabiles, creabiles, labiles, reparabiles* (Gomarus); *creabilis, condendus, conditus, permittendus in lapsu, & lapsus* (Maccovius). Mastricht's sequence, *creabilis & labilis, creandus & lapsurus, creatus & lapsus, electus & reprobus*, is noticeably different in its inclusion of fallibility or fallenness in all parts of the sequence and, therefore, in not separating *creatus* as a distinct term from *lapsus* to yield a category of created but not yet fallen, or as Maccovius indicated, created and then permitted to fall. Mastricht also declined to include in his own sequence the category of *redemptus & vocatus* that he attributed to the "Universalist Reformed"

---

147. Note here, John Davenant, *Animadversions written by the Right Reverend Father in God, John, Lord Bishop of Sarisbury, upon a Treatise Intituled, Gods Love to Mankinde* (London: Iohn Partridge, 1641), pp. 160–61: "Whereas [Samuel Hoard] troubleth himself with distinguishing the Supralapsarian, and the [Sublapsarian] Doctrine, calling them *Supralapsarians*, who in ordering the eternall decrees of God concerning Election and Preterition or Reprobation place them before the consideration of the fall, and those *Sublapsarians*,who place them after; this pains might well have been spared. For Priorities and Posteriorities in the eternall immanent decrees of God are but imaginations of mans weak reason." Davenant's arguments concerning the variant views, and his own resolution, are worthy of a major analysis.

although, arguably, it could be added, with reference to election, as a final instant in the sequence.

Given this paradigm, both rigid supralapsarians and rigid infralapsarians are shown to be lacking and, therefore, incapable of refuting each other. Even so, if the infralapsarians allege against the supralapsarians a series of texts that identify the object of predestination as human beings lost in sin and then claim that the object of predestination is simply man as created and fallen, they have, in effect, identified the third act of predestination as the first and only act. The infralapsarians fail, accordingly, to consider God's universal predestination, omitting the first act, which addresses man as *creabilis & labilis*, and losing sight of the ultimate end of God's glory in the salvation and damnation of individuals known in the first act as *indefinite*, namely, as possibles. If, on the other hand, the rigid supralapsarians accuse the infralapsarians of losing sight of the end of predestination in the manifestation of God's glory and justice, the infralapsarians can respond that they respect the end or goal of divine glory in creation and permission to fall, in effect, allowing for man as *creandus & lapsurus* as the object of the manifestation of God's grace and justice and man as *creatus & lapsus* as the object of election and reprobation.[148] By implication, the supra- and infralapsarians agree that human beings in their reception of the means of salvation are either elect or reprobate.

Mastricht proposes that his mediating orthodoxy resolves the debate by incorporating all four acts concerning the object of divine willing—*creabilis & labilis, creandus & lapsurus, creatus & lapsus*, and *electus & reprobus*—into a single inclusive paradigm, and by distinguishing the ultimate object of predestination from the object of election and reprobation. The ultimate object of predestination is man *creabilis & labilis*, capable of being created and capable of falling; the object of election is man *creatus & lapsus*, created and fallen.[149]

Mastricht's own supralapsarian logic is clear in his advocacy of the logical formula "first in intention, last in execution," which defined the order of the decree as beginning with the divine intention to manifest God's glory in grace and justice, followed by the intention to create

---

148. Mastricht, *Theoretico-practica theol.*, III.ii.12.
149. Mastricht, *Theoretico-practica theol.*, III.ii.13; cf. III.iii.7.

human beings in order to bring about this end.[150] What Mastricht does not provide is a full rationale of how and why his paradigm of four acts and four distinct understandings of the objects of divine willing comports with the Reformed understanding of the eternal divine knowledge of all possibles and actuals. In other words, unlike Junius, Ames, Maccovius, and other predecessors, he does not deploy the distinctions between the eternal divine *scientia simplicis intelligentiae* concerning all possibles and the eternal divine *scientia voluntaria* concerning future actuals. This, despite the fact that Mastricht elsewhere discussed all of these aspects of the full argument, including an overtly Amesian understanding of the idea of all things absolutely in the divine essence,[151] the distinction between the two kinds of divine knowledge,[152] the distinction between absolute and ordained power,[153] and a grounding of possibility in the divine "all-sufficiency and infinite perfection."[154]

The remaining question concerning Mastricht's solution to the so-called lapsarian issue is how it should be seen as "mediating." It clearly does incorporate what Mastricht defined as a rigid supralapsarian position (*creabilis & labilis*) with what he identified as the rigid infralapsarian position (*creatus & lapsus*), if only because he incorporated both of these "rigid" definitions of the object of predestination into his definition. His definition of predestination as consisting in election and reprobation follows the double predestinarian pattern which, taken by itself, would have been congenial to supralapsarians and most infralapsarians. It is difficult to say, moreover, whether the rigid supralapsarians would have objected to Mastricht's inclusion of *lapsurus* with *creandus* as well as *creatus & lapsus* in the sequence, although a supralapsarian might find it objectionable to place human objects considered as *electus & reprobus* at the end of the sequence. A "rigid" supralapsarian would also probably object to Mastricht's distinction between objects of predestination and objects of election and reprobation. What is clearer is that Mastricht's approach would not be acceptable to infralapsarians of the stamp of Pierre Du Moulin or

---

150. Mastricht, *Theoretico-practica theol.*, III.ii.21.
151. Mastricht, *Theoretico-practica theol.*, II.xiii.7–10, citing Ames, *Medulla*, I.vii.14.
152. Mastricht, *Theoretico-practica theol.*, III.xiii.14.
153. Mastricht, *Theoretico-practica theol.*, II.xx.15.
154. Mastricht, *Theoretico-practica theol.*, II.xiii.23.

Francis Turretin who adamantly denied that God can will particular attributes in or destinies for pure possibles.[155] Nor would Mastricht's appeal to the logical formula "first in intention, last in execution" be acceptable to the infralapsarians.[156]

Mastricht's solution to the question of the object of predestination can be identified as mediating if (and only if) it is placed as Mastricht himself positioned it between a rigid supralapsarianism that allows only a *creabilis & labilis* object of predestination and a rigid infralapsarianism that allows only a *creatus & lapsus* object. The background and premises of the solution, however, belong to the trajectory of Junian supralapsarianism, and Mastricht himself was foundationally supralapsarian in the identification of the object of predestination, although he included an infralapsarian definition in his specific identification of the objects of election and reprobation. In short, Mastricht's view is mediating if understood as drawing on both supra- and infralapsarian definitions, but not if it is taken to be a solution that would be fully acceptable to either side of the debate.

Patterns of Argument among Eighteenth-Century British Theologians: Gill, Brown, and Hill

The vicissitudes of eighteenth-century Reformed or Calvinist thought in Britain brought a series of responses to the issue of a supra- or infralapsarian definition of the decrees ranging from fairly traditional acceptance of one definition or the other, to attempts reminiscent of the language of Junius, Maccovius, Hoornbeeck, and Mastricht to reconcile the two approaches, to refusals to raise the question and repudiations of the entire debate—all from theologians belonging to what can be loosely defined as late orthodoxy in the Reformed tradition.

John Gill's *Body of Doctrinal and Practical Divinity* and his *Cause of God and Truth*, an extended defense of predestination against Daniel Whitby, both contain rather even-handed analyses of the supra- and infralapsarian definitions of the decree. Given the intensity of debate in the preceding century, of which Gill was well aware,[157] this balance is

---

155. Du Moulin, *Anatomy*, xiii.13, 15 (pp. 97, 98); Turretin, *Institutio*, IV.ix.9.

156. Turretin, *Institutio*, IV.ix.23.

157. On Gill's sources, see Richard A. Muller, "John Gill and the Reformed Tradition: A Study in the Reception of Protestant Orthodoxy in the Eighteenth

quite remarkable. One might interpret the balance of Gill's definitions and defenses as indicative of his interest in defending the Reformed doctrine of predestination in general rather than his own particular form of definition. And that might be so. But it is also the case that Gill did not see the infralapsarian and supralapsarian definitions as necessarily opposed. He remarks that "the difference" between the two views "is not so great as many have thought at first sight; for both agree in the main and material things in the doctrine of election."[158] He goes on to note five fundamental points of agreement between supra- and infralapsarians: that election is particular and personal, that it is "absolute and unconditional," that it rests entirely on the divine good pleasure, that the "elect" and the "non-elect" are viewed impartially in the decree and predestined apart from any consideration of what is in them, and that the decree is an eternal, not a temporal act. Gill specifically notes that the infralapsarian view is often misunderstood as a temporal act of God following the fall. He then indicates that the difference between the supra- and infralapsarian positions has to do with the definitions of the objects of the decree as it is willed eternally in the mind of God.[159]

Gill cites Twisse, "who was as great a Supralapsarian as perhaps ever was, and carried things as high as any man ever did," as recognizing, for all his distance from the infralapsarian position, that the difference was over an *"apex logicus"* and lay only "in the ordering and ranging of the decrees of God."[160] Gill then offers his own summation:

> For my own part, I think both may be taken in; that in the decree of the end, the ultimate end, the glory of God, for which he does all things, men might be considered in the divine mind as createable, not yet created and fallen; and that in the decree of the means, which, among other things, takes in the mediation of Christ, redemption by him, and the sanctification of the Spirit; they might be considered as created, fallen, and sinful,

---

Century," in *The Life and Thought of John Gill (1697–1771): A Tercentennial Appreciation*, ed. Michael A. G. Haykin (Leiden: Brill, 1997), pp. 51–68.

158. John Gill, *A Complete Body of Doctrinal and Practical Divinity*, 3 vols. (London: W. Winterbotham, 1796), vol. 1, p. 269.

159. Gill, *Body of Divinity*, vol. 1, p. 270.

160. Gill, *Body of Divinity*, vol. 1, p. 270.

> which these things imply; nor does this suppose separate acts and
> decrees in God, or any priority and posteriority in them; which
> in God are but one and together; but our finite minds are obliged
> to consider them one after another, not being able to take them
> in together and at once.[161]

Gill has here, in fact, pointed out the primary grounds for formulating the doctrine one way or the other. Is it to be formulated with attention to the final goal or end of the decree and the logical priority of ends over means, or is it to be formulated in view of the temporal means on which the earthly life of the believer ought to be focused? Gill notes that the two positions can be reconciled by allowing both a "decree of the end" and a "decree of means," but he ultimately chooses against a model that distinguishes and orders decrees. Such orderings reflect the need of finite minds to divide topics and set the parts in order, but he favors moving past such distinctions and recognizing a single decree without priority or posteriority. In Gill's view, given the eternity and simplicity of God, the formulation need not press in one direction or the other but can easily incorporate both perspectives.

John Brown of Haddington (1722–1787), perhaps influenced by lines of argument already present in Mastricht and Gill, carried the point still farther. He noted that "it is not agreed among divines, how God considered men in his predestinating purpose,—Whether as *creatable* and *fallible*; or as *to be created* and *to fall*; or as *created* and *fallen*; or as *converted*; or as having persevered in holiness till their death."[162] Brown declared the latter two views—as converted and as having persevered—absurd. The first of these two may have an antecedent in a model like Trelcatius' where *restauratus* appears in the sequence, and the second may reflect the view of Philip Doddridge. The first three views, which could have been drawn directly from Mastricht, he declared to be "reconcilable," commenting that each arose as an effort to understand the infinite and simple divine purpose on the part of finite minds, specifically from the use of each of three human

---

161. Gill, *Body of Divinity*, vol. 1, p. 270.

162. John Brown of Haddington, *A Compendious View of Natural and Revealed Religion. In seven books*, 2nd ed., revised (Edinburgh: Murray and Cochrane, 1796), II.iii (p. 144).

perspectives as an "exact exemplar" of God's knowledge and willing.[163] The result of such specification of objects, in these three cases, Brown avers, was not error so much as partial truth.

The partial truth and the reconcilability of each of the approaches appear from an analysis of the doctrine in terms of four different aspects of God's purpose. In Brown's words,

> In God's infinite mind, his whole purpose of predestination is but one simple thought, which, by our finite and weak minds, may be apprehended in the four following steps: 1. His purpose of manifesting the glory of his own perfections, particularly of his mercy and justice in his dealings with men. In respect of this, men can only be considered as *creatable* and *fallible*. 2. His purpose of creating men and permitting them to fall in their common Head, in order to promote or occasion the glorification of his mercy and justice. In respect of this step, men must be considered as *to be created* and *to fall*. 3. His fore-appointment of some particular men for the manifestation of his *mercy*, and others as objects for the manifestation of the glory of his *justice*. In respect of this step, men must be viewed as *created* and *fallen*. 4. His fixing the proper means for rendering the former vessels of mercy, and the latter vessels of his everlasting, but just indignation. In respect of this step, men must be considered as *chosen* or as *passed by*.[164]

The paradigm appears to be drawn directly from Mastricht, with the single exception that Brown replaces Mastricht's active *reprobus*, condemned or rejected, with the passive "passed by," more clearly approaching the infralapsarians. All of these statements concerning the divine purpose, in Brown's view, are exegetically and doctrinally sound, and all represent correctly one aspect of the eternal, simple, divine purpose. The supralapsarians, he continues, rightly understand the "objects of predestination" in terms of the first two aspects noted, namely, "as *creatable* and *fallible*, or *to be created* and *to fall*." As in the case of Mastricht, the addition of "fallible" to the first "step" may indicate an attempt at rapprochement with the infralapsarian position. If the second "step" is taken from Mastricht, Brown has chosen to remove the implication of a likely pending event by translating Mastricht's

---

163. Brown, *Compendious View*, II.iii (p. 144).
164. Brown, *Compendious View*, II.iii (pp. 144–45).

future participle (*lapsurus*) as a simple future infinitive. Brown's third "step" is still more clearly a point of approach to an infralapsarian argument since, again like Mastricht, it reserves the acts of election and reprobation to the created and fallen objects of the decree—an argument that would displease supralapsarians. Having stated these four steps, Brown indicates that the infra- or sublapsarians, equally rightly, define the human objects of predestination "as *created* and *fallen*" and, by extension, in view of the decree, as either "*chosen* or as *passed by*." Thus, in this larger understanding of the four aspects of the doctrine, taken as a whole, the supra- and infralapsarians "may cordially agree": "The glory of God's perfections, at the last end of the whole purpose, is first presented to view; and the decree appears *whole* and *uniform* as Supralapsarians need wish. And men, as sinners, are chosen to salvation in Christ, as Sublapsarians contend."[165]

The Scottish Presbyterian George Hill (1750–1819) also developed the inclusive argument at considerable length, grounding his argument on the Reformed understanding of the divine *scientia simplicis intelligentiae* and the divine *scientia voluntaria* as eternally comprehending all possibility and all future actuality. The "disputes about the order of the Divine Decrees, and the controversy between the Supra-lapsarians and the Sub-lapsarians," he argued, "are insignificant."[166] Hill argued that the doctrine of predestination, properly understood, needed to be formulated in recognition of God as "the Supreme Being" and "cause of every thing that now exists, or…is to exist at any future time." In particular, this recognition of the nature of God would yield a "view of the divine prescience which is the ground-work of the doctrine of predestination."[167]

Hill begins, therefore, by addressing the issue of divine knowledge and does so in a manner reflective of the older orthodoxy and its approach to possibles. Absolute impossibles, such that cannot be brought into existence even by an omnipotent God, are also

---

165. Brown, *Compendious View*, II.iii (p. 145); cf. Mastricht, *Theoretico-practica theol.*, III.ii.12–13.

166. Hill, *Heads of Lectures in Divinity* (St. Andrews: at the University press, 1796), IV.vii.3 (p. 79); cf. idem, *Lectures in Divinity* (Philadelphia: Herman Hooker, 1842), IV.vii.3 (pp. 520–24).

167. Hill, *Lectures in Divinity*, IV.vii.3 (p. 520).

impossible of conception. By contrast, possibles or possible things are conceivable—indeed, perfectly conceivable by God: "To the Supreme mind, therefore, there are distinctly represented, not only all the single objects which may be brought into existence, but also all the possible combinations of single objects, their relations, and their mutual influences on the systems of which they may compose a part."[168] God does not, however, will all possibilities into existence, but only one order of compossibles, including the circumstances and "manner of existence" of all things in the order: all things accordingly depend on the will of God and, as willed by Him according to His knowledge of all possibles, must also be known by Him as a particular order of possibles that is to be actualized.

These two kinds of divine knowing, Hill adds, have been traditionally called *scientia simplicis intelligentiae* and *scientia visionis*, indicating on the one hand the divine knowledge of all possibility and, on the other, "the knowledge which God, from eternity, had of all that he was to produce."[169] Given that God is the sole creator, these two kinds of divine knowledge account for all that can be known. That this *scientia visionis* is "from eternity," Hill adds, requires "particular attention." God, as infinitely perfect and omniscient, is not subject to change and knows, unchangingly, the entire plan of His creation. Prior to creation the entire content of the *scientia visionis* is known by God as to be made; in the temporal realization of God's plan things "pass in succession from the state of possibility into the state of existence" and then some pass out of existence. In time there is past, present, and future, but in the "divine mind," given that the things and events belonging to the *scientia visionis* are eternally known, all things past, present, and future to human beings are "equally in view."[170] The supralapsarian definition "considered God as regarding men before they were created"; the infralapsarian "as regarding men in the wretched situation to which [the fall] had reduced them."[171] Debate over these views, Hill concludes, is "insignificant" in view of a full understanding of how an eternal and omnipotent God knows all things, inasmuch as the entirety

---

168. Hill, *Lectures in Divinity*, IV.vii.3 (p. 520).
169. Hill, *Lectures in Divinity*, IV.vii.3 (p. 521).
170. Hill, *Lectures in Divinity*, IV.vii.3 (p. 521).
171. Hill, *Lectures in Divinity*, IV.vii.3 (p. 524).

of possible and actual existence is eternally known to God. By implication, the supralapsarian definition reflects the divine *scientia simplicis intelligentiae*; the infralapsarian definition, the divine *scientia visionis*.[172]

Conclusion

A series of Reformed theologians in the seventeenth and eighteenth centuries took up Franciscus Junius' original rejoinder to Arminius and made the point, against Arminius' argument that there was a fundamental disagreement of the varied Reformed definitions of predestination, that the supra- and infralapsarian definitions are not, in fact, incompatible. Each may be viewed, given the boundaries supplied by the Reformed confessions and by the Reformed doctrine of God, as taking a legitimate perspective on the doctrine. Junius' fundamental contribution was to point out that the supralapsarian view takes the perspective of the divine *scientia necessaria*, understanding the human objects of predestination as *possibilia*, while the infralapsarian view takes the perspective of the divine *scientia voluntaria*, understanding the human objects of predestination as *actualia*.

What is ruled out by these perspectives is the Arminian understanding of the objects of predestination as future contingents lying outside of the divine willing, specifically the perspective of a divine *scientia media*, as advocated by the Arminians and the Molinists. This view, moreover, would be the engine that ran Arminius' conception of predestination.[173] Given that the supralapsarian construction of predestination drew directly on a view of the objects of the decree according to God's knowledge of all possibility (the *scientia necessaria*) and the infralapsarian construction drew on a view of the objects of the decree according to God's knowledge of all willed actuality (the *scientia voluntaria*), not only were both of these constructions viable in the Reformed context, they were also as compatible as the pair of legitimate distinctions in the divine knowing. Arminius' view, as resting on *scientia media*, the rejected third member of the distinction, fell outside

---

172. Hill, *Lectures in Divinity*, IV.vii.3 (p. 524).

173. Cf. Eef Dekker, *Rijker dan Midas: Vrijheid, genade en predestinatie in de theologie van Jacobus Arminius, 1559–1609* (Zoetermeer: Boekencentrum, 1993), pp. 76–132; with Muller, *God, Creation, and Providence*, pp. 150–56; and idem, *PRRD*, III, 5.3 (E.1–3; F.3–4).

of the Reformed model for the proper understanding of the ways in which God can know objects. Junius, as we have seen, recognized the problem, and he, with those who took up variations on his argument in the seventeenth and eighteenth centuries, also saw past the debates among the Reformed between supra- and infralapsarian formulations of the doctrine of predestination. None of the views noted obliges the typical pattern of distinguishing supra- from infralapsarianism by the location of a distinct decree to create as prior or posterior to a decree to predestinate or to elect and reprobate: the entire series of the divine knowing and willing of objects includes at each gradation or degree the divine knowing and willing with respect to their creation. Among the later formulations, those of Mastricht and Brown are more clearly mediating, given their distinction between objects of predestination and objects of election and reprobation. The historical and doctrinal outcome of these arguments, however, was not the cordial agreement projected by proponents of the several inclusive variants. In particular, proponents of strictly infralapsarian formulae—like Turretin—were not swayed to allow any form of the *creabilis* designation, even though they typically held the distinction between the necessary and voluntary knowledge of God and identified the necessary knowledge as a knowledge of pure possibles.

CHAPTER 5

Defending Dort:
John Robinson and the Separatist Predestinarian Controversy

John Robinson (ca. 1575–1625), a central figure among the English Separatists of the late sixteenth and early seventeenth centuries, has been the subject of a significant scholarly literature,[1] notably for his congregational ecclesiology and his role in the Pilgrim migration to Massachusetts. His doctrinal debates, however, have received considerably less attention.[2] One ongoing debate in particular deserves further attention, especially given the different readings found among the few writers who have considered it, namely, his debate with others in the Separatist community over predestination and related points of

---

1. On Robinson's life and work, see Timothy George, *John Robinson and the English Separatist Tradition* (Macon, Ga.: Mercer University Press, 1982); Ozora S. Davis, *John Robinson: The Pilgrim Pastor* (Boston: Pilgrim, 1903); Frederick James Powicke, *John Robinson (1575?–1625)* (London: Hodder and Stoughton, 1920); and Walter H. Burgess, *John Robinson, Pastor of the Pilgrim Fathers: A Study of His Life and Times* (London: Williams and Norgate, 1920). Also note Robert Ashton, *Memoir of Rev. John Robinson*, in *The Works of John Robinson, Pastor of the Pilgrim Fathers*, 3 vols. (London: John Snow, 1851), vol. 1, pp. xiii–lxxxii, and the appendixes in vol. 3, pp. 437–91. In what follows, I have provided references to the original printings of Robinson's works, but have also included references to the relevant pages in the 1851 *Works*.

2. See Stephen Brachlow, *The Communion of Saints: Radical Puritan and Separatist Ecclesiology, 1570–1625* (Oxford: Oxford University Press, 1988); A. C. Carter, "John Robinson and the Dutch Reformed Church," in *Studies in Church History*, 3 (1966), pp. 232–41; also Frederick James Powicke, "John Robinson and the Beginnings of the Pilgrim Movement," in *Harvard Theological Review*, 13 (1920), pp. 252–89; and idem, *Henry Barrow, Separatist (1550?–1593) and the Exiled Church of Amsterdam (1593–1622)* (London: James Clarke, 1900), pp. 272–93, et passim.

doctrine. That debate is significant for understanding the theological relationship of the Separatists to the Church of England, the Arminian controversy in the Reformed churches, and the immediate context of the English Separatist churches in the Netherlands, in which Robinson was one of the more eminent preachers and teachers.[3]

The few who have written on Robinson's doctrine of predestination are agreed that it stands within what had been generally identified as "Calvinism" but, that being said, there is considerable disagreement on the content and implication of his thought. His early twentieth-century biographer, Ozora Davis, presents Robinson's thought as a form of Calvinism that "squarely faces the two facts of God's sovereignty and man's freedom," recognizes the resulting "dilemma," and proposes two distinctions as a way of resolving the issue—the first between necessity and compulsion, the second between the temporal act caused by God, as an act, and the sinfulness of the act arising from the human will.[4] Timothy George's two presentations of Robinson's views on predestination are in accord with Davis' interpretation, also noting in more detail the scholastic distinctions employed by Robinson to explain his position, and adding that Robinson argued an asymmetrical view of election and reprobation.[5] Both Davis and George interpret Robinson's understanding of Christian doctrine as in accord with and explanatory of the confessional statement of his fellow Separatists in Amsterdam, a document written in large part by Henry Ainsworth.[6] Further, they argue that, apart from the specific

---

3. Timothy George, "Predestination in a Separatist Context: The Case of John Robinson," in *Sixteenth Century Journal*, 15/1 (1984), pp. 73–85, here pp. 75–77, 79–80.

4. Davis, *John Robinson*, pp. 153–54.

5. George, *John Robinson*, pp. 191–201; and idem, "Predestination," pp. 81–82.

6. *A True Confession of the Faith, and humble acknovvledgement of the alegeance, vvhich vvee hir Maiesties subjects, falsely called Brovvnists, doo hould tovvards God, and yeild to hir Majestie and all other that are ouer vs in the Lord Set dovvn in articles or positions, for the better & more easie vnderstanding of those that shall read yt: and published for the cleering of our selues from those vnchristian slanders of heresie, schisme, pryde, obstinacie, disloyaltie, sedicion, &c. vvhich by our adversaries are in all places given out against vs* (Amsterdam: s.n., 1596). And note the modern text in James T. Dennison Jr., ed., *Reformed Confessions of the 16th and 17th Centuries in English Translation*, 4 vols. (Grand Rapids: Reformation Heritage Books, 2008–2014), vol. 3, pp. 748–64; and the critical text with introduction in Williston Walker, *The Creeds and Platforms of Congregationalism* (1893; repr., New York: Pilgrim, 1991), pp. 41–74. Ainsworth's work is often

issue of ecclesial separation, Robinson was also in accord with the English Reformed tradition as expressed in the Thirty-Nine Articles and the Lambeth Articles.[7] A similar conclusion was reached by Stephen Johnson, who argues Robinson's agreement with the Canons of Dort and the clarity with which Robinson rebuts the charge that the canons rendered God the author of sin.[8]

A diametrically opposed reading of Robinson's views has been argued by Jeremy Bangs:

> Robinson did not expressly deny that this system [i.e., the "Perkinsian" Reformed theology against which Arminius argued] made God the author of sin. Rather, when repeatedly confronted with the problem of evil, Robinson maintained the evil itself must be essentially good in a superior way that imperfect men are too ignorant to understand. No doubt Robinson sought to include Isaiah 45:7, according to which (in the Geneva translation of the Bible) God said, "I forme the light and create darkness: I make peace and create evill: I the Lord doe all these things." Any theology that incorporated freedom of choice (and thus placed responsibility for evil on the choice of the actor) was considered a heretical attack on the divine property of omnipotent omniscience.[9]

---

identified as "The Second Confession of the London-Amsterdam Church," inasmuch as it was preceded by *A True Description out of the Word of God* (1589), by Henry Barrow and John Greenwood, identified as "The First Confession of the London-Amsterdam Church." The *True Description*, however, is not a full doctrinal confession but what Walker calls "an ideal sketch" of Congregationalist polity (*Creeds and Platforms*, p. 30). Robinson attested his accord with the *Confession* in a letter to Ainsworth on the power of the church, in *Works*, vol. 3, p. 480.

7. Cf. Davis, *John Robinson*, pp. 149–50; with George, "Predestination," p. 75, citing Charles H. George and Katherine George, *The Protestant Mind of the English Reformation, 1570–1640* (Princeton: Princeton University Press, 1961), p. 46; also note Frank Hugh Foster, "The History of the Original Puritan Theology of New England, 1620–1720," in *American Journal of Theology*, 1/3 (1897), pp. 700–727, here pp. 701–2.

8. Stephen M. Johnson, "The Soteriology of John Robinson, Pilgrim Pastor and Advocate of the Reformed Faith," in *Westminster Theological Journal*, 44/1 (1982), pp. 31–57; also M. Jerry Davis, "John Robinson, the Pilgrim Pastor: His Polity and Theology" (PhD diss., Claremont School of Theology, 1967), pp. 98–107.

9. Jeremy D. Bangs, "Beyond Luther, beyond Calvin, beyond Arminius: The Pilgrims and the Remonstrants in Leiden, 1609–1620," in *Reconsidering Arminius: Beyond the Reformed and Wesleyan Divide*, ed. Keith D. Stanglin, Mark G. Bilby, and Mark H. Mann (Nashville: Abingdon, 2014), pp. 46–47, offering no documentation for his comments.

If Bangs' assessment of Robinson's theology can be elicited from Robinson's varied writings, Robinson's thought would stand outside the boundaries set by the Reformed confessions of the era—indeed, beyond the limits of the Canons of Dort that Robinson undertook to defend in a treatise of 1624. It would also defy one of the most fundamental tenets of Augustinian theology, namely, that evil is a defect in the essentially good substances created by God. Given these disparate assessments of Robinson's thought and its place in the debates of its time as well as in the history of Reformed theology, some further examination of his work is required.

Theological Preparation and Theological Allegiances: Cambridge (1592–1604) and Leiden (1609–1624)

John Robinson began his studies at Corpus Christi College, Cambridge, in 1592.[10] William Perkins, then catechist of Christ's College, had recently published *Armilla Aurea* or *Golden Chaine*, which saw its second printing in the year of Robinson's matriculation.[11] Robinson would later praise Perkins as a theologian of "great account" and would write an appendix (posthumously published) to Perkins' *Foundation of the Christian Religion*.[12] Robinson was awarded the BA in 1595, elected fellow of the college in 1598, and awarded the MA in 1599. During that time he was also ordained in the Church of England.[13] Robinson left the university in 1604, resigned his fellowship, and shortly thereafter was attached to St. Andrew's Church in Norwich.[14]

The controversy that exercised Cambridge during his years as a fellow is directly relevant to Robinson's later formulation and polemic. On April 29, 1595, William Barrett, a fellow of Gonville and Caius College and a student of the Huguenot refugee and Lady Margaret

---

10. Cf. Davis, *John Robinson*, pp. 60–61; Burgess, *John Robinson*, p. 34.

11. William Perkins, *Armilla Aurea, id est, theologiae descriptio mirandam seriem causarum & salutis & damnationis juxta verbum Dei proponens* (Cambridge: John Legat, 1590); and *A Golden Chaine: or, Description of Theologie. Containing the Order of the Causes of Salvation and Damnation, According to Gods Woord* (Cambridge: Iohn Legat, 1591).

12. John Robinson, *An Appendix to Mr Perkins his Six Principles of Christian Religion. Touching the more solemn Fellowship of Christians, (the Church of God) as being a Divine Institution* (London: J. L. for N. Bourn, 1656), in *Works*, vol. 3, pp. 421–36.

13. Burgess, *John Robinson*, pp. 37–39.

14. George, *John Robinson*, pp. 60–61; Burgess, *John Robinson*, p. 60.

Professor of Divinity at Cambridge, Peter Baro, preached a sermon intended to finalize his BD, in which he denounced the notion of security in salvation, argued that sin was the "proper" cause of reprobation, and specifically attacked the teachings of Calvin, Vermigli, Beza, Zanchi, and Junius.[15] Within six days of his sermon, Barrett was required to deliver publicly a recantation drafted by Robert Some, master of Peterhouse. This result was protested by Barrett and viewed as less than adequate by John Whitgift, Archbishop of Canterbury, leading to the drafting of the Lambeth Articles by the Regius Professor of Divinity, William Whitaker. After the finalization of the articles in November 1595, Baro joined the debate with a sermon grounding reprobation in the sinner's rejection of grace, which led to the accusation that he had disagreed with the Lambeth Articles. Baro contested the accusation, but his tenure as professor was rendered questionable, and he was not reelected to the position in 1596.[16] Robinson's biographer, Walter Burgess, commented, "The fact that Robinson was at Cambridge when these questions of predestination, election, reprobation, and justifying faith were so eagerly debated was not without effect on his mind. The influence of this period is strongly marked in his writings."[17]

After Cambridge, while he was serving a parish in Norwich, Robinson's Puritan tendencies led to conflict, probably over use of the Prayer Book, and ultimately to his suspension from the ministry. By his own testimony, on a return trip to Cambridge, Robinson heard lectures by Laurence Chaderton and Paul Baynes that inclined him

---

15. The controversy has been surveyed and analyzed, with varied interpretations, in H. C. Porter, *Reformation and Reaction in Tudor Cambridge* (Cambridge: Cambridge University Press, 1958), pp. 376–90; Peter G. Lake, *Moderate Puritans and the Elizabethan Church* (New York: Cambridge University Press, 1982), pp. 201–42; Nicholas R. N. Tyacke, *Anti-Calvinists: The Rise of English Arminianism, c. 1590–1640* (Oxford: Clarendon, 1990), pp. 35–38; and Peter White, *Predestination, Policy and Polemic: Conflict and Consensus in the English Church from the Reformation to the Civil War* (Cambridge: Cambridge University Press, 1992), pp. 110–17.

16. The course of the debate and the contours of Baro's theology as well as the varied interpretations in the scholarship on the controversy are detailed in Keith D. Stanglin, "Arminius *Avant la Lettre*': Peter Baro, Jacob Arminius, and the Bond of Predestinarian Polemic," in *Westminster Theological Journal*, 67 (2005), pp. 51–74.

17. Burgess, *John Robinson*, p. 55; cf. George, *John Robinson*, pp. 68–69.

toward Separatism, ultimately on the basis of the difference Robinson perceived between the forms of prayer used in "the reformed Churches" and those used in "the unreformed Church of England."[18] Probably in 1605, Robinson became associated with local nonconformists.[19] He associated with a like-minded group of believers at Scrooby and, when they gave up any hope of being permitted to exercise unperturbed worship separate from the Church of England, emigrated with them first to Amsterdam and subsequently to Leiden.[20]

Once established in Leiden, in addition to his ministerial duties, Robinson also associated himself with the theological faculty of the university, enrolled as a theological student, and engaged in disputations. A brief account of Robinson's university connection is found in Edward Winslow's defense of the theological orthodoxy of the New England Plantations and their communion with the French and Dutch Reformed Churches. Winslow referred to Robinson's time as minister to the Separatist church in Leiden: "Our Pastor Mr. *Robinson* in the time when Arminianisme had prevailed so much, at the request of the most Orthodox Divines, as *Poliander, Festus Homlius, &c.* disputed daily against *Episcopius* (in the Academy at *Leyden*) and others the grand champions of that error, and had as good respect amongst them, as any of their own Divines."[21] Inasmuch as this association

---

18. John Robinson, *A Manumission to a Manuduction, or Answer to a letter inferring publique communion in the parrish assemblies upon private with godly persons there* (Amsterdam: G. Thorpe, 1615), pp. 20–21.

19. George, *John Robinson*, p. 79.

20. On Robinson's work as a Separatist pastor in England and the emigration to the Netherlands, see George, *John Robinson*, pp. 69–86; and Burgess, *John Robinson*, pp. 67–109.

21. Edward Winslow, *Hypocrisie Unmasked: by a true relation of the proceedings of the Governour and company of the Massachusets against Samuel Gorton (and his accomplices) a notorious disturber of the peace and quiet of the severall governments wherein he lived: with the grounds and reasons thereof, examined and allowed by their Generall Court holden at Boston in New-England in November last, 1646* (London: Rich. Cotes, for John Bellamy, 1647), p. 95, referencing Johannes Polyander and Festus Hommius, both delegates to the Synod of Dort. The former was one of the authors of the orthodox *Synopsis purioris theologiae, disputationibus quinquaginta duabus comprehensa ac conscripta per Johannem Polyandrum, Andream Rivetum, Antonium Walaeum, Antonium Thysium, S.S. theologiae doctores et professores in Academia Leidensi* (Leiden: Elsevir, 1625); the latter was a minister in Leiden. Note the extended account in George, *John Robinson*, pp. 174–77; cf. Burgess, *John Robinson*, pp. 55–57.

began in 1609, Robinson experienced the university in the aftermath of the internal controversy over Arminius, and of the faculty who had been involved in the controversy, Robinson would have had contact only with Gomarus. As will become clear, Robinson's supralapsarian understanding of predestination was more akin to that of Perkins and the Leiden theology of Junius, Gomarus, and Lucas Trelcatius Jr. than to the generally infralapsarian theology of Polyander and the next generation of Leiden theologians.

Robinson's later theological efforts demonstrate that he deployed a version of Reformed theology that he imbibed at Cambridge in the 1590s, which was augmented and refined through his connection with the Leiden faculty of theology and through conflict with supporters of an Arminian or synergistic soteriology among the English Separatists in Amsterdam and Leiden both before and after the Synod of Dort.[22] He also identified his theology as in accord with predecessors in the Reformed tradition, notably, Bucer, Musculus, Bullinger, Vermigli, Beza, Perkins, Jeremias Bastingius, and David Pareus.[23] Robinson also indicated agreement with the Belgic Confession, the Thirty-Nine Articles, and the other confessions in the 1586 *Harmony of the Confessions*.[24]

With William Brewster, he declared in their confession of 1617, "To ye confession of fayth published in ye name of ye Church of England & to every artikell theerof wee do wth ye reformed churches wheer wee live & also els where assent wholy."[25] Then, in 1624, he published

---

22. Cf. Burgess, *John Robinson*, pp. 55–57; with Davis, *John Robinson*, pp. 149–61.

23. E.g., John Robinson, *A Iustification of Separation from the Church of England Against Mr Richard Bernard His Invective, Intituled; the Separatists Schisme* (Amsterdam: G. Thorp, 1610), in *Works*, vol. 2, p. 218; also *Essays*, in *Works*, vol. 1, pp. 57, 94, 202, 210, 242, 417, 467–68; and "Mr Robinson's Letter on Church Power," in *Works*, vol. 3, p. 484.

24. John Robinson, *A Just and Necessary Apologie of Certain Christians, no Lesse Contumeliously Then Common Called Brownists, or Barrowists* (Amsterdam: Successors of G. Thorp, 1625), in *Works*, vol. 3, p. 64, indicating assent to the Belgic Confession, the Thirty-Nine Articles, and other confessions found in the *Harmony of the Confessions of the Faith of the Christian and Reformed churches, which purlie professe the holy doctrine of the Gospell in all the chiefe Kingdoms, Nations, and Provinces of Europe* (Cambridge: Thomas Thomas, 1586).

25. John Robinson and William Brewster, *The Seven Articles from the Church of*

his extended defense of the Canons of Dort.[26] Both of these statements bore ecclesio-political implications. In the former, Robinson identified himself as being in accord with the confession of the Dutch Republic where his congregation had gathered and with the English Church from which they had separated on grounds of polity. In the latter, written as part of negotiations with the king to settle in North America, he maintained allegiance to the confession of the English Church.[27] Robinson, who remained in the Netherlands with a portion of the Leiden congregation, declared his and, accordingly, his congregation's agreement with the confessional declaration of the Dutch against the Arminianizing arguments of another Separatist living in the Netherlands, John Murton.[28] For both theological and political reasons, Robinson was and remained overtly committed to Reformed confessional orthodoxy and its defense.

Robinson's Rejoinder to the Followers of Smyth and Helwys

Robinson's development from critical reformist within the Church of England to Separatist and ultimately, in 1608, to expatriate has been detailed.[29] The English Separatists were hardly a unified community. Some of the Separatists, notably those belonging to the "Ancient London Church" in Amsterdam, followed the direction set by Francis Johnson and Henry Ainsworth.[30] The group led by John Smyth

---

Leyden, 1617, with an introductory letter by George Bancroft (New York: New York Historical Society, 1856), p. 9.

26. John Robinson, *A Defence of the Doctrine Propounded by the Synode at Dort: Against Iohn Murton and His Associates, in a Treatise Intituled; a Description of What God, &c.*. (S.l.: s.n., 1624); also in *Works*, vol. 1, pp. 261–471.

27. On the complexity of the negotiations with the king, the Virginia Company, and the Dutch, see Davis, *John Robinson*, pp. 227–38.

28. On Murton, his connection with Smyth and Helwys, and his debates with Robinson, see Walter H. Burgess, *John Smith, the Se-Baptist, Thomas Helwys and the First Baptist Church in England with Fresh Light upon the Pilgrim Fathers' Church* (London: James Clarke, 1911), pp. 276–89, 298–302.

29. Stephen Brachlow, "John Robinson and the Lure of Separatism in Pre-Revolutionary England," in *Church History*, 50/3 (1981), pp. 288–301; cf. Burgess, *John Robinson*, pp. 61–72, 82–84, 94–102.

30. On Ainsworth, see Michael E. Moody, "The Apostasy of Henry Ainsworth: A Case Study in Early Separatist Historiography," in *Proceedings of the American Philosophical Society*, 131/1 (1987), pp. 15–31; idem, "'A Man of a Thousand': The

that emigrated in 1608 differed with the Ancient Church over the issues of soteriology and baptism—with Smyth and his group advocating, by 1608, a more synergistic soteriology and adult baptism.[31] Robinson, who also emigrated with his congregation in 1608, stood with the Ancient Church and its more strictly Reformed theology but, by spring 1609, had established itself as a distinct congregation in Leiden.[32] The fundamental theological differences among the separatists fairly quickly led to controversy.

The final chapter of Robinson's *Of Religious Communion* (1614) is devoted to a substantial refutation of the "Confession of Faith, published in certain Conclusions by the remaynders of Mr. Smithes Company after his death," the title given by Robinson to the *Propositions and Conclusions, Concerning True Christian Religion* (1613).[33]

Reputation and Character of Henry Ainsworth, 1569/70–1622," in *Huntington Library Quarterly*, 45/3 (1982), pp. 200–214; and Raymond A. Blacketer, "Henry Ainsworth, Harried Hebraist (1570–1622)," in *Biblical Interpretation and Doctrinal Formulation in the Reformed Tradition: Essays in Honor of James A. De Jong*, ed. Arie C. Leder and Richard A. Muller (Grand Rapids: Reformation Heritage Books, 2014), pp. 129–55.

31. On Smyth see B. R. White, *The English Separatists from the Marian Martyrs to the Pilgrim Fathers* (Oxford: Oxford University Press, 1971), pp. 116–41; and see the subsequent debate among Douglas Shantz, "The Place of the Resurrection in the Writings of John Smith," in *Baptist Quarterly*, 30/5 (1984), pp. 199–203; James Coggins, "The Theological Positions of John Smyth," in *Baptist Quarterly*, 30/6 (1984), pp. 247–64; Stephen Brachlow, "John Smith and the Ghost of Anabaptism: A Rejoinder," *Baptist Quarterly*, 30/7 (1984), pp. 296–300; and B. R. White, "The English Separatists and John Smyth Revisited," in *Baptist Quarterly*, 30/8 (1984), pp. 344–47.

32. Cf. Burgess, *John Robinson*, pp. 82–93, 143–52; and Johnson, "Soteriology," pp. 36–38; the differences among the Separatist groups are detailed by Henk Bakker, "Baptists in Amsterdam," in *Baptist Quarterly*, 43/4 (2009–2010), pp. 229–34.

33. John Robinson, *Of Religious Communion Private, & Publique. With the silenceing of the clamours raysed by Mr. Thomas Helwisse agaynst our reteyning the Baptism receaved in Engl: & administering of Bapt: unto infants. As also a survey of the confession of fayth published in certayne conclusions by the remaynders of Mr. Smithes company* (S.l.: s.n., 1614), p. 100; in *Works*, vol. 3, p. 237. Contrary to the editorial note in Robinson's *Works*, vol. 3, p. 237, the argument is not against Thomas Helwys, *A Declaration of the Faith of the English People remaining at Amsterdam, in Holland* (S.l.: s.n., 1611), nor is it against John Smyth's (unpublished) confession of ca. 1609–1610. The document singled out by Robinson is the *Propositions and Conclusions, Concerning True Christian Religion, conteyning a confesion of faith of certaine English people, liuinge at Amsterdam* (Amsterdam: s.n., 1613), published in a pamphlet with Smyth's *Last booke…called the Retractions* and *The Life and Death of Iohn Smith*. There is an account of the history of the document, followed by the text, in William Joseph McGlothlin, ed., *Baptist*

The *Propositions and Conclusions*, probably by Smyth, are the last in a series of confessions emanating from the English Separatist churches in Amsterdam and Leiden, in which Robinson was a minister. Ainsworth's *True Confession of the Faith* (1596) was the earliest full theological confession of the Separatists, followed by the confessions of John Smyth (1609/10 and 1613) and Thomas Helwys (1611), both of which veered toward Arminianism and anti-paedobaptism.[34] Robinson, writing at the time of a major debate between Reformed and Remonstrant theologians, clearly took the Reformed side, arguing both the justice of God's will to redeem some and pass by others and the limited efficacy of Christ's satisfaction.[35]

Still, Robinson's reply to Smyth's *Propositions* was not altogether negative. His intention in critically examining Smyth's work was "to passe by (as approving it) what I fynd agreable to the Scriptures, albeit not set down in so convenient termes: to explain, & clear what may seem doubtful, & so to evince by the same Scriptures, what I deem contrarie to the wholesome doctrine of godlines & forme thereof."[36] Beyond what he held to be Smyth's doctrinal errors, Robinson took exception to the imprecision of Smyth's language—in several instances, not only to Smyth's failure to consider a suitable battery of biblical texts, but also to his lack of sophistication in deploying the distinctions requisite to careful formulation.[37]

Confessions of Faith (Philadelphia and Boston: American Baptist Publication Society, 1911), pp. 66–84; also found in William L. Lumpkin, ed., *Baptist Confessions of Faith* (Valley Forge, Pa.: Judson, 1969), pp. 123–42. Smyth's confession of 1609 and a further confessional document of 1610 are also found in Lumpkin, *Baptist Confessions of Faith*, pp. 97–113.

34. Cf. Burgess, *John Smith*, pp. 285–89, 314–17; with Antony D. Rich, "Thomas Helwys' First Confession of Faith 1610," in *Baptist Quarterly*, 43/4 (2009–2010), pp. 235–41, which includes a translation of the 1610 Latin text of Helwys' confession; and note M. Dorothea Jordan, "John Smyth and Thomas Helwys: The Two First English Preachers of Religious Liberty. Resemblances and Contrasts," in *Baptist Quarterly*, 12/6–7 (1947), pp. 187–95.

35. Robinson, *Of Religious Communion*, pp. 116, 117; *Works*, vol. 3, pp. 250–51.

36. Robinson, *Of Religious Communion*, p. 100; *Works*, vol. 3, p. 237; cf. Burgess, *John Robinson*, p. 151.

37. Davis, *John Robinson*, p. 155, notes Robinson's use of "subtle distinctions" with some disapproval.

With these intentions spelled out, Robinson omitted comment on the first six of Smyth's propositions. To the seventh proposition, which began "That to understand & conceive of God in the mynde is not the saving knowledge of God," Robinson took partial exception, given the potential anti-intellectualistic implication of Smyth's argument, noting that salvation is impossible without the faith "which is wrought in the mynde & understanding" and that the "renewing of Gods Image in us, [is] first in the understanding."[38]

Robinson, however, took major exception to a series of Smyth's subsequent propositions, among them the ninth, tenth, and seventeenth, which were concerned with the eternal decrees of God concerning sin and the issue of Adam's continuing freedom of will after the fall. Robinson cited the ninth proposition only in part: "That God before the foundation of the world did foresee, & determine the issue & event of all his workes. Act. 15.18,"[39] after which Smyth added (not quoted by Robinson), "and that actually in time he worketh all things by his providence, according to the good pleasure of his will. Eph.1.11. and therfor we abhorre the opinion of them, that avouch, that all things happen by fortune of chance. Acts.4.27.28. Mat.10.29.30."[40] The proposition, Robinson declared, contained "no untruth," but still came "much shorte of the trueth," inasmuch as God did not merely foresee and determine "the issues, & events of his workes" but had also eternally "decreed & purposed" them.[41] What Smyth did not make clear is that all of the events in time that God foresees and determines in their issue and event were also eternally purposed—namely, that God's foreknowledge of temporal events and His determination of their "issue" rests on His eternal purpose and decree. Specifically, it is not as if God predestines (and thereby determines the end of) particular human beings because He foresaw their belief in Christ.[42] Smyth, in other words, had not stated his proposition in such a way as to rule out an Arminian doctrine of election grounded in divine

---

38. Robinson, *Of Religious Communion*, p. 100; *Works*, vol. 3, pp. 237–38.

39. Robinson, *Of Religious Communion*, p. 100; *Works*, vol. 3, p. 238.

40. Smyth, *Propositions and Conclusions*, sig. A1v; also, slightly modernized, in McGlothlin, *Baptist Confessions*, p. 67.

41. Robinson, *Of Religious Communion*, p. 100; *Works*, vol. 3, p. 238.

42. Robinson, *Of Religious Communion*, p. 101; *Works*, vol. 3, p. 239.

foreknowledge. Indeed, the way in which Smyth stated his proposition would allow for an Arminian-Molinist view of divine middle knowledge, according to which, prior to His will to actualize the universal order of things, God eternally knows how a person will act under certain circumstances and, given that knowledge, actualizes those circumstances as part of the universal order that He brings into being.[43]

Robinson's reaction to Smyth's tenth proposition is partially positive and partially negative—and on the negative side, largely because of the lack of detail, nuance, and distinction in Smyth's wording and the possibility of what might be inferred from the proposition in the absence of further qualification:

> The beginning & end of the 10th Position : viz: *That God is not the Author, or worker of sin: & that he geves no influence, instinct, motion, or inclination to the least sin*, I embrace: But the middle parte thereof, viz: *That God onely did foresee, & determyne what evil the free will of men, & Angels would do*, I except against, as derogatory to the infinitenes of Gods power, & wisdom: neyther indeed is it sensible to say, that God determyned, what the will of others would do.[44]

As in Robinson's preceding objection to Smyth, much of Robinson's exception relates to the use of "determine" and "determined," which might seem curious given Robinson's insistence that all things come to pass by reason of the eternal purpose and decree. What appears to be at issue here is an implication of "determine," taken not in the sense of a general willing that something be so, but in the specific sense of the appointment of an effect, end, or result,[45] as in the sense of an action

---

43. On Arminius' Molinist conception of divine *scientia media*, see Eef Dekker, "Was Arminius a Molinist?," in *Sixteenth Century Journal*, 27/2 (1996), pp. 337–52; also idem, *Rijker dan Midas: Vrijheid, genade en predestinatie in de theologie van Jacobus Arminius, 1559–1609* (Zoetermeer: Boekencentrum, 1993); and Richard A. Muller, "Arminius's 'Conference' with Junius and the Protestant Reception of Molina's *Concordia*," in *Beyond Dordt and De Auxiliis: The Dynamics of Protestant and Catholic Soteriology in the Sixteenth and Seventeenth Centuries*, ed. Jordan J. Ballor, Matthew T. Gaetano, and David S. Sytsma (Leiden: Brill, 2019), pp. 103–26.

44. Robinson, *Of Religious Communion*, p. 101; *Works*, vol. 3, p. 239.

45. Cf. "To Determine," s.v., in John Rider, *Bibliotheca scholastica. A double dictionarie, penned for all those that would haue within short space the vse of the Latin tongue, either to speake, or write. Verie profitable and necessarie for scholars, courtiers, lawyers and*

of will to "accept or reject" by reason of "an antecedent disposition or object, that inclines or moves the will to Good, or to Evil."[46] Unqualified use of "determine" in this sense would imply that God moves a creature's will to evil.

That it was Robinson's intention to deny this specific sense of "determine" is apparent from his focus on the relationship of the foreknowledge, purposes, and providence of God to the problem of human sin. Robinson's argument hinges on two assumptions. Since "sin is the worke of men & Angels, it followeth that sin is from them, who are themselves from God: though the sin be not, but of themselves." Thus, all creatures are from God and dependent on God's will, but their sin is entirely their own:

> Yea, not onely the natures, & persons, but even the naturall powers, faculties, and instruments together with their naturall motions & actions, in, & by which sin is wrought, are of God also: by him susteyned, & upheld, & acted by his almighty power, which is the cause of every creature, & upholdeth all things, & so of every action, as an action [marg., Acts xvii.28; Rom. xi.30; Col. i.17; Heb. i.8]: Sin not being created of God, nor any part or power of man, or Angel, nor any motion or action, but only the depravation, corruption, crooked & inordinate abuse & application of the same created part, power, or motion.[47]

Adam, in his creation, was given by God the capacity to see and partake of the fruit of the tree of the knowledge of good and evil. Even so, Adam was created with the natural desire of pleasant things as well as "the power & ability of taking" them. All of these powers belong to the nature created by God. All of these powers are sustained by God, indeed, in an ultimate sense moved by God as the ultimate source of all motion in the universe. What God does not will is "the inordinateness, & abuse of the sense, appetite, & power upon that, which was

---

their clarkes, apprentices of London, travellers, factors for marchants, and briefly for all discontinuers within her Majesties realmes of England and Ireland (Oxford: Ioseph Barnes, 1589); and note Robinson's own usage of "destinate" as to "ordain beforehand, a person or thing to its end" in *Defence of the Doctrine*, in *Works*, vol. 1, p. 272.

46. "Determinare," s.v., in Rudolph Goclenius, *Lexicon philosophicum, quo tanquam clave philosophiae fores aperiuntur* (Frankfurt: Matthias Becker, 1613), p. 525, col. 1.

47. Robinson, *Of Religious Communion*, pp. 101–2; *Works*, vol. 3, pp. 239–40.

forbidden" by Him: the same actions, directed toward any fruit not forbidden by God, would not have been sinful.[48]

Far from accepting a definition of divine determination that could be developed from Goclenius' *Lexicon* as "an antecedent disposition or object, that inclines or moves the will to Good, or to Evil," Robinson argued that "God doth administer the occasions by which the creature through his own default, is provoked, & incited unto sin."[49] Further he argued that God "willingly, & wisely" permits sin, "not by geving the creature leave to sin, for that is impossible: but by not putting the effectual impediments which might hinder sin, as he both could and lawfully might, if he would."[50] God, in His freedom, might have refrained from creating beings who could and would fall into sin, and He could also have prevented sin by the administration of an irresistible grace. God, then, "permitteth [sin] willingly."[51] Robinson's argument, including its terms, directly parallel and echo the understanding of Calvin, Vermigli, Beza, Perkins, and other Reformed thinkers of the era who held, not an otiose permission, as if some acts and effects can occur outside or beyond the sphere of divine willing, but a "willing permission" or as Robinson also indicates, a "permitting will."[52] The point is clarified by positing not different wills in God but different "degrees" in the divine willing *ad extra*:

---

48. Robinson, *Of Religious Communion*, p. 102; *Works*, vol. 3, p. 240.

49. Robinson, *Of Religious Communion*, p. 102; *Works*, vol. 3, p. 240.

50. Robinson, *Of Religious Communion*, p. 102; *Works*, vol. 3, p. 241.

51. Robinson, *Of Religious Communion*, p. 102; *Works*, vol. 3, p. 241.

52. Cf. John Calvin, *Institutio christianae religionis* (Geneva: Stephanus, 1559), I.xvi.8; Peter Martyr Vermigli, *Loci communes D. Petri Martyris Vermigli…ex variis ipsius authoris scriptis, in unum librum collecti* (London: Thomas Vautrollerius, 1583), I.xiv.10, 15 (pp. 101, 103); Theodore Beza, *Iobus, Theodori Bezae partim commentarijs partim paraphrasi illustratus. Cui etiam additus est Ecclesiastes, Solomonis concio de summo bono, ab eodem Th. B. paraphrasticè explicata* (London: George Bishop, 1589), axiom 7 (p. 79); idem, *Quaestionum & responsionum christianarum libellus: In quo praecipua Christianae religionis capita proponuntur* (Geneva: Jean Crespin, 1570), p. 99; William Perkins, *A Treatise of Gods Free Grace and Mans Free-Will*, in *The Works of that Famous and Worthie Minister of Christ, in the Universitie of Cambridge, M. W. Perkins: Gathered into one volume, and newly corrected according to his owne copies* (Cambridge: Iohn Legat, 1603), p. 874, col. 2–p. 875, col. 1; idem, *A Treatise of the Manner and Order of Predestination, and of the Largenes of Gods Grace*, trans. Francis Cacot and Thomas Tuke (London: William Welby, 1606), p. 60.

And thus sin (though it be alwayes agaynst the degrees of the commanding, approveing, & effecting will of God) yet it is not at all, agaynst his permitting will, or agaynst that degree of manifestation of that one in it self, & simple will of God: neither is it wrought, he absolutely nilling it. This sin he doth also suffer, not (as men oft suffer thinges to come to passe) without care, or consideration of it, but of purpose & with infinite wisdom, as knowing how to bring light out of darknes, & by the creatures sin, to effect his most holy worke, according to his unsearchable counsayle: the depth whereof may swallow up the mind, but cannot be sounded by it, & in the meditation whereof, the best bound, & bottom is for man to consider, & confesse, that God is both more wise, & more holy than he.[53]

All acts and effects, then, belong to God's eternal purpose, but (given the several degrees of willing) all are not willed by God in the same way: some, indeed, are willed to occur by the exercise of will on the part of rational creatures.

Robinson never so much as implied that "the evil itself must be essentially good in a superior way that imperfect men are too ignorant to understand."[54] Rather, as he also argued in his *New Essayes*, and in accord with virtually the entire Western tradition of Christian theology, "Everie thing that *is*, and hath *being* is, in that regard *good*, and of God," to the end that "the naturall parts and powers of body, and Soul of the most wicked men remain in themselvs (notwithstanding all infection of evil in them) God's good *Creatures*."[55] Inasmuch as God is the source of all the essential goodness of created being, "sin is nothing that hath being in nature, but an absence of, and crossnesse to that which should be."[56] In a sizeable citation from Peter Lombard, Robinson did make a series of distinctions concerning human acts, which may or may not be good in themselves, good in the doer of the

---

53. Robinson, *Of Religious Communion*, pp. 102–3; *Works*, vol. 3, p. 241. Note that the editor of the *Works* here mistakes Robinson's argument and alters "degree" to "decree."

54. Contra Bangs, "Beyond Luther," pp. 46–47. George, *John Robinson*, p. 195, underestimates the force of Robinson's argument against the accusation.

55. John Robinson, *New Essayes; or Observations Divine and Morall. Collected out of the Holy Scriptures, ancient and modern writers, both divine and humane* (S.l.: s.n., 1628), v (p. 21); *Works*, vol. 1, p. 17; cf. *Synopsis purioris*, x.18–19.

56. Robinson, *New Essayes*, v (p. 22); *Works*, vol. 1, p. 18; cf. *Synopsis purioris*, xiv.34.

act, or good in the person who is the object of the action. Among such acts, then, according to Lombard, there can be an act "neither good in it self, nor in the doer, nor for him to whom it is done; as an evill, or injurie: yet good, as it is ordered by God to an end supernaturally good"—but, as Augustine argued, God permits evil because He knows how "to work good out of it."[57]

Rather than unwillingly permit sin, God "doth most wisely, & most powerfully determine, order, & direct the sins of men, & Angels in respect of the continuance, extent, & use thereof by him to be made: bringing light out of darknes," as is eminently illustrated in the work of Christ, where "the envy of the *Pharises*, the malice of *Satan*, the treason of *Iudas*, & the injustice of *Pontius Pilate*" all were used by God to bring about the greater good of the satisfaction for sin in the death of Christ.[58] In such divine providential work, the absolute and infinite goodness of God demonstrates "that nothing is absolutely, & infinitely evill."[59]

Smyth's seventeenth proposition, "that Adam being fallen did not loose any naturall power, or facultie, which God created in his soul, because the work of the Devill, which is sinne, cannot abolish Gods Workes, & Creatures; and therefore being fallen he still reteyned freedom of will," Robinson judged to be "in parte doubtfully set down, and in parte, untrue."[60] It is quite true, Robinson begins, that Adam had free will both before and after the fall, inasmuch as Adam in falling into sin did not cease to be a human being: "Take away will from a man, & he ceaseth to be a man: and take away freedom from the will, in that which it willeth, & it ceaseth to be will."[61] In accord with what he argued concerning Smyth's tenth proposition, Robinson indicates that sin does not destroy the "naturall powers" of the body and soul. Rather, it corrupts them, so that which was "rightly ordered, & disposed onely to good" prior to the fall, albeit mutable, is corrupted and disordered by sin so as to be no longer disposed to the good. In other

---

57. Robinson, *New Essayes*, v (p. 23); *Works*, vol. 1, p. 19.

58. Robinson, *Of Religious Communion*, p. 103; *Works*, vol. 3, p. 241.

59. Robinson, *Of Religious Communion*, p. 103; *Works*, vol. 3, p. 242; again, contra Bangs, "Beyond Luther," p. 46.

60. Robinson, *Of Religious Communion*, p. 106; *Works*, vol. 3, p. 245.

61. Robinson, *Of Religious Communion*, p. 106; *Works*, vol. 3, p. 245.

words, the fallen human being retains the powers bestowed in creation, but can no longer perfectly will the good unless renewed by grace.[62] Robinson also allowed that human begins have it in their power to reject the work of the Holy Spirit. What they cannot do is will to receive the work of the Spirit prior to the gift of grace that changes or regenerates the will.[63]

Robinson versus Murton on the Divine Will and Decree

Robinson's defense of the Canons of Dort is a major work extending to 203 pages in its seventeenth-century printing. It was written in response to a polemical treatise by another Separatist, John Murton, an associate and ally of Thomas Helwys. Murton's treatise was directed in six of its seven chapters against the teachings of the synod and in its seventh and final chapter against Robinson's doctrine of baptism.[64] Robinson's work takes the form of a response to Murton, following the line of Murton's argument rather than the outline of the Canons of Dort.[65] Given his comments on Smyth's propositions of 1613, Robinson's response to Murton is unsurprising, although its selection of arguments from Murton provided an opportunity for Robinson to display his knowledge of technical, scholastic distinctions with which Murton was probably unfamiliar. Robinson's work has major parallels in Ainsworth's later and somewhat less detailed response to Murton, albeit several differences: whereas Robinson was most concerned to defend the Canons of Dort against Murton's arguments, Ainsworth was more overtly concerned to defend the orthodoxy of John Knox's

---

62. Robinson, *Of Religious Communion*, p. 106; *Works*, vol. 3, pp. 245–46.

63. Robinson, *Of Religious Communion*, p. 122; *Works*, vol. 3, p. 267.

64. John Murton, *A Discription of What God Hath Predestinated Concerning Man in His Creation, Transgression, & Regeneration: as Also an Answere to Iohn Robinson, Touching Baptisme* (S.l.: s.n., 1620).

65. The order and arrangement of the Canons' five "heads" of doctrine is (1) election and reprobation; (2) the death of Christ; (3–4) the fall, human sin and corruption, conversion and regeneration; and (5) perseverance. Murton's order is (1) predestination; (2) election and reprobation; (3) falling away, i.e., against perseverance; (4) free will; (5) the original state of man; (6) being in Christ as the foundation of salvation; and (7) on baptism against Robinson. Murton's two final topics, although clearly articulated in the initial "contents" of the book, are not marked out as sections in the text.

treatise on predestination, given that Murton had singled out Knox as his primary "Calvinist" opponent.[66]

Robinson took immediate issue with Murton's basic definitions, which indicated that "God predestinated to make the world, and man &c."[67] Scripture, Robinson responded, never states that "God predestinated to make the world and man"—rather God "purposed from eternity" to create but "destinated" or predestinated the world and man "considered as (to be) made, to their ends."[68] The distinction between being eternally purposed and eternally predestined is important inasmuch as some things are predestined but not created, while others are created but not predestined. The Synod of Dort quite clearly defined predestination in relation to "reasonable creatures" only while at the same time "referring the decree of creation, and permission of the fall, to a more general work of divine providence."[69] As distinct from the Canons, however, Robinson's identification of the objects of predestination as the world and man "considered as (to be) made" has a supralapsarian accent, but he focuses his defense on the infralapsarian definition found in the Canons of Dort, "which considers *man as fallen in Gods account.*"[70]

---

66. Henry Ainsworth, *A Censure vpon a Dialogue of the Anabaptists, intituled, A description of what God hath predestinated concerning man. &c. In 7 poynts. Of predestination. Of election. Of reprobation. Of falling away. Of freewill. Of originall sinne. Of baptizing infants* (S.l: s.n., 1623), p. 5; cf. Murton, *Discription*, sig. A3v–A4r. The treatise by Knox is his *An Answer to a Great Nomber of blasphemous Cavillations written by an Anabaptist, and Adversarie to Gods eternal Predestination. And confuted by John Knox…wherein the Author so discovereth the craft and falsehood of that sect, that the godly knowing that error, may be confirmed in the truth by the evident word of God* (Geneva: Jean Crespin, 1560; London: Thomas Charde, 1591).

67. Robinson, *Defence of the Doctrine*, i.1 (p. 1); *Works*, vol. 1, p. 271; cf. Murton, *Discription*, p. 3, at greater length, "We holde, that before the foundation of the World, the most holy God, of his meere love, without any cause out of himselfe, Predestinated to make the World; and Man, and all good thinges that are made: to make man a reasonable soule; to give him a righteous Law; to give him abilitie to keep it or breake it; if hee brake it to punish him, yet so as not to forsake him" and to elect those who "receive…his *Grace* by *Faith* in his Son."

68. Robinson, *Defence of the Doctrine*, i (p. 1); *Works*, vol. 1, p. 272; N.B., bracketed text is Robinson's.

69. Robinson, *Defence of the Doctrine*, i (p. 2); *Works*, vol. 1, p. 272.

70. Robinson, *Defence of the Doctrine*, i (p. 3); *Works*, vol. 1, p. 272; cf. Johnson,

The first point of contention in Murton's *Discription* is the Reformed view that God decreed the sin of Adam. Murton and his associates "insinuate" that those who subscribe to the Canons of Dort "made *God the Authour*, yea, *the principall Author of all the evill* of sin *in the world*."[71] What Murton stated directly is that the Reformed identify God as the principal cause and author of all things, "appointing" all things, whether damnation or salvation, vice or virtue, as opposed to the assumption, held by Murton and his associates, that only good comes from God and all evil from the devil. Insofar as the Reformed claim both that Adam has free will such that he could have chosen not to sin and that sin occurred by necessity as decreed by God, they contradict themselves. So also is it a contradiction to claim that God commanded Adam not to sin but also decreed that Adam would sin. As a specific instance of the contradictions implicit in Reformed theology, Murton noted the theses published in Geneva under the supervision of Beza and Faius.[72]

The synod itself responded to such insinuations which, Robinson adds, arise from the adversaries' "want of skill, to put difference between Gods working of the sinne, as author thereof; and his appointing, and ordering, both of sin, and sinner to his own holy ends."[73] Robinson might also have cited the Genevan theses which, contrary to Murton's claim, read as follows:

> It behooved also, that this man should be indued with a free and voluntarie power, to moove himselfe. It is so far then, that God bereaved our first Parents of the libertie of will, and the voluntarie inclination to bee caried both wayes. Otherwise as God was the Author, so he might be accounted the destroyer thereof. For the aeternall purpose of God, doeth impose no other necessitie upon the events which he hath determined, then such as he will have second causes, to be mooved according to their owne nature:

"Soteriology," who mistakes Robinson's approach to his defense of Dort as an indication of Robinson's own infralapsrianism.

71. Robinson, *Defence of the Doctrine*, i (p. 2); *Works*, vol. 1, p. 274.

72. Murton, *Discription*, pp. 4–5, citing *Propositions and Principles of Divinitie Propounded and Disputed in the University of Geneva. under M. Theod. Beza and M. Anthonie Faius*, trans. John Penry (Edinburgh: Robert Waldegrave, 1595), p. 26; cf. Robinson, *Defence of the Doctrine*, i (p. 3); in *Works*, vol. 1, p. 274.

73. Robinson, *Defence of the Doctrine*, i (p. 2); *Works*, vol. 1, p. 273.

whence it followeth, that it doth not take away the contingency
or voluntarines of mans will.[74]

Robinson's response parallels the Genevan theses, insisting in several places that God is not the author of sin. He devotes an entire section of his *Defence of the Doctrine* to the topic "God suffered, and so decreed to suffer" sins, but did not decree the sinfulness of the actions, where he quite explicitly states, "We do not hold, that God decreed *Adams* sin, as they conceive, that is, either to approve it, or command it, or compel unto it, nothing lesse: but this we affirm, that God decreed to leave *Adam* to himself in the temptation, and not to assist him."[75] Adam's sin was decreed by God in such a way that it followed the decree "not as an effect, upon a cause working it (God forbid); but as a consequent upon an antecedent; or as effect necessarily following upon a most holy, wise and powerfull providence," in such a way that it "should so come to pass infallibly, though performed by Adam's free, and freely working will."[76] Adam's sin, then, although occurring (as must everything that occurs) within the divine will, nonetheless arises "infallibly" as a consequent upon the antecedent both of God's providential governance and of Adam's "freely working will."

Arguably, Robinson here draws on the distinctions, first, between a necessity of the consequent thing (*necessitas consequentis*) and a necessity of the consequence (*necessitas consequentiae*) or hypothetical necessity and, second, between a causal necessity and a necessity of infallibility. The latter term in both cases indicates a contingency, given that the antecedent or antecedents could be otherwise and, accordingly, the present necessity of the consequence is necessary in the sense only that it must be what it is when it is. In this case, there are two levels of causality operative. As first cause, God freely wills that Adam fall by freely willing to sin. As second cause having a power of self-determination, Adam freely wills to sin. Robinson's further distinction (already noted in his response to Smyth) between the divine moving of creaturely actions as actions and the creature acting deficiently by sinning, both places the sin under the category of divine permission and indicates

---

74. Beza and Faius, *Propositions and Principles*, xi.7–8 (p. 26).
75. Robinson, *Defence of the Doctrine*, i (p. 10); *Works*, vol. 1, p. 280.
76. Robinson, *Defence of the Doctrine*, i (p. 3); *Works*, vol. 1, p. 274.

how it is infallibly known by God.[77] Given the antecedent willing, there is the consequence that things be as they are, but given Adam's freedom, Adam did not sin necessarily.

Murton and other adversaries of the Reformed view agree with the Reformed that "God foreseeth all evil to come," that this foresight or foreknowledge is certain, and that God cannot be deceived. From this it follows that the foreseen evils will "necessarily and unavoydably come to passe."[78] Just as it is true that "Gods foresight is not the cause of the evill," Robinson adds, it is equally so that God's decree and providence are not the cause. Again, the evil follows as the consequence of an antecedent, not as the effect of a divine cause. In order to clarify his point Robinson appeals to a distinction concerning the divine knowledge:

> This knowledge, or fore-knowledge of God, is two-fold: naturall and indefinite, by which God knowes all possible things, and whatsoever in any respect, or upon any supposition, can possibly be: or definite and determinate, by which of things possible he knows what shall and what shall not be. Now howsoever this fore-knowledge (as all other things in God) be one, and that infinite and eternall; yet in our conception, the former of those acts of Gods fore-knowledge, goes before the decree, the latter presupposeth it. For therefore God certainly and infallibly foresees a thing shall be, because he unchangeably decrees it shall be in and according to its kind: if good, by his working it: if evill, by his suffering it, and governing the creature in working it.[79]

Again, Robinson has recourse to a pattern of argument characteristic of the supralapsarian understanding of the decrees, in this instance resting on the distinction between the absolute or simple divine knowledge of

---

77. Cf. George, *John Robinson*, pp. 196–97, where George explains the distinction properly, except for his comment (in n. 100) that a necessity of the consequence "follows inevitably from a prior condition, but allows for contingency"; rather, the necessity of the consequence is a contingency because the prior condition is not an inevitability. See the discussion of *necessitas consequentiae* in Willem J. van Asselt, J. Martin Bac, and Roelf T. te Velde, trans., ed., and commentary, *Reformed Thought on Freedom: The Concept of Free Choice in Early Modern Reformed Theology* (Grand Rapids: Baker Academic, 2010), pp. 35–39.

78. Robinson, *Defence of the Doctrine*, i (p. 8); *Works*, vol. 1, p. 279.

79. Robinson, *Defence of the Doctrine*, i (p. 8); *Works*, vol. 1, p. 279.

all possibles or indefinites (*scientia simplicis intelligentiae*) and the voluntary or visionary divine knowledge of all actuals or definites (*scientia voluntaria* or *scientia visionis*).[80] The divine willing or decree intervenes between God's knowledge of possibles and God's knowledge of actuals, given that their actuality depends on the divine will—and, by way of extension, the divine willing explains why the divine knowledge of actuals is identified as a voluntary or volitional knowledge.[81]

This pattern of argument concerning the decrees emerged as a significant aspect of Reformed doctrinal formulation in Junius' epistolary debate with Arminius and became a staple in the argumentation of his Leiden colleagues and successors, Gomarus and Trelcatius.[82] Robinson's use of the language indicates his intellectual proximity to the Leiden faculty of theology in the years leading up to the Synod of Dort and his retention of their patterns of argument and formulation after the synod and in its defense.

Robinson explains, taking the biblical case of Absalom as his point of reference, how this distinction between the two species of

80. George, *John Robinson*, pp. 195–96, mistakenly identifies this argument as the transposition of a nominalist reading of the *potentia absoluta–potentia ordinata* distinction into an epistemological construct. It is the case that the divine *scientia simplicis intelligentiae* is the knowledge that stands in relation to the *potentia absoluta* and the *scientia libera sive voluntaria* stands in relation to the *potentia ordinata*, but Robinson's distinction is epistemological in its basic assumptions—i.e., not a transposition—and the *potentia absoluta–potentia ordinata* distinction is not the simple property of nominalists. George also mistakes the issue when he comments (p. 195), "Robinson takes it as axiomatic that the certainty of God's decree follows from the infallibility of His foreknowledge." The infallibility of God's foreknowledge of actuals rests on the decree to create them.

81. Cf. *Syntagma disputationum theologicarum, in Academia Lugduni-Batava quarto repetitarum.... Francisco Gomaro, Jacobo Arminio, Luca Trelcatio juniore praesidibus* (Rotterdam: Joannes Leonardi à Berewout, 1615), iii (p. 51), a disputation of Trelcatius; with Franciscus Gomarus, *Theses theologicae de praedestinatione Dei...Samuel Gruterus; sub praesidio Franc. Gomari* (Leiden: Joannes Patius, 1604), x.

82. Cf. Gomarus, *Theses theologicae de praedestinatione*, ix; idem, *Disputationum theologicarum quinto repetitarum trigesima quarta: de Dei praedestinatione...sub praesidio...D.Francisci Gomari* (Leiden: Joannis Patius, 1609), xlv–xlvi; Lucas Trelcatius Jr., *Disputationum theologicarum quarto repetitarum trigesima, de aeterna Dei praedestinatione* (Leiden: Joannes Patius, 1606), vii, where the possibles are identified as human beings understood as *creabilis* and *condendus*—i.e., as creatible and to be created. And see the essay "Inclusive Supralapsarianism," chapter 4 in this volume.

divine knowing, between which the divine will intervenes, illustrates the way in which God wills all things without being the direct efficient cause or author of sin and evil. God must have "certainly and infallibly" foreseen Absalom's incestuous conduct with his father's concubines "because *Absalom* would certainly and undoubtedly practise it in time."[83] This is a point on which Murton would agree. But, asks Robinson, how might this infallible divine foreknowledge arise? Neither Absalom's birth, nor his survival through the vicissitudes of youth, nor his having the "naturall ability, and opportunitie" to commit his sin were absolutely necessary in themselves. David might have taken his wives with him when he fled Jerusalem, or his wives might have fled or hidden themselves. Further, Absalom had "libertie of will," might not have taken David's concubines and might "have exercised his lust upon some other object."[84] Still, God eternally foreknew Absalom's sins. Robinson concludes with rhetorical questions and a blunt answer: "How then could that particular event follow unchangeably from his changeable will? How necessarily and unavoydably, from his choyce of will which was free in it self either to that act, or to another of that kinde, or to neither? Either therefore Gods decree from eternitie (and so his work in time) must be acknowledged for the disposing and ordering of all events unavoydably, or his knowledge be denied in foreseeing them infallibly."[85] Ainsworth would state more clearly the point that foreknowledge is a matter of certainty that "imposeth no necessity on things."[86]

Robinson does not expand further on his illustration, but the implication is that the life-history and freely willed sins of Absalom stood as indefinites or possibles known to God in His simple or absolute knowledge, willed by God, and consequently known infallibly in God's free or voluntary knowledge of all actuals. God, then, is the ultimate cause of the existence of Absalom, antecedent to Absalom's commission of sin in a world disposed and ordered by God to God's

---

83. Robinson, *Defence of the Doctrine*, i (p. 8); *Works*, vol. 1, p. 279; N.B. regularizing the spelling of "Absalom."

84. Robinson, *Defence of the Doctrine*, i (p. 9); *Works*, vol. 1, pp. 279–80; cf. 2 Sam. 16:20–22.

85. Robinson, *Defence of the Doctrine*, i (p. 9); *Works*, vol. 1, p. 280.

86. Ainsworth, *Censure vpon a Dialogue*, p. 6.

own ends. Murton's alternative that things are done "against Gods will, fore-knowledge, and foretelling" and, as well, "against Gods counsell," and that, accordingly, "God fore-seeth all thinges, yet doth he not will all thinges, for his foresight doth extend both to good and evill, but his will is onely of thinges that be good, as God fore-seeth the death of a sinner, and the cause thereof, namely his wickedness, but willeth it not, as he saith,"[87] is, in Robinson's view, simplistic and only serves to create a further problem. Such attempts to relieve God of the authorship of sin and evil by arguing that evil occurs "without Gods providence ordering and governing it" set the creature outside of divine governance and "shut God out of the earth, whilst men do as they list in it."[88]

Murton alleged, further, that the Reformed way of including sin within the compass of the divine will and governance rests on a confused notion of two wills in God, one secret that decrees sin, the other revealed that forbids sin. If the former is secret, Murton adds, how can anyone know of it? And if the other, the revealed will, is God's, it must also be hidden in God before it is revealed. There are, then, according to Murton's account of the Reformed view, two hidden or secret wills in God, the one opposed to the other.[89] Robinson responded that Murton had misunderstood the distinction between the secret and revealed will of God. In the first place, the fact of a secret will has been made known either by God's Word in Scripture or by inference from God's works. In the latter case, given what Scripture has revealed about God's will, when a particular event occurs that itself has not been revealed in Scripture, it should be recognized as the work of God if the event is good or understood as something suffered or permitted by God and ordered to God's ultimate end if "the worker thereof is evill."[90]

Accordingly, the distinction between God's secret and revealed will does not imply two wills in God. All it indicates is that some aspects of God's willing are hidden and some are revealed. In itself,

---

87. Murton, *Discription*, pp. 18, 20, citing Ezek. 18:32; 33:11.
88. Robinson, *Defence of the Doctrine*, i (p. 9); in *Works*, vol. 1, p. 280; and cf. Ainsworth, *Censure vpon a Dialogue*, p. 4.
89. Murton, *Discription*, pp. 11–12.
90. Robinson, *Defence of the Doctrine*, i (p. 10); in *Works*, vol. 1, p. 281.

as it is in God, the divine will is one and simple, as is affirmed of the divine essence in general. So also is the divine will conceived by human beings as "divers, according to the diversity of objects upon which it is set."[91] Murton also made a logical mistake in his accusation of a contradiction: that sin is both forbidden and willed by God is not contradictory inasmuch as God forbids sin in one sense and wills it in another: contradiction or "contrariety" consists in "the willing and nilling of the same thing in the same respect."[92]

If, then, the Reformed do not posit two wills in God, they nonetheless recognize that there are "differences of the will of God in the exercising of itself towards the creature."[93] Murton is guilty of ambiguous language concerning the will.[94] Robinson, by way of response, and paralleling the Leiden *Synopsis*, indicates three "degrees" of divine willing. According to "the first and weakest degree" of which human beings can conceive, God wills to permit or suffer "sin, as sin." Robinson adds that when God permits or suffers something to occur, He permits it willingly inasmuch as He both knows the event and, given His omnipotence, could hinder or prevent it.[95] The "second degree" of divine willing (which corresponds to the so-called preceptive will of God) concerns the divine command that something "be done," and according to which God approves of the action if it is done. The third degree of God's willing is "that according to which he workes all things by his omnipotent power."[96] There can be disobedience to God's command but this disobedience nonetheless occurs according to divine permission and within the omnipotent will of God concerning all things. Given that finite human beings, who have a single faculty of will, can will in ways analogous to these degrees of divine willing,

---

91. Robinson, *Defence of the Doctrine*, i (p. 11); in *Works*, vol. 1, pp. 281–82; cf. Ainsworth, *Censure vpon a Dialogue*, p. 3.

92. Robinson, *Defence of the Doctrine*, i (p. 11); in *Works*, vol. 1, p. 282; cf. Murton, *Discription*, pp. 11–12.

93. Robinson, *Defence of the Doctrine*, i (p. 19); in *Works*, vol. 1, p. 290.

94. Ainsworth, *Censure vpon a Dialogue*, pp. 5–6.

95. Cf. Johnson, "Soteriology," pp. 39–41.

96. Robinson, *Defence of the Doctrine*, i (pp. 18–19); in *Works*, vol. 1, p. 289; cf. *Synopsis purioris theologiae*, vi.34; also note the same distinction of degrees in Robinson, *New Essayes*, iv (pp. 14–15); in *Works*, vol. 1, pp. 12–13.

it should be eminently clear that God's will, as infinite, can operate "more intensly or remisly."[97]

Further, the Reformed postulate a distinction between necessity and compulsion. This is also misunderstood by Murton, who fails to recognize the difference between God decreeing something and God forcing something to occur, and therefore Murton fails to see that something may occur in a sense necessarily but also freely. In making this distinction, Robinson also returns to his initial point against Murton's definition: the divine purpose, decree, or predestination is eternal, but the divine work is temporal and belongs to providence. It is not the decree that "works" in the temporal order but the divine "power according to [God's] will."[98] That will, moreover, is exercised differently in relation to diverse objects in the temporal order. With respect to God's providence, there is a necessity that corresponds with the ultimate divine causality at the same time that there is freedom and contingency in the order of finite or secondary causality. Underlying the issues of freedom, contingency, and necessity is the nature and character of all divine acts: they are both free and necessarily done well. So also all of the good angels "do the will of God most voluntarily, and yet most necessarily."[99] Causality, accordingly, operates at two levels, the divine or primary and the creaturely or secondary, with God and the rational creature both willing the act, albeit at different levels, in different ways, and with different ends or goals.[100]

> Neither will seem strange unto us, that one and the same action comes under so divers considerations, as in one regard, to be voluntary, contingent and casual; and in another, necessary: if we consider, how divers agents concur and meet together in producing it. No work of man, is so mans alone, as that God hath not some hand in it, in sustaining and ordering the person and work, yea in effecting that which is good in it, as all that is, which hath in it any created being or order. What hinders then, but that the same thing may, in regard of man as the particular and immediate

---

97. Robinson, *Defence of the Doctrine*, i (p. 19); in *Works*, vol. 1, p. 289; cf. Ainsworth, *Censure vpon a Dialogue*, p. 4.

98. Robinson, *Defence of the Doctrine*, i (p. 20); in *Works*, vol. 1, p. 290.

99. Robinson, *Defence of the Doctrine*, i (p. 20); in *Works*, vol. 1, p. 290.

100. Cf. *Synopsis purioris theologiae*, xi.10.

cause, be voluntary and contingent; and yet in regard of God, the highest and generall cause, necessary?[101]

Robinson does not, at this point, return to the different kinds of necessity—absolute and hypothetical, of the consequent thing and of the consequence. Rather, he rests content in observing that there are two levels of causality, one that can evidence contingencies at the same time that the other sets forth a necessity.

An arguably more telling argument that Robinson draws out of his views on providence concerns the way in which "God is the author of the action, or fact, but not of the sin of the fact or crime."[102] In response to the charge that the Reformed make God the author of sin, Robinson states somewhat more precisely what he had argued in response to Smyth, now explicitly resting his case on the concept of a divine "physical premotion" that explains the manner of providential concurrence in the relationship of the two orders of causality, primary and secondary:

> We deny their charge, and answer by distinction; that *Adams* taking and eating the Forbidden fruit, *Davids* adultery, *Joabs* murther, and the like, are to be considered in two waies: First, naturally, and as they are motions in nature, performed by mans natural & created faculties and powers of soul and body: secondly, morally, as those motions are misapplyed, and abused to wrong objects, by mans blinde mind and corrupt will. In the former respect, & materially, as we speak, they are of God and created nature; in the latter and formally, of mans proper corruption. Now the sinne is not the natural action of the motion, but the pravity and abuse of the action.[103]

Robinson argued, much like various Reformed predecessors and contemporaries, that even as "we live, and move, and have our being" in God (Acts 17:28), all of our natural "motions" arise from God, but that the sinfulness of the act does not arise from God, but from the moral contrariety of the human being.[104] The divine provision of motion is

---

101. Robinson, *Defence of the Doctrine*, i (pp. 20–21); in *Works*, vol. 1, p. 291; cf. Robinson, *New Essayes*, iv (pp. 16–17); in *Works*, vol. 1, p. 14.

102. Robinson, *Defence of the Doctrine*, i (p. 22); in *Works*, vol. 1, p. 293.

103. Robinson, *Defence of the Doctrine*, i (p. 23); in *Works*, vol. 1, p. 293.

104. See Richard A. Muller, *Grace and Freedom: William Perkins and the Early Modern Reformed Understanding of Free Choice and Divine Grace* (New York: Oxford

natural or physical, not moral: "The same naturall motion of man in which great sin is committed, if it were exercised upon another object, might be without sin, and lawfull; and therefore not the very action or motion, but the misapplying of it, is the sin; from which the action hath its morall, but not its naturall being."[105] There is, then, a divine providential conveyance of motion to finite, creaturely movers that concurs in their actions as well as a divine "sufferance" or "permission" that allows for human free choice in sin. This permission, therefore, is a willing or willed permission, not a "bare permission" that would place some creaturely actions outside of the providential governance of God—nor, Robinson adds, is it legitimate for Murton to cite Ursinus against Calvin. Ursinus did not, as Murton implies, set divine permission apart from divine willing.[106]

God's Election, Conditional Promises, and Human Freedom

The fundamental difference between Murton and Robinson on the nature of divine permission was paralleled by their differences over the way in which divine election and the conditional promises of God relate to the capabilities and limits of human freedom. Murton conjoined divine promise with election, arguing "that as the Promise of God's *Election* is Free, without any desert in us originally, yet upon condition of Faith and obedience to CHRISTS *Gospell*; so the same free promise of Gods *Election*, is continued unto us, upon continuance of the same condition, from the which men may fall away."[107] In response, Robinson indicated that it was a mistake to put promise

---

University Press, 2020), pp. 17–18, 117–18, 145–46, 156–61, 169–72, 183–84; and on premotion, idem, *Providence, Freedom, and the Will in Early Modern Reformed Theology* (Grand Rapids: Reformation Heritage Books, 2022), pp. 7–8, 40–43, 51–52 (Vermigli); 59–73 (Beza); 117 (Rollock); 192–93, 196–205 (Charnock).

105. Robinson, *Defence of the Doctrine*, i (p. 25); in *Works*, vol. 1, p. 295.

106. Robinson, *Defence of the Doctrine*, i (pp. 36–39); in *Works*, vol. 1, pp. 306–9. I have not identified the edition of Ursinus' catechetical lectures cited by Murton, but the reference is clear enough: see Zacharias Ursinus, *The Summe of Christian Religion, delivered by Zacharias Ursinus in his Lectures upon the Catechism…Wherein are debated and resolved the questions of whatsoever points of moment which have beene or are controverted in divinity*, trans. Henry Parry (Oxford: Joseph Barnes, 1595), pp. 961–62, commenting on the sixth petition of the Lord's Prayer.

107. Murton, *Discription*, p. 78.

prior to election. Election is the eternal purpose of God before the foundation of the world, and therefore it is necessarily prior to what God promises in time: "He but promiseth in time, what he purposed from eternity."[108] By reversing the order and setting promise before election, Murton is "driven" to the "absurd" conclusion that "actual and particular election, is not of men living, but dead," inasmuch as when election is promised on fulfillment of the condition of perseverance in faith, the election can only be finalized when falling away has become impossible. And that impossibility, on Arminian terms, occurs only at death.[109] From Robinson's perspective, Murton correctly understood that God has not promised to save anyone who fails to persevere in repentance and faith, but what he failed to grasp is that repentance and faith depend on God's election, which is a predestination to the means as well as to the end. Salvation and damnation, Robinson continued, are conditional. In the former case the conditions are fulfilled by God, in the latter by human beings themselves:

> We affirm, that God predestinates none to salvation but with condition of the death of Christ, and the persons (coming to years of discretion) faith, and repentance, and continuance therein to the end, to goe before that their salvation: nor to damnation, but with condition of sin and impenitency therein to goe before that their damnation…. Onely, these two things we further hold in this case. First, that the former conditions (Christ, and faith in him) are God's free gifts also, infallibly and effectually obtained by the former persons: the latter condition (impenitency in sin) the certain effects of Satans malice, and their own corruption, being left of God thereunto.[110]

Murton's polemic against the "Calvinist" understanding of free will, like his comments on permission, included an attempt to set some of the earlier Reformed writers against both Calvin and the Canons of Dort—in this case, Bastingius and, once again, the *Theses Genevensis.*

---

108. Robinson, *Defence of the Doctrine*, iii (p. 99); in *Works*, vol. 1, p. 368.

109. Robinson, *Defence of the Doctrine*, iii (p. 100); in *Works*, vol. 1, p. 368.

110. Robinson, *Defence of the Doctrine*, iii (p. 118); in *Works*, vol. 1, p. 386; cf. Ainsworth, *Censure vpon a Dialogue*, p. 6, who states that God wills some things absolutely and other things conditionally, which, therefore "are not effected unlesse the condition be observed." And note Johnson, "Soteriology," pp. 43–45.

According to Murton, "Calvinists" typically insist on several "undeniable consequences of their *Predestination*," namely, that God is both the "principall cause of all things" and the immediate "Author," such that "the wicked are compelled by the power, force, and compulsion of Gods predestination, to commit all those wicked and cruell crimes" for which they must be punished.[111] Inasmuch as they are predestined, the wicked cannot refuse wicked acts, nor can the "Godly" refuse the good.[112] Murton cites Bastingius and the Genevan *Propositions and Principles* as offering a somewhat different view—that freedom of will in "Naturall, civill, morall, and Iudiciall" matters remains after the fall, and that there is also freedom to will evil. What Bastingius and the Genevans insist, however, is that freedom to do good is lacking in spiritual things. Murton also notes Bernard of Clairvaux's view that the power to will remains after the fall, but not the power to will well.[113]

Robinson regarded these claims as "a false, and foul accusation," nor did he regard Bastingius and the *Theses Genevensis* as providing anything other than Calvinist or Reformed theological arguments quite in agreement with the Canons of Dort.[114] Bastingius allowed a standard scholastic definition of free will, or as he notes, *liberum arbitrium*, according to which "the word *arbitrium* must be referred to reason, whose office it is to discerne between good & evil, the word *Liberum* unto wil, which is flexible unto either." He adds "that seeing these two powers of the soul, understanding and wil (which remaining sound and intire, man had been able to doe good) are now perished and corrupted, he is therefore now utterlie unfit to doe well, and prone to all vice."[115] Equally clear is the argument in the *Theses Genevensis*: "[As created] therefore, man was indeed the Lord of his owe actions, that is, endued with free wil. Yet because he was mutable & changeable both waies, he did so incline from good to evil, that as Augustine saith, by sinning he lost both himself, and his libertie. Not that he

---

111. Murton, *Discription*, pp. 94–95.

112. Murton, *Discription*, p. 95.

113. Murton, *Discription*, p. 95.

114. Robinson, *Defence of the Doctrine*, iv (p. 125); in *Works*, vol. 1, p. 393; citing Murton, *Discription*, pp. 94–95.

115. Jeremias Bastingius, *An Exposition or Commentarie upon the Catechism taught in the Lowe Countryes* (Cambridge: Iohn Legatt, 1589), fol. 12r–v.

was turned unto a stock, and so bereved of judgment and will: For sinne hath not utterly abolished nature although it hath lamentablie polluted the same: but such libertie remaineth, as can wil nothing but what is evill, and that evillie."[116]

Murton implies that the definitions of Bastingius and the *Theses Genevensis* are nearly satisfactory, but then goes on to argue "that there is left in man, the facultie of will, to chuse or refuse" such that, just as in civil matters where threats of punishment presume the ability of human beings to choose what is right, so also in spiritual matters the divine threats of punishment presume the ability to choose: "If some cannot repent, and others cannot choose but repent, to what end are these threatenings?"[117] The "Calvinists," however, insist "that man lyeth so bound in the cordes of sin, that he can doe nothing, without the compelling *Grace* of God; God must draw him up without Free-will and liberty; and he cannot resist the drawing of God, and yet God standeth threatening Hell, to all those that will not ascend up."[118] Whether in the divine commands in Scripture or in the exhortations of "Christian Preachers," the clear intention is to "bend the will of man," to induce "him to change opinion, and leave his former determinations."[119] According to Murton, therefore, Calvinist doctrine runs counter to the intention of divine commandments and of sound preaching.

The point in debate, Robinson responded, was not about freedom to choose as a basic human capacity, as evidenced in "good, natural, civill, morall, and judiciall things," which the Reformed do not deny, but "about *freedom of will in spirtuall things*; which we alone deny."[120] Further, Murton's mistake was to "unskilfully confound *necessity & compulsion*": an action or event can be free "in it selfe" and yet be "determined necessarily this way, or that" by divine providence, in such a way that a person's free choice of sin can "stand together" with God's

---

116. Beza and Faius, *Propositions and Principles*, xxi.5–6 (p. 68).

117. Murton, *Discription*, pp. 97–98.

118. Murton, *Discription*, p. 98.

119. Murton, *Discription*, p. 99.

120. Robinson, *Defence of the Doctrine*, iv (p. 125); in *Works*, vol. 1, p. 393; Robinson here echoes the position of Reformed predecessors and contemporaries like Ursinus, Pareus, and Perkins, as well as Bastingius and the *Theses Genevensis*: see Muller, *Grace and Freedom*, pp. 111–19.

providential governance of the human choice toward "his holy ends."[121] In the case of human choice of the good, God works by "inclination" not "compulsion": there would be compulsion if God acted preventively against a person's specific inclination, but there is no compulsion in God's working toward the "inclining" of a choice toward the good. This bestowing of an inclination is not a matter of forcing a person toward the good but rather a gift of an "inward will and strength of grace" by which the person himself can choose the good.[122]

Robinson concludes his point by somewhat obliquely distinguishing between a necessity of the consequent thing and necessity of the consequence, the latter being not an absolute or causal necessity, but a hypothetical or implicative necessity, namely, a contingency: "And if all kind of necessity abolish all kind of freedom, then in truth a man doth nothing freely; for whatsoever he doth, he doth it necessarily, when he doth it."[123] There are, in other words, different kinds of necessity, one of which does not abolish freedom. In the case of a person doing something, the necessity is simply the fact that the doing is (and must be) when it is, although it is not ultimately necessary that it is. Thus it is a necessity of the consequence.[124]

This understanding of necessity of the consequence as identifying a contingency is fundamental to Robinson's further arguments concerning the relationship between predestination, human choice, and the one case—freedom of will in spiritual things—in which the human ability to do otherwise is drastically limited by sin:

> We acknowledg that whatsoever good or evill a man doth outwardly, or inwardly, where the will comes to work (for there may be acts of the understanding, and motions of the affections before and without the wills working), he useth liberty and freedom in chusing, or refusing: that is, he doth it not by any violence or compulsion, but from the inward principles of his mind; the understanding directing, and the will consenting; though yet the wicked, being left of God, cannot but doe wickedly, any more than *the Aethiopian can change his skin, or the Leopard his spots*

---

121. Robinson, *Defence of the Doctrine*, iv (p. 125); in *Works*, vol. 1, p. 393.
122. Robinson, *Defence of the Doctrine*, iv (p. 126); in *Works*, vol. 1, p. 394.
123. Robinson, *Defence of the Doctrine*, iv (p. 126); in *Works*, vol. 1, p. 394.
124. Cf. Van Asselt et al., *Reformed Thought on Freedom*, pp. 35–36.

> [marg. Jer. xiii. 23]; nor the godly but doe godlily, by the grace of
> God effectually inclining him thereunto.[125]

Inasmuch as God inclines the will, without coercing it, the divine "threatenings, and promises, and precepts" are understood by Calvinists to be effectual, contrary to Murton's allegations. God, by the inward work of the Holy Spirit gives "increase to the outward preaching" and opens the human heart to receive it. Scripture consistently teaches that the Holy Spirit works in human beings both with and without means. Murton's arguments would appear to deny that the Spirit can and does work as God pleases.[126] In the case of those who do not, even cannot, respond to divine threatenings, promises, and precepts, it is true that God has not provided them with the inward inclination to believe and obey, but the actual fault lies neither with God or in a "defect of his grace," but in the wicked themselves. By analogy, Robinson adds, "It is not my fault, that a drunkard fals and lyes in the street, though he cannot but both fall and ly there, except I hold, and help him up; except withal I be bound so to help him." God is not "bound" to give grace to all.[127]

Conclusions

Robinson's theological concerns and formulations on the issues of predestination, human freedom, good, and evil, have been shown to conform to the assumptions and doctrines characteristic of early modern Reformed confessional orthodoxy. His approach to doctrinal argument also exhibits characteristics of the early orthodox scholastic development, notable for its appeal to distinctions between necessity and certainty, absolute necessity and necessity of the consequence, and *scientia simplicis intelligentiae* and *scientia voluntaria*. Robinson also drew on the kind of argument for a supralapsarian doctrine of predestination that can be traced to Franciscus Junius and other members of the Leiden faculty of theology in Robinson's era, namely, the

---

125. Robinson, *Defence of the Doctrine*, iv (p. 126); in *Works*, vol. 1, p. 394; on the issue of grace and human freedom among Robinson's contemporaries, see Muller, *Grace and Freedom*, pp. 97–153.

126. Robinson, *Defence of the Doctrine*, iv (pp. 126–27); in *Works*, vol. 1, pp. 394–95.

127. Robinson, *Defence of the Doctrine*, iv (p. 127); in *Works*, vol. 1, p. 395.

identification of possibles known to God in his *scientia simplicis intelligentiae* as objects of divine willing and the concept of divine physical premotion. Accordingly, Johnson's, Davis', and George's conclusions about the way in which Robinson formulated his theological concerns in the context of both English and Dutch Reformed confessionality are confirmed and amplified. As adumbrated by both Davis and George, the nuances and distinctions found in Robinson's formulations have been shown to belong to the early orthodox scholastic development of Reformed thought, although in neither case is the impact of Robinson's use of scholastic distinctions fully recognized.

By contrast, Bangs' comments have been shown to lack basis in the documents. To make the point somewhat more bluntly, Bangs reduplicates Murton's rather naive objections to Dort and transfers them to his criticism of Robinson. Quite opposite to Bangs' remarks, Robinson repeatedly and rather strenuously denied that God is the author of sin—and did so in carefully argued scholastic distinctions that allowed him to recognize God as the omnipotent ultimate source of all physical motion in the universe but nonetheless not the cause of the sinfulness of creaturely acts. Nor did Robinson draw on Isaiah 45:7 to imply any evil done on God's part—indeed, Robinson appears not to have cited the text at all. A search through Robinson's works for citations from Isaiah reveals that he did cite Isaiah 45, but not verse 7. Robinson cited verse 9, "Woe unto him that striveth with his maker… shall the clay say to him that fashioneth it, What makest thou?" but only because his adversary, John Murton, had claimed Jeremiah 18:21 was the source of Paul's words in Romans 9:21, "making a vessel of dishonor." Robinson noted that the actual Old Testament parallel to Paul's words was Isaiah 45:9, which, however, spoke not to the issue of Romans 9:21 but "of another matter."[128]

Contrary to Bangs' genuinely odd (and ontologically bizarre) claim, Robinson certainly did not declare that evil is "essentially good" nor did he imply that this might be so in a manner too difficult for human beings to understand. Robinson adhered to the Augustinian view of sin and evil as a defect in otherwise good being; the notion that evil might be considered essentially good—indeed, the notion that evil

---

128. Robinson, *Defence of the Doctrine*, ii (p. 96); in *Works*, vol. 1, p. 365.

could be "essential"—is utterly foreign to his thought. Bangs' further claim that Robinson either declared or implied that "any theology that incorporated freedom of choice (and thus placed responsibility for evil on the choice of the actor) was considered a heretical attack on the divine property of omnipotent omniscience" borders the absurd. It is quite the opposite of Robinson's documentable formulations. Robinson, like other Reformed writers of the era, placed responsibility for sin squarely on the sinful human actor and did so on the basis of his assumptions concerning free choice. Nor did Robinson consider freedom of choice to be incompossible with either divine omnipotence or divine omniscience. He did, of course, espouse a view of free choice and grace inimical to Arminian and Remonstrant theology.

CHAPTER 6

Joseph Hall (1574–1656): Toward Peace in the Church and a Reformed *Via Media*

The confessional position and theological views of the prolific Joseph Hall, fellow of Emmanuel College Cambridge, Dean of Worcester, delegate to the Synod of Dort, Bishop of Exeter, prisoner in the Tower, and later Bishop of Norwich, have been subject to various interpretations. Indeed, the nature of Hall's attempt to find a *via media* has been subject to varied readings—as has the whole notion of a *via media* theology in the seventeenth century. Hall's nineteenth-century biographer, George Lewis, described him as a moderate who began his intellectual life as a "sponsor for Calvinism" and of strongly Puritan sentiment, but who eschewed extremism and sectarianism and who "in his maturity [was] almost a High Churchman, with only the remnants of Calvinism still clinging to him."[1]

---

1. George Lewis, *A Life of Joseph Hall, D.D., Bishop of Exeter and Norwich* (London: Hodder and Stoughton, 1886), p. 245. See also the more recent biography, Frank Livingstone Huntley, *Bishop Joseph Hall (1574–1656): A Biographical and Critical Study* (Cambridge, Mass.: Harvard University Press, 1979). Also note John Jones, *Bishop Hall, His Life and Times, Or, Memoirs of the Life, Writings, and Sufferings, of the Right Rev. Joseph Hall, D.D. Successively Bishop of Exeter and Norwich: With a View of the Times in which He Lived, and an Appendix Containing Some of His Unpublished Writings, His Funeral Sermon, &c.* (London: L. B. Seeley, 1826); James Hamilton, *Life of Joseph Hall, D.D., Bishop of Norwich* (New York: Robert Carter, 1850); and Michael Willoughby Dewar, "Bishop Joseph Hall, 1574–1656: An Ecumenical Calvinist Churchman," in *Churchman*, 80/3 (1966), pp. 194–200; idem, "An Ecumenical Calvinist, Bishop Joseph Hall (1574–1656)," in *Evangelical Quarterly*, 40/2 (1968), pp. 110–15. Hall's works were much published, seeing at least three distinct editions in the nineteenth century: *The Works of the Right Reverend Father in God, Joseph Hall, D.D.*

This reading of Hall coincides with the fairly typical nineteenth- and twentieth-century reading of an Anglican *via media*. Hall has been described as exemplifying "the conciliatory position of the Anglican church" by pointing out "the mistake of the Catholics without sub-scribing himself to the extreme view of Puritans and Calvinists,"[2] just as the Church of England has been described as "a *via media*, a quiet rational middle course between Presbyterianism and popery."[3] One author has gone so far as to describe Hall's "opposition to the rigid stand of the Calvinists" at the Synod of Dort as inclining on issues of grace and predestination "toward the liberal view of the Armin-ians, whose theology was close to that of the Church of England."[4] Hall's *via media* has also been interpreted as opposing English Puri-tanism "in its extreme forms," as not at all inclined toward a doctrine of double predestination, and, because of this stance, as significant to dialogue between Continental Reformed and Lutheran thinkers, including Leibniz.[5]

---

successively Bishop of Exeter and Norwich: now first collected. With some account of his life and sufferings, written by himself, ed. Josiah Pratt, 10 vols. (London: C. Whittingham for Williams and Smith, 1808); *The Works of Joseph Hall, D.D. successively Bishop of Exeter and Norwich: with some account of his life and sufferings, written by himself*, new ed., 12 vols. (Oxford: D. A. Talboys, 1837–1839); and *The Works of the Right Reverend Joseph Hall, D.D. Bishop of Exeter and afterwards of Norwich*, ed. Philip Wynter, new ed., 10 vols. (Oxford: Oxford University Press, 1863). The 1837–1839 edition will be cited (hereinafter as *Works*) unless otherwise noted, as preferable, since it is better indexed and includes the translations that are not entirely given in the other editions.

2. Marco Orrù, "Anomy and Reason in the English Renaissance," in *Journal of the History of Ideas*, 47/2 (1986), p. 187, referring specifically to the issue of sin as *anomia* or, alternatively, as *adikia* as debated in the exegesis of 1 John 3:4.

3. Hugh Thomas Swedenberg, *England in the Restoration and Early Eighteenth Century: Essays on Culture and Society* (Berkeley: University of California Press, 1972), p. 76; note how the same framework is found in John Henry Newman's 1834 essay, "Via Media," in *The Via Media of the Anglican Church. Illustrated in Lectures, Letters, and Tracts written between 1830 and 1841*, 2 vols. (London: Longmans, Green, 1891), vol. 2, p. 28; cf. John F. Russell, *The Judgment of the Anglican Church (Posterior to the Reformation) on the Sufficiency of Holy Scripture and the Authority of the Holy Catholic Church in Matters of Faith* (London: A. H. Baily, 1838), p. 279.

4. Rudolf Kirk, "A Seventeenth-Century Controversy: Extremism vs. Modera-tion," in *Texas Studies in Literature and Language*, 9/1 (1967), pp. 5–35, here p. 5.

5. Irena Backus, *Leibniz: Protestant Theologian* (New York: Oxford University Press, 2016), p. 64.

Quite to the contrary, Michael Dewar has noted the Calvinist or Reformed direction taken by "most" Elizabethan theology, the problems caused for this Reformed lineage in the English church by "non-church Puritans," and concluded that whereas various of Hall's contemporaries had emerged out of these struggles as Arminians, "Hall lived on as an Anglican Calvinist, which had not before been a contradiction in terms."[6] Similarly, in a carefully framed essay on Joseph Hall's epistolary debates over Puritanism, Kenneth Fincham and Peter Lake comment that Hall's middle way "lay not between Rome and Geneva, but between popery and Protestant sectarianism" and that it rested on the assumption that "Reformed" religion was both the only true religion and the only religion of the Church of England.[7] A similar conclusion has been argued by Dan Steere.[8]

Debate over the character of Hall's *via media* also raises the question of the nature of confessionality and of orthodoxy in the early modern era. Was confessional orthodoxy, whether in its theological or church-political aspects, a consistently precisionistic scholasticism that disavowed nearly any deviation in doctrinal statement, as is often argued particularly in an older scholarship,[9] or was it, at least in the view of some of its exponents, a more variegated movement that could and did allow for varieties of formulation within the framework of the confessional documents?[10]

---

6. Dewar, "Bishop Joseph Hall," pp. 194–200, here pp. 194, 196, 197; cf. Jonathan M. Atkins, "Calvinist Bishops, Church Unity, and the Rise of Arminianism," in *Albion: A Quarterly Journal Concerned with British Studies*, 18/3 (1986), pp. 411–27.

7. Kenneth Fincham and Peter Lake, "Popularity, Prelacy and Puritanism in the 1630s: Joseph Hall Explains Himself," in *English Historical Review*, 111/443 (1996), pp. 856–81; here p. 863.

8. Dan Steere, "'For the Peace of Both, for the Humour of Neither': Bishop Joseph Hall Defends the Via Media in an Age of Extremes, 1601–1656," in *Sixteenth Century Journal*, 27/3 (1996), pp. 749–65.

9. E.g., Brian G. Armstrong, *Calvinism and the Amyraut Heresy: Protestant Scholasticism and Humanism in Seventeenth-Century France* (Madison: University of Wisconsin Press, 1969).

10. E.g., Emidio Campi, "Calvin, the Swiss Reformed Churches, and the European Reformation," in *Calvin and His Influence, 1509–2009*, ed. Irena Backus and Philip Benedict (New York: Oxford University Press, 2011), pp. 119–43, here pp. 132–33; idem, *Shifting Patterns of Reformed Tradition* (Göttingen: Vandenhoeck &

The following essay will argue that Hall's understanding of a middle way ought to be understood as an aspect of a confessionally Reformed and broadly irenic approach that sought peace in the church catholic and among what Hall identified as "particular Churches," allowing for differences among the churches without undermining either a particular confessionality or the more detailed or speculative formulations of individual theologians. With John Davenant, John Dury and others, Hall worked to avoid extremes across a wide spectrum of issues and to find different paths to churchly and theological dialogue in differing circumstances, albeit resting on clearly stated foundational premises. Hall's own identification of his theology as occupying a *via media*, then, does not fit well into the popular nineteenth- and twentieth-century portrait of an Anglicanism poised midway either between the Arminians and the Calvinists or, indeed, between Rome and Protestantism.[11] Rather, it can be shown to fit within the specific compass of an early modern attempt to secure peace among Protestants of differing confessional allegiances. Once, moreover, Hall's own understanding of a middle way and its attendant irenic dialogue has been clarified, identification of his thought as confessionally Reformed (rather than as either for or against a stereotyped "Calvinism"),[12] thoroughly Anglican, and intentionally catholic also becomes clear.

Ruprecht, 2014), p. 7, et passim; Jonathan D. Moore, *English Hypothetical Universalism: John Preston and the Softening of Reformed Theology* (Grand Rapids: Eerdmans, 2007).

11. See the discussions of this line of scholarship in W. J. Torrance Kirby, *Richard Hooker: Reformer and Platonist* (Burlington, Vt.: Ashgate, 2005), pp. 11–12; also note, with reference to Hall, Anthony Milton, *Catholic and Reformed: The Roman and Protestant Churches in English Protestant Thought, 1600–1640* (Cambridge: Cambridge University Press, 1995), pp. 348, 377–78.

12. Rejecting the term "Calvinist" as of limited value as an identifier of varieties of early modern Reformed theology: see Richard A. Muller, *Calvin and the Reformed Tradition: On the Work of Christ and the Order of Salvation* (Grand Rapids: Baker Academic, 2012), pp. 51–69; and idem, "Reception and Response: Referencing and Understanding Calvin in Seventeenth-Century Calvinism," in Backus and Benedict, *Calvin and His Influence*, pp. 182–201.

Principial Matters: Hall's "Right Way of Peace in Matters of Religion"

Throughout his career, Hall worked to define his own theological stance. He had a clear sense of the nature of the Church of England as a Reformed church that had turned away from the gross errors of Rome. He also had a broad, irenic, and genuinely ecumenical understanding of the church catholic and of the need to overcome schism—although, as Anthony Milton has shown, the ecumenism or irenicism of the seventeenth century needs to be rather carefully parsed, particularly so as not to be misread as "shibboleths of liberal-minded tolerationists."[13] Hall refused to separate his Protestantism from an assumption of catholicity and took up the argument made famous in his time by the debates over William Perkins' *Reformed Catholike* and Thomas Morton's *Catholike Appeale for Protestants*, that the Protestant faith was a Reformed catholicism—and that Rome itself was "the chiefe cause and originall" of "dissentions" and, indeed, a schismatic body.[14] Nonetheless, he insisted—quite controversially in his time—on the "common Sisterhood of all Christian Churches" and held that despite the "manifold enormities, and depravations...enough to deforme any

---

13. Anthony Milton, "'The Unchanged Peacemaker'?: John Dury and the Politics of Irenicism in England, 1628–1643," in *Samuel Hartlib and Universal Reformation: Studies in Intellectual Communication*, ed. Mark Greengrass, Michael Leslie, and Timothy Raylor (Cambridge: Cambridge University Press, 1994), pp. 95–117, here p. 97. Some account of Hall's connections with Hartlib are discussed in G. H. Turnbull, "John Hall's Letters to Samuel Hartlib," in *Review of English Studies*, 4/15 (1953), pp. 221–33.

14. Joseph Hall, *The Old Religion: a Treatise, wherein is laid downe the true state of the difference betwixt the Reformed, and Romane Church; and the blame of this schisme is cast upon the true authors*, 2nd ed. (London: Nathaniell Butter and Richard Hawkins, 1628), p. 21; cf. Lewis, *Life of Joseph Hall*, p. 252. Note William Perkins' *A Reformed Catholike: or, A declaration shewing how neere we may come to the present Church of Rome in sundrie points of religion: and vvherein we must for euer depart from them* (Cambridge: Iohn Legat, 1598); and Thomas Morton, *A Catholike Appeale for Protestants, out of the Confessions of the Romane Doctors Particularly Answering the Mis-named Catholike Apologie for the Romane Faith, out of the Protestants: manifesting the antiquitie of our religion, and satisfying all scrupulous obiections which haue bene vrged against it* (London: Richard Field, 1609). Perkins' work was attacked in a series of volumes by William Bishop (two against Perkins and two more against Robert Abbot), and defended at length in four volumes by Robert Abbot and in another by Anthony Wotton, continued in print as far as 1611—a debate and an issue that could not have escaped Hall's notice.

Church," that even in the case of the Roman communion these were "not enough to Dis-church it."[15] Despite the schism and the depth of Roman abuse, "the Roman Church" and the "English Church" remained "but the several limms of one large and universal body."[16] Indeed the Roman Church was not so utterly corrupt as to cease to be a part of the visible church.[17]

Hall also penned a series of works devoted to finding grounds of agreement among what he identified as the "particular Churches" belonging to the church catholic.[18] His foundational assumption intended to achieve peace among the churches was that truths, albeit equal in trueness, are not equal in value. "Theological Truths," he declared, "are…more precious than all others," but even in theology there are degrees of value or importance: "amongst divine Truths those are most important, which are requisite to the regulating of Religion, both in the Theorye, and Practise thereof."[19] But even among these regulative truths, a distinction must be made between "Truths of Christian Doctrine" and "Truths of Catholick Faith," inasmuch as the former allow "great latitude and variety" whereas the latter are characterized by "more narrownesse and restraint."[20] Catholic or universal truths of the faith can also be identified as "Fundamentall points of

---

15. Joseph Hall, *The Shaking of the Olive-Tree. The Remaining Works of that incomparable prelate Joseph Hall, D.D.… with some specialties of divine providence in his life, noted by his own hand* (London: J. Cadwel, 1660), p. 408.

16. Joseph Hall, *A Letter Paraenetical, to a Worthy Knight Ready to Revolt from the Religion Established*, in *Shaking of the Olive-Tree*, p. 403.

17. Hall, *Old Religion*, p. 7. Hall was almost immediately opposed by Henry Burton, *The Seuen Vials or a Briefe and Plaine Exposition upon the 15: and 16: Chapters of the Revelation Very Pertinent and Profitable for the Church of God in These Last Times* (London: William Iones, 1628), pp. 33–34, 51–52; cf. Milton, *Catholic and Reformed*, pp. 142–46, on the controversy over Hall's argument.

18. Joseph Hall, *The Peace-Maker: Laying forth the Right Way of Peace, in Matter of Religion* (London: Nathaniel Butter, 1645) (also in *Works*, vol. 7, pp. 43–108); idem, *Via Media. The Way of Peace in the five busy articles commonly known by the name of Arminius*, published posthumously in Hall, *Shaking of the Olive-Tree*, pp. 351–88 (also in *Works*, vol. 10, pp. 471–98); and *Certain Catholic Propositions, Which a Devout Son of the Church humbly Offers to the Serious consideration of All Ingenuous Christians, Wheresoever Dispersed All the World Over*, in *Works*, vol. 9, pp. 427–32.

19. Hall, *Peace-Maker*, i (p. 2).

20. Hall, *Peace-Maker*, i (p. 2).

Religion," such are found in the Apostles' Creed and the Decalogue and, by implication, "a joynt-use and celebration of the holy Sacraments."[21]

In response to his critics, Hall nuanced his view that Rome, despite its errors and abuses, should be recognized as part of the visible church, arguing that it was not the Protestant churches that departed from catholicity: Rome "could…never name any one Articles of all the anciently approved Creeds, which we have denied; any one fundamentall errour which we have maintained."[22] Rather, Rome departed from the ancient catholic faith with "novell impositions, which they would injuriously obtrude upon Gods Church, as matters of faith," as evidenced in the teachings of the Council of Trent and in the claims of Rome to render new decisions that "shall passe for matters of Faith."[23] The way to peace with Rome was blocked by Rome itself, and Hall did not envision rapprochement with Rome in his irenic efforts.

Thus, Hall's argument concerning the Roman Church did not merely rest on the assumption that Rome had erred in its doctrinal innovations. Even if the disputed doctrines were valid representations of aspects of the Christian religion, they could not legitimately be imposed on the church. The "sum of the Christian Faith," he declared, is "contained and laid down in the Canonical Scriptures, whether in express terms or by necessary consequence; and in the Ancient Creeds, universally received and allowed by the whole Church of God."[24] Despite his own subscription to the Thirty-Nine Articles, he insisted that, insofar as no "creature under heaven" can make a new article of faith, there can be no new rules of faith—and heretics are only those who deny the ancient rules of Scripture and the creeds. This definition would not, however, rule out the formulation of doctrine in the church: "There are and may be many theological points, which are wont to be believed and maintained, and so may lawfully be, of this or that particular Church, or the Doctors thereof, or their Followers, as godly doctrines and probably truths, besides those other essential and main matters of Faith, without any prejudice at all of the common peace of the Church."[25]

---

21. Hall, *Peace-Maker*, iii (pp. 12–13).
22. Hall, *Peace-Maker*, iii (p. 28).
23. Hall, *Peace-Maker*, iii (pp. 28–29).
24. Hall, *Certain Catholic Propositions*, iii, in *Works*, vol. 9, p. 429.
25. Hall, *Certain Catholic Propositions*, vii (*Works*, vol. 9, pp. 429–30).

Given these definitions, Hall could rule out the possibility of rapprochement with Rome at the same time that he could present as a basis for dialogue with the Lutherans the principle that no theologian or particular church could be justified in imposing their own particular doctrines on other legitimate churches or on individual persons.[26] A concern for the identification of the catholic faith upon which all ought to agree in contrast to particular "points of Scholasticall disquisition" that ought to belong to "Academicall disputations, not worthy to trouble the publique peace, or to perplexe the heads, much lesse the hearts of Christian people," becomes the focus of Hall's comments on division between the Lutheran and Reformed churches.[27] What is evident from Hall's comments about scholastic argumentation is that his approach to such theological niceties was rather different from what has often been claimed in modern scholarship— namely, that scholastic argumentation as such lay at the root of early modern antagonisms.[28] Quite to the contrary, Hall saw the problem not with scholastic disputation *per se* but with the confusion of tight scholastic argumentation with confessional norms and with basic, required Christian belief. Whereas he was clear that there was a necessary separation of the English Church from "the Roman party," Hall was convinced that the highly technical antagonisms between the Lutherans and the Reformed could not be justified, despite the heated, detailed, and scholastic disputes that had taken place between Lutheran and Reformed theologians over such topics as predestination and the Lord's Supper.[29] Discord and debate might well be the norm for the university classroom, but in Hall's view such academic and speculative matters ought not dictate interconfessional relationships or personal piety.

Hall's Letter to John Dury—a Way of Peace in Protestant Ecumenism

As noted by Backus, Hall's irenic approach to various doctrines debated between Lutheran and Reformed theologians had a significant appeal

---

26. Hall, *Certain Catholic Propositions*, viii–ix (*Works*, vol. 9, p. 430).
27. Hall, *Peace-Maker*, v (p. 39).
28. Thus, e.g., Armstrong, *Calvinism and the Amyraut Heresy*, pp. 132–38.
29. Hall, *Peace-Maker*, v (pp. 32–33).

in the seventeenth century, from shortly after the Leipzig Colloquy of 1631 to the end of the century and Leibniz's ecumenical efforts. Hall penned his initial letter on peace among "evangelicals" at the invitation of the ecumenist John Dury.[30] It was published in Amsterdam in 1634 and again in 1635 with the intention of finding agreement between the Reformed and Lutheran churches,[31] and it was reissued with a modified title in England in 1638.[32] Another letter by Hall was published together with a similar missive from John Davanent in 1642 in an irenic treatise by the Bremen theologian Hermann Hildebrand.[33] Similar sentiments are expressed in two other theological epistles of Hall, also sent to Bremen theologians, namely, Baltasar Willius and Ludovicus Crocius, this time defending the Bremen theology as a legitimate Reformed post-Dort position against Reformed detractors overly worried about Arminian tendencies.[34] Excerpts from Hall's first

---

30. On Dury, see Milton, "'Unchanged Peacemaker'?"; Thomas H. H. Rae, *John Dury and the Royal Road to Piety* (New York: Peter Lang, 1998); also J. Minton Batten, *John Dury: Advocate of Christian Reunion* (Chicago: University of Chicago Press, 1944).

31. John Dury, *De pacis ecclesiasticae rationibus inter evangelicos usurpandis, et de theologorum fundamentali consensu in Colloquio Lipsiensi inito, trium in Ecclesia Anglicana venerabilium Episcoporum Johannis Davenantii, Episcopi Sarisburiensis, Thomae Mortoni, Episcopi Dunelmensis, Josephi Halli, Episcopi Exoniensis, Sententiae Iohanni Duraeo ab ipsis ad Ecclesiarum Evangelicarum aedificationem et reconciliationem promovendam traditae* (Amsterdam: s.n., 1634).

32. John Dury, *De pace inter evangelicos procuranda sententiae quatuor quarum tres a Reverendis Dominis Episcopis Tho. Dunelmensi. Io. Sarisburiensi. Ios. Exoniensi. Vltima ab eximijs quibusdam in Gallia theologis conscripta est. Traditae pridem fuerint Johanni Duraeo Scoto viro docto ac prudenti qui in opere hoc pijssimo jam per aliquot annos non infeliciter desudavit. Prodeunt vero hae (praesertim tres priores) istis Amstelodami anteà editis non paulo pulchiores, utpote quae ab autoribus revisae sunt, nec non proprijs ipsorum manibus tam auctae tum emendatae. Accessit syllabus brevis Dorum qui de hac argumente antehac scripserunt* (London: G. M[iller] for Walter Hammond, 1638), pp. 135–51. The letter is reproduced, with a translation on the facing page, in Hall, *Works*, vol. 11, pp. 489–511; Hall's letter hereinafter cited as Hall, *De pace inter evangelicos*.

33. Hermann Hildebrand, *Orthodoxa declaratio articulorum trium, de Mortis Christi sufficientia et efficacia, Reprobationis causa meritoria, Privata denique communione, conscio & instante venerando ministerio Bremensi, pro sopiendis inter quosdam collegas hinc exortis controversiis concepta* (Bremen: Berthold Villieranus, 1642); the letter can also be found in Hall, *Works*, vol. 11, pp. 450–63; hereinafter cited from Hall's *Works* as *Epistola ad Hildebrandum*.

34. Joseph Hall, *Clarissimo viro D. Baltasari Willio S. Theol. D. et im Bremensi ecclesia professori celeberrimo*, in *Shaking of the Olive-Tree*, pp. 317–20; also in *Works*, vol. 11,

letter were also published in the appendix of a treatise of Johannes Bergius, published in 1653, in which Bergius hoped to show grounds of agreement of major Reformed figures (including himself) with the Lutheran position that had been enunciated by the Saxon delegates to the Leipzig Colloquy of 1631.[35]

In Backus' view, the letter, as excerpted by Bergius, underscores Hall's *via media* and illustrates not only his distance from a doctrine of double predestination but that, most probably, he was "a moderate figure that could be formally classified as Reformed," albeit not a close follower of Calvinistic teachings.[36] These conclusions are open to question inasmuch as neither the excerpted passage nor the full document presents Hall's own theological views in detail or identifies the extent of his differences with the Lutherans. When examined in full, the letter presents a path toward agreement between the Reformed and the "most dignified Theologians of Saxony," Matthias Hoe, Polycarp Leiser, and Heinrich Hofner[37]—a path based on Hall's sense of the breadth of catholicity of Reformed theology, the limited usefulness of dogmatic disputation in the life of the church, and probably a perception shared with Dury of the potential role of the Church of England in achieving a form of Protestant unity.[38]

Hall, at Dury's request and with his copy of the Leipzig Colloquy "in hand," actually addressed three controverted issues, namely, the *communicatio idiomatum*, the presence of Christ in the Lord's Supper, and the doctrine of predestination. On the first two topics, Hall argues what is basically a single point. The Lutherans affirm that, given the personal union of the divine and human natures, Christ is omniscient

---

pp. 422–31 (with translation); and Joseph Hall, *Reverendo in Christo fratri, viro clarissimo, D. Ludovico Crocio S. Theologiae D. et in illustri schola Bremensi professori*, in *Shaking of the Olive-Tree*, pp. 320–30; also in *Works*, vol. 11, pp. 430–51 (with translation).

35. Johannes Bergius, *Der Wille Gottes von aller Menschen Seligkeit: Aus dem Spruch des Apostels Pauli in der ersten Epistel zu Timotheo am andern Capitel. Wider allerhand alte und newe Irrungen erkläret und Zur Vergleichung der mißhelligen Theologen…gerichtet* (Berlin: Runge, 1653), pp. 299–300; cf. Backus, *Leibniz*, p. 64.

36. Backus, *Leibniz*, p. 64. Note that Backus makes the rather common mistake of interpreting the Canons of Dort as condemning not only the Arminian but also the supralapsarian position; see Backus, *Leibniz*, p. 69.

37. Hall, *De pace inter evangelicos*, pp. 137, 148; also in *Works*, vol. 11, pp. 492, 498.

38. Cf. Milton, "'Unchanged Peacemaker'?," pp. 97–100.

according to his human as well as his divine nature—a doctrine that the Reformed deny. So also, in their doctrine of the Lord's Supper, the Lutherans affirm that unworthy recipients receive the body of Christ—which the Reformed also deny. Neither of these debates, Hall indicates, can be resolved from Scripture, and neither is a matter that ought to disturb either the individual believer or the church. Both, if they must be discussed, belong to the theological schools. As to the christological point, it pertains to "the devotion of faith" not to "the necessity of faith," and as to the second, Christians ought to be concerned that they participate in the Supper worthily and not be concerned over participation by the unworthy.[39]

On the third topic, predestination, Hall indicated that there were differences, but that the Reformed and the Lutherans at Leipzig had both stated their views "modestly and prudently," with agreement on what he took to be the most significant issues, specifically that election "is the free and gracious act of a merciful God," that it is not caused by anything in the elect, and that those sinners who "continue in sin and unbelief" are eternally "reprobated to damnation," not absolutely, but with respect to their sin.[40] The Saxons disagree in that they "place the foreknowledge of faith and perseverance prior to the act of divine Election," arguing specifically "that God foreordained from eternity such as he foresaw would in time believe."[41] This was definitely not Hall's own view—nor was it what he held to be that of the Anglican Church.[42] Nor, indeed, did Hall consider establishing a middle theological ground on the point between himself and the Lutherans: here the *via media* would be framed in minimalist confessional terms.

In approaching the Saxon position, Hall made no attempt to accommodate it to his own. Rather, he took the view that the disagreement arose out of diverging understandings of the highly recondite question of the nontemporal or logical "order of the decree." Much

---

39. Hall, *De pace inter evangelicos procuranda*, pp. 142–47; also in *Works*, vol. 11, pp. 494–99.

40. Hall, *De pace inter evangelicos procuranda*, pp. 136, 147–48; also in *Works*, vol. 11, pp. 492, 496, 498.

41. Hall, *De pace inter evangelicos procuranda*, p. 148; also in *Works*, vol. 11, p. 498.

42. See Joseph Hall, *A Letter Concerning Falling Away from Grace*, in *Shaking of the Olive-Tree*, pp. 389, 392.

like his colleague John Davenant, Hall understood that this aspect of debate could be avoided inasmuch as all recognized that the eternal decree was "a single and most simple act…accomplished by the infinite and most wise ruler of the world."[43] Setting aside the issue of determining the order or relation between divine foreknowledge of faith and perseverance and the decree of election, Hall could note that all were agreed that election is a free and utterly gracious act of God, that there is no cause of election in those chosen by God, and that God has "from eternity predestined and condemned to eternal damnation those who persevere in sin and unbelief," with the entire cause of this damnation being in those who are damned.[44]

Once the issue of the order of the decree is set aside, all might easily agree—indeed, "Nothing is more certain," Hall opines, "than that God has foreseen those who would believe and has predestined those who will be saved" and "that faith is the unique gift of God himself."[45] On the latter point, that faith is the unique gift of God, there could be straightforward agreement. On the other points, however, agreement could only be by way of omission of further explanation. Specifically, does God foresee faith as the antecedent to His election (the Saxons) or as the consequence of His election (the Reformed)? And similarly, does God predestine to salvation in view of faith (the Saxons), or is faith an aspect of the outworking of predestination (the Reformed)? Hall's approach is to propose agreement and to omit the further explanation on which there would be major disagreement.

---

43. Hall, *De pace inter evangelicos procuranda*, p. 149: "uno & simplicissimo actu… ab infinito & sapientissimo rerum moderatore peragi"; also in *Works*, vol. 11, p. 498; cf. John Davenant, *Dissertationes duae: prima De morte Christi…altera De praedestinatione & reprobatione. Quibus subnectitur ejusdem sententia de Gallicana controversia* (Cambridge: Roger Daniels, 1650), p. 108.

44. Hall, *De pace inter evangelicos procuranda*, p. 149: "ab aeterno Deum, in peccatis et infidelitate perseverantes, ad aeternam damnationem praedestinasse et reprobasse"; also in *Works*, vol. 11, p. 498; rendering *reprobasse* as "to have condemned" rather than as "to have reprobated" inasmuch as Hall is referencing a decree to damn and not a decree, coordinate with election, to reject. He has used a word typical of Reformed formulations but in such a way as to be acceptable to the Lutherans.

45. Hall, *De pace inter evangelicos*, pp. 149–50; also in *Works*, vol. 11, p. 498: "Nihil certius est, quam Deum praevidisse credituros, & salvandos praedestinasse: Detur hoc modo, quod iidem Saxonici non illibentes profitentur, Fidem esse unicum Dei ipsius Donum"; differing with the translation in Backus, *Leibniz*, p. 64.

The excerpts published by Bergius, therefore, obscure somewhat Hall's intention, almost demanding the passage to be read as an example of a *via media* theology that avoids a Reformed understanding of predestination, specifically as double predestination. But here the basis for agreement is a very limited *via media* constructed in the broadest terms for the case of finding common ground and representing the full theological position neither of Hall nor of the Saxons. The quotation from Hall's letter concludes "God shall have foreseen from eternity what he will have decreed to or bestow in time [*dare decreverit in tempore*] on those who would believe; therefore all is secure and there is no reason to extend this quarrel."[46] Rightly rendered, Hall is here making the standard scholastic distinction between the eternal decree and its temporal execution, and his use of the verb to foresee (*praevideo*) echoes Romans 8:29, "For whom he did foreknow, he also did predestinate." His final clause, indicating that there is no reason to extend the debate, reflects his previous strictures in relation to the eucharistic debate: contention had occurred over doctrinal formulae not necessary to the faith. As in his writings concerning the peace of the church, Hall was ready to distinguish between what he regarded as catholic truths and those theological truths held by either "particular Churches" or individual theologians: the former should be grounds of agreement, the latter should never become grounds for separation.

Although in the letter to Dury, he did not specify how to read Romans 8:29, he did do so when he paraphrased the text. There he clearly took the Reformed rather than the Arminian approach and read God's foreknowledge as "his eternal counsel" in which God "did…own for his…those did he preappoint and predestinate."[47] When making a somewhat fuller statement, then, Hall did not advocate an election grounded in foreknowledge, but understood the foreknowledge referenced in Romans 8:29 much as Calvin, Beza, and Reformed writers in general had taken it, namely, as an eternal knowing of those who

---

46. Hall, *De pace inter evangelicos procuranda*, p. 150: "Praeviderit ab aeterno Deus, quod ipse ab aeterno dare decreverit in tempore credituris; tuta sunt isthic omnia, nec est quod iste contentionis funis ultra protrahatur"; again differing from the translation in Backus, *Leibniz*, p. 64.

47. Joseph Hall, *A Paraphrase Upon the Hard Texts of the Whole Divine Scripture*, in *Works*, vol. 4, p. 318.

would be the objects of divine election. How then should his letter to Dury be explained? Surely, it was intended as a broadly stated irenic position that could be accepted by either Reformed or Lutheran theologians. It was not intended as a detailed or specific statement of Hall's own teaching or even as a declaration of the full doctrine of the Church of England on the disputed points, but it was fully in accord with Hall's own assumptions, stated in his *Certain Catholic Propositions*, concerning the relationship between catholic doctrine required for belief and the doctrinal positions of "particular Churches" and individual theologians.

Hall's *Via Media*—the Tract and Its Intention

Like several other of the more irenic thinkers of the seventeenth century, Hall used the notion of a middle way as the theme of one of his irenic theological proposals, and he wrote a work entitled *Via Media. The Way of Peace in the Five Busy Articles Commonly Known by the Name of Arminius*.[48] Although the treatise reflects concerns that Hall expressed as a delegate to the Synod of Dort and that are reflected in the statement of the British delegation to the synod, written after Hall's departure, Hall's *Via Media* was published only in 1659, some three years after his death.

Given its theological concerns, the composition of Hall's *Via Media* was placed by John Jones, Hall's first nineteenth-century biographer, "during the broils and disputes about the dogmas of Calvin and Arminius" that took place in England after the Synod of Dort and "probably previous to [King James'] injunctions, set forth in August

---

48. For other versions of the "middle way," cf., e.g., Francis Duke, *The fulnesse and freenesse of Gods grace in Iesus Christ; declared in the point of Election, by a middle way between Calvin and Arminius, and different from both, in a uniform Body of Divinity* (London: Richard Oulton and Gregory Dexter, 1642); George Gillespie, *VVholesome severity reconciled with Christian liberty. Or, the true resolution of a present controversie concerning liberty of conscience. Here you have the question stated, the middle way betwixt popish tyrannie and schismatizing liberty approved* (London: for Christopher Meredith, 1645); John Humfrey, *The middle-way in one paper of election & redemption, with indifferency between the Arminian & Calvinist* (London: for T. Parkhurst, 1673) (Humfrey penned more than a half dozen treatises claiming a "mediocria" or a "middle-way"); John Turner, *The Middle Way betwixt Necessity and Freedom. A discourse containing Two Sermons preached at St. Mary's in Cambridge* (London: for Samuel Sympson, 1683).

1622," whereas George Lewis, toward the end of the nineteenth century and on the basis of better evidence, sets its composition several years later, after the suppression of Richard Montague's *Gagg for the New Gospell* and shortly after Hall's elevation to the see of Exeter.[49] Lewis also infers from Hall's reminiscences that the treatise was not then printed but passed in manuscript through various hands—and after King James' injunction of 1628 against further debate, left unpublished or, as Hall himself commented, "buried…in secure silence" until its posthumous publication.[50]

In his autobiographical *Observations*, Hall wrote that his "little project of Pacification" arose in the wake not of the Dutch controversies and the Synod of Dort but as a reaction to the "broil" in the Church of England following "Mr. Montagues tart and vehement assertions… neer of kin to the Remonstrants of Netherland," as Lewis noted, following Montagu's *Gagg*, and perhaps even after Montagu's response to his critics.[51] Hall further comments—revealing a more nuanced paradigm of English theology than a simple Calvinst-versus-Arminian model—that Montagu was wrongly accused of being Arminian and had "meant to express, not *Arminius*, but *B. Overall*, a more moderate and safe Author."[52] John Overall, Bishop of Norwich, Hall continued,

---

49. Richard Montagu, *A Gagg for the New Gospell? No: a new gagg for an old goose: who would needes undertake to stop all Protestant mouths for ever, with 276 places out of their owne English Bibles. Or an answere to a late abridger of controversies, and belyar of Protestants doctrine* (London: Thomas Snodham, 1624). Jones, *Bishop Hall*, p. 108; but cf. Lewis, *Life of Joseph Hall*, p. 226, who references Jones' dating indicating that this is "almost certainly much too early."

50. Lewis, *Life of Joseph Hall*, pp. 226–31, citing Hall's *Specialties* at length; cf. Wynter, the editor of the 1863 edition of Hall's works followed Jones, indicating that the *Via Media* was actually published in or before 1622, cf. *Works* (1863), vol. 9, p. 488; and note the *Specialties*, or *Observations of Some Specialties of Divine Providence in the Life of Joseph Hall, Bishop of Norwich, Written by His Own Hand*, in *Works*, vol. 1, pp. xxxii–xxxiii. The earliest publication of the *Via Media* that I have identified is posthumous, i.e., 1659; in *Shaking of the Olive-Tree*, together with the *Specialties* and other remains of Bishop Hall.

51. Richard Montagu, *Appello Caesarem: A iust appeale from two vniust informers* (London: Humphrey Lownes, 1625).

52. Joseph Hall, *Observations of Some Specialties of Divine Providence in the Life of Jos. Hall, Bishop of Norwich. Written by His Own Hand*, in *Shaking of the Olive-Tree*, p. 37; also cited in Lewis, *Life of Joseph Hall*, p. 226. The presence of a more nuanced and detailed paradigm is suggested in Peter White, "The Rise of Arminianism

had positioned himself "mid-way, betwixt the two opinions which he held extream."[53]

Hall described his "project of Pacification" as a gathering of "common propositions" drawn "out of *B. Overall* on the one side, and out of our English Divines at *Dort* on the other," designed as a basis for agreement and, equally importantly, cessation of dispute in English pulpits. Drafts of the project were sent to various parties, with the result that Montagu indicated a willingness to "subscribe" to Hall's proposal and various "contrarily minded, both English, Scotish, and French Divines, profered their hands to a no less ready subscription."[54] Others who, as Hall claimed, had not read the document, complained about the process. A royal injunction against debate was issued, and the document was left unpublished.[55]

The posthumous publication of "the project of Pacification" as *Via Media* is replete with citations from the relevant sections of the Thirty-Nine Articles, from the *Collegiat Suffrage* of the British delegation to the Synod of Dort, and from a short work by John Overall. Hall references Overall's work without title. The editors of the nineteenth-century editions of Hall's works identify it as Overall's *De v Artic. in Belgio Controversis.*[56] Use of this document is significant not only because Hall respected Overall's reading of English theology in relation to the Arminian controversy but also because Overall had specifically identified the position of the Church of England as a *via media*—and had defined his *via media* as standing not between Arminian theology and the Canons of Dort or between Arminianism and Calvinism but between the Remonstrant and Contra-Remonstrant views of predestination.[57] Overall's definition of his stance not only carries over

---

Reconsidered," in *Past and Present*, 101 (1983), pp. 45–51; on Montagu's position as other than neatly Arminian, see Jay T. Collier, *Debating Perseverance: The Augustinian Heritage in Post-Reformation England* (New York: Oxford University Press, 2018), pp. 93–123.

53. Hall, *Specialties*, p. 38.

54. Hall, *Specialties*, p. 38.

55. Hall, *Specialties*, p. 39.

56. Hall, *Via Media* (1660), p. 357; cf. *Works* (1837), vol. 10, p. 471, note b.

57. John Overall, *On the Five Articles disputed in the Low Countries*, critical Latin text in Anthony Milton, ed., *The British Delegation and the Synod of Dort (1618–1619)* (Woodbridge, U.K.: Boydell, 2005), p. 67. The Latin original seems not to have been

into Hall's *Via Media*, but it is also, arguably, characteristic of Thomas Goad's position, described by John Goodwin as "betwixt the *Remonstrants* and *Contra-Remonstrants*."[58] Hall himself denied accusations of Arminianism: in a letter written during his time of imprisonment in the Tower in early 1642, he queried, "Can they challenge me as a close and back-stair friend to popery or Arminianism, who have in so many pulpits and so many presses cried down both?"[59]

A Specific Case: Hall's Approach to Predestination

One of the conclusions that becomes clear from an examination of Joseph Hall's efforts to find a "way of peace" or a *via media* is his attention to the levels or gradations of doctrinal truths that related, respectively, to catholicity, to Protestant unity (including the Lutherans), and to doctrinal integrity within "particular Churches" or among "particular Churches" of a shared confessionality. His efforts to defend a *via media* in the latter category more clearly reveal his own sense of the doctrinal formulae to which he subscribed and the doctrinal boundaries within which he framed his own thought. A case of particular interest is Hall's intervention on behalf of a Reformed colleague whose views had come under fire from other Reformed theologians who feared a slippage toward Arminianism. Thus, in his letter to Baltasar Willius, a Reformed theologian of Bremen, in response to Willius' queries about the perceived theological implications of his commentaries, Hall responded positively, noting initially one point

---

published; a translation was printed in John Plaifere, *Appello Evangelium for the True Doctrine of the Divine Predestination, concorded with the Orthodox Doctrine of Gods Free-Grace, and Mans Free Will. Hereunto is added Dr. Chr. Potter his owne Vindication in a Letter to Mr. V touching the same Points* (London: J. G. for John Clark, 1652), pp. 24–31.

58. J. G. in Thomas Goad, *Stimluus* [*sic*] *orthodoxus, sive Goadus redivivus. A disputation partly theological, partly metaphysical, concerning the necessity and contingency of events in the world, in respect of Gods eternal decree. Written above twenty years since by that reverend and learned divine, Thomas Goad, doctor of divinity, and rector of Hadleigh in Suffolk* (London: for William Leak, 1661), preface. On Goad's position, see Richard A. Muller, "Goading the Determinists: Thomas Goad on Necessity, Contingency, and God's Eternal Decree," in *Providence, Freedom, and the Will in Early Modern Reformed Theology* (Grand Rapids: Reformation Heritage Books, 2022), 165–86.

59. Cited in Lewis, *Life of Joseph Hall*, p. 392. Hall and eleven other bishops were charged with treason, ordered imprisoned on December 30, 1641, and released on May 5, 1642; cf. Jones, *Life of Hall*, pp. 279–94, for a clearer narrative of the events.

that should silence Willius' critics: Willius had chosen the right theological "patrons," namely, not Arminius, but theologians from among the "constellations" that sat at Dort, Walaeus, Thysius, and Triglandius.[60] Willius had denied a *praedestinatio absoluta*, had identified Christ as the *fundamentum electionis*, and had defined the "condition to be fulfilled in the saved" as faith—not, however, faith understood as a prerequisite foreseen by God.[61] His denial, Hall comments, was not without consideration of the issue of the decree's execution in time— much after the manner of his colleague, Crocius, who had argued that the "decree of election…is not absolute, but ordained and determined by the merit of Christ and by the means by which it is applied to us."[62] The denial of "absolute predestination," with which Hall concurs, is not, therefore, a denial of the Reformed doctrine of predestination as defined in the various confessions or by the Synod of Dort: the language reflects a distinction between the absolute and ordained will of God and identifies the execution of the decree as belonging to an ordained will that includes means. The recommended alternative to "absolute," then, is not the Arminian "conditional" where the condition is fulfilled by an act of the sinner, but rather "ordained," where the condition is itself fulfilled by God's grace through faith.

Hall's comments on Willius' view of reprobation identify the Reformed position equally clearly, as well as once again indicating Hall's location of the *via media*. It is quite in accord with the Canons of Dort, Hall argues, to state that the "absolute will" of God neither excludes anyone from grace nor consigns anyone to eternal destruction apart from sin: the blame for reprobation arises from human "impenitence and unbelief." Controversy would have been avoided, Hall comments, had the delegates at Dort followed his advice on the interpretation of Romans 9, steering a middle course between those

---

60. Note that two of these writers, Walaeus and Thysius, were authors of the *Synopsis purioris theologiae, disputationibus quinquaginta duabus comprehensa ac conscripta per Johannem Polyandrum, Andream Rivetum, Antonium Walaeum, Antonium Thysium, S.S. theologiae doctores et professores in Academia Leidensi* (Leiden: Elzevir, 1625), a fully orthodox Reformed post-Dort body of doctrine.

61. Hall, *Clarissimo viro D. Baltasari Willio*, in *Works*, vol. 11, pp. 424–25.

62. Ludovicus Crocius, *Syntagma sacrae theologiae quatuor libris adornatum: quo exhibetur idea dogmatum ecclesiasticorum* (Bremen: Bertholdus Villerianus, 1636), IV.i.3 (p. 978).

who ground "the perdition of multitudes" on "the absolute power and will of God" and those who flatter "human freedom" by according human beings "a jurisdiction of their own, as if they were subjected to no decree at all." Both extremes are perilous.[63] Hall expressed some regret that his advice was not completely followed by the synod and that some "inconvenient and incongruous expressions" remained in the canons despite the wishes of various delegates.[64]

Nonetheless, Hall argues that a correct way of formulating the doctrine could be framed with the boundaries set by the Canons of Dort. That middle way could be identified in thesis 5 of the first article on reprobation of the *Collegiat Suffrage* of the British delegation to the synod and in the articles submitted by the Hessian and Bremen delegations.[65] As the synod rightly held, God freely and justly passes over those who "by their own fault" remain in the misery of sin. Even so, it is a matter of sound doctrine to hold, with Dort, that God decrees eternal punishment for "unbelief and other sins." The problem often asserted with these points is, moreover, easily resolved by making a proper distinction between negative and positive reprobation: the former is God's nonelection; the latter is the decree to punish those who, "left in a state of corruption," consequent on nonelection, "procure for themselves a most worthy condemnation."[66]

The explanation of the doctrine of predestination found in Hall's *Paraphrase* of Romans 8:29–30, published in 1633 when Hall was bishop

---

63. Hall, *Clarissimo viro D. Baltasari Willio*, in *Works*, vol. 11, pp. 424–25.

64. Hall, *Clarissimo viro, theologo gravissimo, D. Hermanno Hildebrando*, in *Works*, vol. 11, pp. 460–61; cf. *Clarissimo viro D. Baltasari Willio*, in *Works*, vol. 11, pp. 424–25.

65. Hall, *Clarissimo viro D. Baltasari Willio*, in *Works*, vol. 11, pp. 426–27. See the *Iudicia theologorum exterorum*, separate pagination, pp. 3–14, here p. 13 (British), pp. 24–35 (Hessian), pp. 54–59 (Bremen), in *Acta synodi nationalis: in nomine Domini nostri Iesu Christi autoritate illustr. et praepotentum DD. Ordinum generalium Foederati Belgii provinciarum, Dordrechti habitae anno 1618 et 1619; accedunt plenissima, de quinque articulis, theologorum judicia*, 3 parts (Leiden: Isaac Elzevir, 1620); the judgment of the British delegation is also in translation, *The Collegiat Suffrage of the Divines of Great Britaine, concerning the Five Articles controverted in the Low Countries. Which Suffrage was delivered by them in the Synod of Dort, March 6. Anno 1619. Being their vote or voice foregoing the joint and publique judgment of that Synod* (London: Robert Milbourne, 1629).

66. Hall, *Clarissimo viro D. Baltasari Willio*, in *Works*, vol. 11, pp. 426–27; similarly in Hall, *Viro clarissimo D. Ludovico Crocio*, in *Works*, vol. 11, pp. 448–49.

of Exeter, confirms our interpretation of his letters to Willius and Bergius: it is unabashedly Reformed, in a clearly infralapsarian form:

> For those whom God did, in his eternal counsel, own for his, out of that corrupt mass of mankind, those he did preappoint and predestinate to be conformable to the image of his Son; both in their holiness and in their patient sufferings: that so, he being the Son of God by nature, might be the first born and the ring-leader of many brethren, by adoption and grace. Moreover, there is a strong and indissoluble chain of mercy and grace in God towards his elect, the links whereof can never be either broken or severed: for those, whom he did predestinate, them also in his due time he effectually calleth; and those, whom he thus calleth, he also justifieth; and those, whom he justifieth from their sins, he also doth fully, at last, glorify.[67]

So also in paraphrasing Romans 9:11, Hall indicates that the "will of God" is such that "calleth or refuseth whom he pleaseth"; and on Romans 9:21, Hall comments, "And shall not God have power over the clay of mankind, out of the same mass of perdition, to make up one man a vessel of honour, and to pass over another as a vessel of dishonour?"[68] Similarly, at verse 18, Hall states, "Therefore he hath mercy, on whom he will have mercy…and, whom he will, he passeth over, leaving them to themselves."[69] The implication of Hall's reading of Romans 9, then, is that his infralpsarianism implies a positive willing of election and a negative willing of reprobation. This is not a mere passing over, but a will to pass over the nonelect. Hall clearly conceived of reprobation as belonging to the divine willing and, accordingly, stands as an advocate of double predestination in an infralapsarian form.

Conclusion

Examination of the work of Joseph Hall provides an illuminating perspective on a fairly broad series of issues in seventeenth-century church and theology. Hall maintained the sense of earlier generations of Reformed writers who saw Protestantism as an exemplar of the church catholic. His irenicism centered on an understanding of the

---

67. Hall, *Paraphrase*, in *Works*, vol. 4, p. 318.
68. Hall, *Paraphrase*, in *Works*, vol. 4, p. 323.
69. Hall, *Paraphrase*, in *Works*, vol. 4, p. 322.

Church of England as a Reformed confessionality well-suited to mediating debates among the various Reformed communities, and as such his irenicism ran against tendencies within the Reformed communities, both British and Continental, to narrow the field of acceptable doctrine through rigorous definition. His protest against this narrowing of definition, whether in his understanding of the Canons of Dort and his defense of Reformed colleagues in Bremen or in his outreach to the Lutherans, was neither a diminution of his sense of confessionality nor a rejection of the scholastic methods of the era. Rather, it represented a carefully defined sense of the roles and limits of various forms of theological discourse.

Hall should not be seen as representing a *via media* between Protestantism and Rome. He understood Protestantism as representing the church catholic and Rome as having departed. Nor can he be defined as a "moderate" thinker occupying a middle position between Calvinism and Arminianism. He quite clearly stood against an Arminian reading of the doctrinal issues. Nor should his position be viewed as at odds with the Canons of Dort. Only a very narrow understanding of "Calvinism" would allow that characterization. Hall's position, in agreement with the conclusions of Fincham, Lake, and Steere, ought to be understood as fully confessionally Reformed—as should his understanding of the Church of England, particularly in light of the *Collegiat Suffrage* of the British delegation to Dort. Also, as we have seen, what Backus understood to be Hall's own theological position was actually his suggestion of an irenic confessional stance that could be accepted by both the Reformed and Lutheran churches, stressing common ground and carefully omitting polarizing differences. Where Hall differed from what could be called a more strict or "hard-line" Reformed position was not in any tendency to divest himself of an English Reformed confessionality, but in his willingness to refrain from identifying detailed doctrinal definitions of predestination or the Lord's Supper as fundamental articles and, accordingly, as barriers to interconfessional connections, specifically with the Lutherans,[70] or as barriers to intraconfessional concord, as in his defense of the Bremen Reformed theologian Baltasar Willius.

---

70. As Milton, "'Unchanged Peacemaker'?," p. 101, indicates of Dury.

Accordingly, his *via media* was also not a middle ground between a Calvinistic or Reformed confessionality and some other confessional position. Rather, Hall's *via media* was an irenic way of dealing with differences among theologians within particular confessionalities and differences between divergent confessionalities, evidencing strong connection with the pan-Protestant irenicism of his contemporaries John Dury and Samuel Hartlib. He was not about to set aside his own theological convictions or what he held to be the confessional stance of his own particular church. Rather, he sought a middle ground of catholic agreement among Protestants, whether Reformed or Lutheran, that was able to respect confessional differences and the variety of formulations offered by various theologians of each confessionality. Finally, then, Hall's position offers an illustration of one of several trajectories of argument found within the confessional orthodoxies of the era that was quite unsuccessful in its attempt to bring together the Reformed and Lutheran confessionalities but capable of some success in identifying the breadth of confessional definitions and therefore the possibility of varied positions within the confessional boundaries of the Reformed churches.

Index